Clouds of Memories

Text and drawings © Mona K.K. Kahele

ISBN: 1-932660-02-X

Kamehameha Schools
567 South King Street
Honolulu, Hawaiʻi 96813

Printed in the United States of America

Cover and book design by Stacey Leong Design

Clouds of Memories

Mona Kahele

KAMEHAMEHA SCHOOLS

Contents

Miloliʻi Stories

Miloliʻi Legends

Fishing Traditions

Glossary

Postscript

Publisher's Note

Mona Kapapaokeali'ioka'alokai Kapule Kahele, born in 1921, was a historian from her earliest years: she would listen carefully to stories told by her kūpuna and those of her kūpuna's generation. As soon as she learned to write she recorded every story she could on any material that availed itself to her: ironed grocery wrapping paper, flattened hala leaves, corn husks, even blank Bible pages. She was raised by her paternal grandmother Lokalia who encouraged her and stressed the importance of an education, doing everything she could to ensure Mona's ability to attend school.

A strong woman with firm convictions, Mona kept writing through school, college, her marriage to Abel Kahele, and the rest of her life as she raised children and maintained careers in farming, teaching, counseling, and healing. She believed that preserving the accurate meaning of place names—no matter how geographically small—was very important. If the kupa o ka 'āina do not tell the story of their land, and all its hills, bays, peaks, plains, and caves, then who will?

In 1995, Megan Mitchell, who organized and typed Mona's collection of notes and drawings, found me and asked if I could get the completed manuscript published. Mona wanted the manuscript neither translated into Hawaiian, nor adapted, segmented, or significantly changed. Kamehameha Schools saw the cultural and educational value in Mona's stories and is pleased to bring this oral history into print.

Hawaiian vocabulary is not italicized or set apart from its English language context because this volume is a Hawaiian story, told by a speaker whose first language was Hawaiian. To help the reader, a glossary of Hawaiian terms is provided on page 253. Modern Hawaiian spelling is used throughout the book except for personal names unless they were spelled with diacritics in Mona's manuscript or are widely known and have been used in other Kamehameha Schools publications.

Definitions for Hawaiian terms are as Mona defined them. Editing of the text—such as making tenses agree, fixing typographical errors, or clarifying a sentence to make it easier for a reader to understand—was undertaken carefully so as not to change the meaning of Mona's work. Making the grammar in *Clouds of Memories* conform to English (or Hawaiian) standards was secondary to preserving Mona's voice and manaʻo. Any failure to meet this goal is mine alone.

Aunty Mona passed away and returned to the loving embrace of Ke Akua on March 15th, 2006 shortly before this volume went to press. It is our hope and prayer that *Clouds of Memories* will honor her memory and her beloved land of Kona Hema.

Lilinoe Andrews

Preface

I collected these stories and legends from my grandmothers, grandfathers and others who in turn learned them from their grandfolks, keeping them within our family for many years.

When I came along at about the age of seven, I was fond of stories and other things of interest which my kūpuna had to offer. As soon as I mastered writing, I wrote these stories down in Hawaiian. The problem I had was translating the stories into the English language. A word in Hawaiian has many different meanings, so the right English word has to be chosen to match the Hawaiian.

The materials I used to write this collection were out of this world. I mean, paper and money were scarce and we couldn't afford to buy materials. My mother kept all the wrapping papers that came with the groceries when she went to the store, and smoothed them out with the hot charcoal iron so I could write on them. I also wrote on wide, smoothed out hala leaves, corn husks, wrapping paper, blank pages from books, and even the blank pages of my grandmother's Bible. To write I used a carpenter's flat pencil. Being raised by my father's mother was something else. Speaking English in the household was forbidden, and she didn't speak English at all. In a way I was glad that she didn't know how to read or write, otherwise I would have been in trouble. Every time she saw me writing, she would ask me if I was writing in Hawaiian. My answer was always "yes," otherwise she would crumple all my work. I know it was a lie, but to save all my written work I had to do it.

I was asked by someone why I used *Clouds of Memories* for my title. My answer was because my material comes from my relatives on a hearsay basis and to me it is just like the clouds: they can really paint an interesting story. The clouds tell more things than you can ever imagine. The formations that take place are out of this world. Clouds that look like cotton balls reveal many things to come. Windswept clouds are thoughts that have to be cleaned out. Clouds with edges that are black or gray mean emotion and un-happiness. Smooth and blue clouds bring happiness and a clear mind. But at eventide when the sun is about to set, those gold, pink, or rosy colors tinted with other pastels and all the different formations tell the most beautiful story of all. Most of all I know our Heavenly Father and his Holy Son Jesus Christ are out there too, to help me enjoy and remember the wonders of their creations. So *Clouds of Memories* became my creation for all to enjoy.

I would like to add that some of these stories may seem similar to what other writers have shared, but upon scrutiny you will see that the core of each story is quite different. The most important thing to me has been to get them down on paper. All through the years, I kept these stories as my trea-sures. To me they mean a lifetime that cannot be repeated. I am indebted to many of my relatives. Here I leave these thoughts with good faith and start out with my early memories...

Mona Kahele's self-portrait

Diary Entries

Excerpts from the 1930s to the 1990s

RECOPIES FROM ALL MY DIARIES

SEPTEMBER 17, 1987

So much has happened during my lifetime. As I look back on all the years, the passing of my time, I wish I could capture all the best, hard, lonely years and bring them forward to this time period. There were also times of happiness which were shared with my family like my mother, father, brothers, and sisters. Most of all my grandmother who never spoke or understood a word of English, who never knew how to read or write, but taught me everything that she knew. The language and the culture were her biggest or greatest concern. Next, education and the lifestyle.

My mother played a very important part, too. Her tedious urging of various learning and her love and patience maintained all my aims during my life. I love and miss my mother so much. Today, as I look back, so much has happened. The inner loneliness is still there.

Marriage, children, and grandchildren are a blessing. But will they grasp the same knowledge I had acquired? Sometimes I often wonder if their understanding will be a continued version of mine going on for generations to come. I have faced so much from hard to easy.

Today there's only my youngest sister and myself. We confided in each other about our problems or misfortunes. Is this what is meant as the "Golden Age?" I hope so! I also love nature and what it offers. The study of its elements is tremendous. Words are hard to explain. But the feelings are there to grasp. Ever since I could read and write English, I have collected all kinds of legends, and have studied what some plants offer for medicinal purposes or other uses. I studied the names of places in my home area; old names are never heard by many people. Events that are connected with these place names are something good to know.

In fact, I was always told to make an effort to use the correct names when you describe a certain area so this becomes a habit. Sometimes you get all frustrated when you hear people say the wrong name or use a pronunciation that is not what it should be.

This is how my life has evolved or developed. I was almost a forgotten child due to some hidden incident before I was born. However, it was not a pretty story. That secret died with my mother whom I love so much. Sometimes the memories of her actions, laughing, and of everything else during her stay here on this earth are very heart warming. I wish I could be the way she was. Well, that's how memories happen.

To get this whole story going, I'll get started with being born at Nāpoʻopoʻo, the same area as my mother and father. During my early years I was with my own family. Just before I started school, I was taken to live with my father's adopted mother, Tūtū Mele. Here I lived until I was treated like a slave. I had to do all the hard work, while my cousins could play and go swimming.

I was made to pack brackish water from Waiʻamaʻu to our house every afternoon and boil that water for the daily baths for the people in the house. But, as for me, I had to take my bath at the pond, of course, with cold water.

I often wondered why I had to bathe with cold water, while my cousins bathed with hot water. But I never asked questions because I was always told never to ask questions. Other times I was made to clean all the thorns from bundles of lau hala leaves. It was a monotonous chore. I ended up with thorns stuck in my fingers or centipede bites. Every time I complained about how it hurt and I couldn't get the thorns out, I ended up being slapped around.

Anyway, one evening, I was sitting by the fireplace waiting for the water to get heated. My Tūtū Mele called me to go get one lau hala bundle and clean the thorns out. I was so engrossed doing this chore that I forgot to add some more wood to the fire. It burned out just at the time my aunt came out and saw the fire burned out. She was so angry with me that she picked up the nīʻau broom, soaked it in a bucket of water sitting there, and beat me up until the welts on my arms and legs were bleeding. She hit me on the head and all over my body.

My screaming brought Tūtū Mele out to the cook house and she rescued me from my aunt. I was crying and blood was all over my clothing. Tūtū Mele wet a towel and wiped the blood off. But the welts were too large to stop bleeding.

Just at that time my other grandmother came to visit. Now, this grandmother, Tūtū Lokalia, was my father's real mother. When she saw what had happened to me, she was so angry with my aunt she started yelling at her. All I know is that she had my bundle of clothes and held my hand tight and walked me to the gate. My aunt was yelling all kinds of dirty words and tried to yank me out of my grandmother's hands.

Tūtū Lokalia, who was just about my height, took a big stick and whacked my aunt with it. She told her if she didn't stop, she would get the police and call my father. That somehow stopped her.

This is where my lifestyle changed. She took me home to her house, made hot water, and bathed me. Then she mashed some kukui nuts, extracted the oil, and applied it to all the open welts on my body. It burned so bad that all the crying didn't stop the hurt. I was so mixed up because I missed Tūtū Mele, the one I knew so well and loved. But as time went on, the wounds all healed and Tūtū Lokalia became the one and only person I trusted.

Where she lived, the coffee mill was in the front of the house. She worked in the mill as a coffee sorter with some of the women folks of the village. She taught me how to weave hats, more of the language, and of course, the culture and living patterns.

Tūtū and I always did everything together. When the wana was fat, she would take me with her to the beach and show me what to pick from the seaside to eat. But the rules I had to learn were just countless and I would tell her it was all so stupid.

Rules like don't say anything to anyone if you're going to the beach, only say holoholo. The first fish you catch must be thrown back into the water, then the next fish you catch goes home. The first full hand of 'opihi you toss back to the sea. In fact, anything you catch or pick is first tossed back to the sea. Never face your back to the sea while picking 'opihi and limu. Never answer if anyone is calling you while you're busy at the seaside. If you do answer, you must quit and go home. Take only enough to eat. If you meet anyone on your way home, offer some of your catch.

I had a cousin we always met on Sundays during church time. She and I became very close. We did everything together. She was a couple of years older than I was, but she had the mind of someone younger than me.

During school days, we went to school and home together. We both had the same handicap: we couldn't speak a word of English. All the other cousins and relatives spoke English and Hawaiian. The reason for not being able to speak English was because we were forbidden at home or anywhere. So Kalani and I had some time learning the language. Kalani and I became inseparable until Tūtū Lokalia and I had to leave Nāpo'opo'o and move to Hilo. Tūtū was getting sick, and it was too far to walk to see the doctor and dentist because we didn't have any transportation and had to walk all the way from Nāpo'opo'o Beach to Kealakekua. We moved to Hilo and stayed with my cousin Violet on Mililani Street.

However, we were not happy because Tūtū could not stand my cousin making me look after her children. Tūtū said, "Nobody is going to treat you like a slave."

For that reason she told me we should go find a place and leave them alone. My Uncle Kikoni, Tūtū Lokalia's brother, was living with them also. I think they took him for granted because he was a lōlō and slow thinker, and she (my cousin) took advantage of him. Even though he worked at the cemetery, he had to babysit, lawn mower the yard, wash dishes, and even do all the laundry and house cleaning.

Many times he and Tūtū got into arguments about him having to do all these chores while my cousin went out with her friends to play cards and came home demanding me and Uncle Kikoni what to do. Her husband, always traveling for gambling games, sometimes came home in an ugly mood, and that's when we knew he had lost quite a lot of money gambling.

Tūtū couldn't stand their attitude. Even my Aunt Amina who was my cousin's mother was no better. She went out and every night came home with different men. Many times Aunty and Tūtū got into big fights. One day my Uncle Moses Moku, who was the minister of Haili Church, came to visit Tūtū. She was so happy to see him and poured out all her dislikes of the household where we were. She asked my uncle to find a house for us where we could live alone and I would have time to study, because I was still attending high school. In that house there was hardly time for me to study because there was so much I had to help out with and she couldn't see me doing it. At first my uncle suggested that we move with him because it was closer to school and Tūtū could always be near him. She liked the idea but still wanted her way.

He told us to wait and have patience till he came again. Tūtū said to not let her wait too long.

Anyway, the very next day when I got home from school, she was so tickled. She told me she had packed all our belongings and for me to go phone my uncle and tell him that we were ready and to come and pick us up. I asked her, "Are we moving with Uncle Moku or what?"

She said, "No. Uncle found a house for us and we are moving."

So, I went upstairs to phone my uncle. He came with Aunty Lumela. He helped us move.

We were just about to leave the house when my cousin, her mother, and her husband came home. When they saw that we had packed our things and were ready to leave, they were so angry, and many words flew back and forth.

Violet wanted to throw our things out from Uncle Moses' car. Uncle told her if she did that he would have to have her arrested. She whirled around and told Uncle to get his car off her property. This he did when we got into the car. But before we left, Tūtū was so angry she turned around and slapped my aunty's mouth and my cousin Violet's face for the dirty words they were saying. Aunty Amina yelled at my Tūtū, "Oh, when you have nothing to eat, don't come to me because I would rather feed the dogs than you."

Tūtū told them, "I came from Kona with our own money and my lau hala. Our money and work are honest and we will never come to you for food. In fact, this past month that we stayed in your house, we brought our own food. Now I'm leaving with my mo'opuna and you can go to hell! You folks only kuhilani my mo'opuna and my lōlō son. I feed my own mouth and my mo'opuna with honest money. Not like you folks, big loafers only gamble."

She turned to my aunty and said, "You never change. Still the wahine ho'okamakama. And you, my mo'opuna, nui kou moloā 'ino (you are very lazy.) Like ana 'oe me kou makuahine (you are just like your mother.)"

Many more words were said, but we got into Uncle's car and left that awful place.

Uncle took us to the house we were to live in. Tūtū was so happy, right away she wanted us to stay there. But Uncle said no, we would leave our ukana in that house but we would have to spend the night with them because the lights were not connected yet. Not till the next day.

Lots had to be accomplished before we were established in our home. Neighbors were very friendly and we lived a good, happy life. The war years were just hectic because of the new laws that were issued and we had to abide by them. Most of our island boys got drafted or volunteered into all branches of the service. Blackouts, ID cards, gas masks were a must, and of course, the curfew hours. Some of the food items, gas, and some medicine were rationed.

Servicemen from the mainland were brought to our shores to protect our islands. Many island girls were involved with these boys. Some of them got married to them, but the rest of the girls were left with babies to take care of or raise. This matter was a widespread issue on all of the Hawaiian Islands. Today, almost all ethnic groups have haole in them.

War years brought lots of jobs for the people. But some of the jobs and certain areas were restricted to all but our Japanese or German people. Especially those who were faithful to their homelands.

These were the people who were taken away from the islands to the mainland and placed in internment camps. How they were treated, we in Hawai'i had no idea.

The young men tried to get into the service with the Nissei J.A. Army. Most of my classmates and playmates whom we grew up with all joined up. Some of them came home disfigured or with limbs missing. Others were missing or dead. Sad, sad, sad. But this is what you call war. This all happened during World War II. Well, so much had happened and more was yet to come.

As the war years wore on, I finished school and went on to college. It wasn't easy working the midnight shift. I finished at 6:00 a.m. the next morning then went off to college. Those days were hectic, but they paid off.

The next step was being married. By this time the war had just ended and all our local boys were returning home. This is when Abel, my husband-to-be, also came home with this wave of servicemen.

I gave up my career to be a full-time wife, then later a full-time mother when we adopted Danford, a nice healthy boy. He was then only twenty-four hours old. The parents who gave this baby to us were just loving. Since I couldn't have any children and I longed to have one, this was the answer to complete our family. I wouldn't mind looking for another little baby someday, but a baby girl. This would really be complete. I made our home in Hilo, to see that my son grew up in a better environment than Miloli'i. I made up my mind, whether my husband liked it or not, that I was never going to raise my son at Miloli'i. The conditions there were not what I wanted for my son. So, we bought a piece of land and built a home.

We lived there for a number of years. Abel went fishing there and we made it through the years. In late 1958 we came back to Kona to live but not at Miloli'i. For a while, we lived with my parents until my brother came home, then the air around the house was not happy. So we packed up again and moved down to Nāpo'opo'o. Abel started to work for a construction company for a while. Later, Sure Save expanded to Kona and he was hired to work at the store. He started as a janitor and retired as an assistant manager for the produce department.

During all those years (nineteen years) he worked there, we bought or leased ten acres of coffee land. There was much work to do but we made it and had a comfortable living. Our son graduated from high school and went into the service. He came home, married, and had two little girls. Later he had another little girl.

Before he left for the service, we had another baby girl, Dolly. We loved her so much we just couldn't give her up. At the time we got her, she was about five months old and a very sickly baby. We took her to the doctor to see what was wrong with her. I almost got arrested because the baby was a malnourished child. I told the doctor I had just gotten this baby from one of my nieces who claimed this child belonged to one of her sisters. The sister left the sick baby with Margie. She couldn't take care of this sick baby because she had two little ones of her own and was expecting another soon. Furthermore she asked me to keep the baby as she was not able to buy milk and medicine for her. That's the reason why I had to take this baby to the doctor. We didn't even know what the baby looked like. Her face was covered with sores, deep cuts under her neck, and cuts behind her ears. Her head was just covered with sores and it was the most pitiful sight I'd ever seen in my life. The doctor gave me some kind of medicine and I had to wash the baby twice a day.

The doctor told me she might live for six hours or less, and asked if I would be able to take care of her. At that time I only felt it was a duty I had to perform. So, I agreed.

The baby had to be fed medication and milk with an eye dropper. It took me seven days and seven nights of going without sleep and doing all my chores around the house with a son who attended high school and a husband who worked. At times I almost collapsed, but every time I looked at that sick baby, I developed more strength. I prayed to our Almighty Father to help and heal this baby, for I knew it was no fault of hers.

She was covered with sores from head to toe. Poor thing! But I didn't give up until she could really suck the milk from the nipple. It was the end of the seventh day. As we know, God Almighty created this world in six days and rested on the seventh day. While my husband and son looked after the baby, I fell into a deep sleep for nearly twenty-six hours, the much-needed rest after seven days and nights without sleep.

When I woke up, the first thing I did was to lift that baby high over my head and thank the Father for all the help He gave me. For the first time I saw her smile, with green eyes and outreached hands. I hugged her so close to me that my tears just poured out with relief. That's when I told my husband and son we were keeping this baby and no one would take her from us. We started procedures of adoption. What we ran into was just enormous, from lawyers to a private detective, until the judge. At the end, we won despite the many obstacles we went through. Thank God, our Father in Heaven, that today, Dolly is a mother of two children, a girl and a boy. Although they are menaces, we love them.

As for my son, Danford, he left and volunteered to go into the service right after graduation. He was wounded in Vietnam and came home with a Purple Heart and Bronze Star and many more medals. Discharged, he got married to an island girl. Two little girls were born on the mainland: Ann Marie was born in Maryland and Tracy Lynn was born in North Carolina. A third little girl, Huapala, was born in Kona, Hawai'i. This marriage ended with a divorce, and Danford got custody of the little girls. I offered to care for them while he went to work. He was an ambulance driver for Kona Hospital and a medic when he was not on the road. He met Sandra (Sandy) Nass, a nurse at the hospital, and married her. They have three sweet children, two sons, and a daughter. Danford has changed a lot: no more scallywagging. He became a good Christian and a God-fearing man. I am so happy for him after all the misfortunes he has had in his lifetime.

Sandy has been such a godsend. She is a loving girl, and I think they have a very bright life ahead of them. With five children, their love is built around them. Ann Marie, Danford's daughter, has gone to be with our Heavenly Father. She had been confined in the hospital from age seven until she was sixteen and died. She had an incurable sickness and nothing could make her well. Poor thing. But it was better that way than suffering all those years. So, that leaves us with seven grandchildren with both Danford's and Dolly's together. I love them so much.

During the years that Dolly was growing up, we moved to Middle Ke'ei to land belonging to my mother. Being that I love farm life, we raised pigs and chickens, and planted corn and vegetables for our table. We also had a small acreage of coffee we took care of. We sold whatever coffee we picked and used the money for fertilizer, bags, and poison to keep the grass down.

Later we acquired ten acres of leased land from Bishop Estate. We planted seven acres of coffee, thirty-two avocado trees, and sixteen mango trees. The avocados and mangos were all grafted and of different varieties. Out of thirty-two avocado trees, only nineteen trees were fruit bearing. Only eleven mango trees were fruit bearing. As for the coffee, it took us seven years before we really made a comeback.

During the latter part of the 1960s to the 1970s, our expenses were paid up and we had a sizable profit left over. We made money from the avocados and stopped selling them because the money was not coming in regularly. We were shipping to Canada and San Francisco.

Inspections and packing were a problem. We were shipping about 2,000 pounds a week until the price per pound dropped and the shipping rate went up. So we quit and sold only to the local markets. Although we didn't make much, it was better than nothing.

Then sickness overtook me. I underwent several major operations and treatments for stomach cancer, heart trouble, and whatever else was just too much pain to bear. I spent most of my days in the hospital, from Kona Hospital to the Queen's Medical Center, for several months. I thought I would never make it. Having to leave Dolly, who was about eight years old, at home with my husband and my son Danford was too much for me because I felt she was my responsibility. Before I knew what was going on, Abel sold the coffee land. He intended that I not get back into that racket again. He later told me, "No more farming for you anymore. You work enough, and you're not going back to the same thing again."

You know, I cried and cried. To me I was then useless. I went as far as asking God to take me. Enough burdens on my family. But somehow I was having flashbacks of my family and it made me realize I needed them and they needed me, too. So I fought back to get well. I underwent therapy even though it was hard. But I made it and came home to Hawai'i Island with much happiness, although I couldn't walk. I had to be in a wheelchair for nearly two-and-a-half years before I really could walk a few steps. I lost a lot of weight which made me so happy. Ten years after I got married I began to gain weight until I was about 409 pounds. I took a lot of tests before I found I had gland trouble. Anyway, in all I had a narrow escape from death.

God Almighty has been ever loving to grant me another chance at life. The pains were just countless and I thought I would lose my mind. A psychiatrist was called in, but I was on the road to recovery.

I was told I might have a lifespan of a year or less. The thoughts that were going through my mind were numerous. I began to think about my daughter who was then nine years of age. How would she be if I were not there? I still had dreams of seeing her through school. How would my husband face problems not being able to read or write or understand? My son had a family of his own. My grandchildren. "Oh God, what am I going to do?" The road ahead was narrow for me. Not able to walk, my right side was almost useless. What would I do?

Night after night I kept pondering and trying to think of a way that would not burden my family. There was only one thing to do, and that was to beg

God for forgiveness and commit my whole being into His hands. Every day I kept begging Him. Little by little there was movement in my right leg and hand. I then knew my prayers were being answered. It took me two years of hard work and prayers to be on both feet again to help people good or bad.

To me, I love them all. As Jesus said, love one another—even if they hate you. In short, I had come a long way to recover.

Now I am involved in so many community activities that sometimes I hardly find time for myself. In a way I do enjoy what I am doing. I never dwell on the thought that death was ever so close. I guess when you put God before you, there is always a chance. After all I experienced, I resolved to take life as it is, and not think how lifeless I might be. I never thought of myself as being handicapped but as someone who can lend a helping hand.

MAY 1946, MILOLIʻI

Dear Diary,

In the three weeks I spent here in Miloliʻi I learned a lot. Yes, fishing is their life existence. Fish caught is trucked to Hilo and sold to the markets there. Money received pays for the ice and food the people order.

Leftover money is saved and goes into buying bonds. Nobody is on welfare support. The old kūpuna who worked for the county have a pension of $12.00 to $23.00 a month. The rest of the people live on fishing, even sending their children away for more education.

There are two churches in the village. A Catholic church and a Kalawina church, which has a touching story. No electricity or running water. People have tubs or wooden barrels to catch their water when it rains. Other than that, brackish water is used for all domestic uses.

JUNE 1946, MILOLIʻI

Dear Diary,

Today I decided to mingle with the kūpuna. Perhaps this time I will be able to converse with them in their mother tongue.

I haven't spoken Hawaiian for a long time, since my grandma died. Maybe now I can test myself if I still can speak the language.

Well, I can see them gathered under the kiawe tree by Kalanihale Awa. So I'm on my way.

Kūpuna greeted me in their native tongue and invited me to sit with them, which I did. I returned the greetings and added more words like how calm the sea was and that it was such a clear day. They looked stunned and glanced at each other without saying a word, then looked back at me. I thought I must have said something wrong to them. But somehow they were surprised at the way I spoke to them. I sat next to the elderly kupunawahine. She turned to me and said, "I thought you were a city girl and could not speak the language." I laughed. I told her I was brought up by my kupunawahine who did not speak English. She said I spoke the language fluently, not like the young people here: if you speak to them, they answer you in English.

One conversation led to another. Before I knew what I was saying, I asked them if there were any stories or places of importance in the village and why it was that no canoes or people mending nets were around the beach on Sundays?

One kupunawahine whom everyone calls Tūtū Kipi responded and these are the actual words she spoke to me. I wrote them down and I'm glad I did. Perhaps someday I will be able to share them with her descendents.

TŪTŪ KIPI: 'O ka Lāpule, he lā kapu loa no kēia wahi. No ka mea, he mo'olelo i pili ana i ka halepule Kalawina 'o ia nō ho'i 'o Hau'oli Kamana'o. He mo'olelo kūpaianaha. Nā kahua hale a pau loa o kēia wahi, ua wāwahi a holoi 'ia a ma'ema'e kēia 'āina. A koe nō kēlā halepule. 'O ia ho'i ua ho'ē'e ka kai a mimiki. Mai ia manawa mai, 'o nā po'e kūpuna o kēia wahi ua ho'olaha mai kēia lā aku 'o nā Lāpule, kapu loa.

1. He lā hele i ka pule.

2. E ho'omaha.

3. 'A'ole he lā e hele i ka lawai'a.

4. 'O nā mea hana pau loa e waiho no kahi lā aku.

5. 'O nā mea'ai e ho'omo'a ma mua o ka nāpo'o 'ana o ka lā ma mua o ka Lāpule.

Inā ʻaʻole e hoʻolohe mai ʻo ka hopena paha nō ka make nō o mākou pau loa. ʻAkā, hoʻonele ʻia nā mea pono o ka poʻe. ʻAe, ua pakele nō mai ka make, a ʻo ia ka moʻolelo liʻiliʻi o ka Lāpule o kēia ʻāina.

Pehea, makemake nō ʻoe a hoʻolohe i ka moʻolelo o kēlā halepule a me ka makahiki i loaʻa kēlā kai mimiki? A pili ana i kēia moʻolelo o ka Lāpule i haʻi aku iā ʻoe.

ʻAe nō au iā ia.

TRANSLATION: *The Sundays are kapu for this place because there is a story which concerns the church Hauʻoli Kamanaʻo (Happy Thoughts). It is a strange story. All the houses and foundations of this place were destroyed and the place seemed as if it were washed clean and only the church was left because there were high waves. From that time the kūpuna of this place made a proclamation that all Sundays are kapu.*

1. *It's a day to go to church.*

2. *Rest.*

3. *You don't go fishing on that day.*

4. *All your work things or whatever you have to do, leave for the next day.*

5. *If you have something to cook, you have to do it one day before Sunday. Everything has to be done before Sunday.*

If we don't listen we might die, who knows? And yet the people were made to go without. At least they were saved from death. And that is the story of Sundays here.

"Do you want to listen to the story about that church and the year they had that tidal wave?"

I said yes to her.

I asked if it was all right for me to write down what she would tell me. She and the other kūpuna sitting there all said, "Why not? Perhaps someday maybe our generations will want to listen to this story if they care."

One kupuna responded, saying, "ʻO ia hoʻi inā makemake au a kamaʻilio i kekahi mau moʻolelo i nā poʻe kamaliʻi a me nā moʻopuna, ʻo kēia nā pane: ʻhe old fashion hoʻi kēlā ʻano moʻolelo.' ʻAkaʻaka nei au. (If I want to tell you the stories and then when I tell my children and grandchildren, their answer is, 'that's old fashioned.' That's when I start to laugh.")

'Ae, ho'opa'a 'oe i kēia mau mo'olelo. Mēia paha, he mau lā aku e ho'olohe ana nō nā 'ohana e ola ana. (Yes, you should write down the stories. Maybe someday some of the families will listen, those who are living and the next generation.)

I kēia manawa, 'o mākou nā po'e kūpuna ola nei ke iho nei nā lā a koe nō nā pua. (Now we are kūpuna that are living here and our days are going down the hill and only our young ones will be left.) "'Ae," ku'u pane. (Then I answered, "Yes.")

I was so thrilled at having an opportunity like this that I didn't waste time taking out my pen and diary which I carried wherever I went. Anyway, I'm writing these stories as they were related to me.

Tūtū Kipi, as known to the village and now to myself, was the one who was telling me these stories in her way. Sitting with her under this kiawe tree were Aunty Kapeka and Uncle Kukulu (my aunt and uncle by marriage), Kūkū Kalani and Kūkū Malaea Kahele (who became my in-laws.)

We sat there listening while all the young people were playing volleyball.

My Aunty Sarah whispered to me, "Good, write it down."

Tūtū Kipi began her story and these are her actual words. I wish tape recorders were in use during that time.

Interview with Tūtū Kipi, June 7, 1946, 2:41 p.m.

I ka wā ma mua, noho au i kēia wahi i ka manawa 'ōpiopio ana nō. Ma hope aku, male au i ke kāne a noho me ia i Ho'ōpūloa. 'O ia ho'i 'o ka inoa pololei 'o Kaumuloa. Ma hope au ha'i aku iā 'oe (i ka mo'olelo 'o Kaumuloa.) I kēia manawa 'o Ho'ōpūloa.

Noho mākou i laila a i loko o ka makahiki 'umikūmāiwa iwakāluakūmāono, iho mai ka pele mai uka. Pau nā kauhale i 'ai 'ia na ka ahi, me ka uhi 'ia me ka lava a komo nō i loko o ke kai. Holo mākou ma kēia 'ao'ao e pakele mai i ka ahi. Ho'okahi nō iho 'ana, a komo i loko o ke kai. Nui nō nā pilikia, akā, no Pele ka 'āina. Nāna nō i hana, a nāna nō ka lawe.

Ne'e mākou ma kēia 'ao'ao. Komo mai ke aupuni a kūkulu hale no mākou. Kahi mau 'ohana ne'e nō lākou i uka. A kekahi 'ohana, no ka maka'u, holo lākou i Honolulu e noho ai. 'O mākou, aia nō ke noho nei ma kēia wahi. 'O ia ka'u mo'olelo i hiki i kēia wahi 'o Miloli'i.

I loko o ka makahiki 'umikūmāwalukanaiwakūmāwalu o Pepeluali, lā 'elima (February 5, 1898) nui ka pilikia o kēia wahi. I kēlā manawa 'ōpiopio nō au.

Loa'a mākou ke kai ho'ē'e a mikimiki pū. 'Ike 'oe i kēlā lae i waho, a 'o Laeloa nō 'o ia. Ma kēlā lae a hiki pau loa he kauhale wale nō. 'A'ohe alanui holo 'ia ke ka'a. He alanui hele wāwae wale nō.

I ka manawa i mimiki ke kai, 'o nā hale po'e wa'a me nā mea lawai'a, pau i ka lilo i ka kai. Koe nō kēlā halepule Kalawina, kēlā po'e kumu paina i kai, ka pā hale kula ma kai aku, ma laila kēia halepule. Ho'okahi nalu nui i pi'i mai, hāpai i kēia halepule a waiho kokoke ma kēlā pā pōhaku. 'A'ohe ho'okahi papa pukaaniani i nōhāhā. 'O nā kū pahu kahi i lawe 'ia e ke kai. Kani kēia pele a hiki ka mālie o ke kai.

Nā wahi a pau, kohu mea ua holoi 'ia a ma'ema'e.

He kupunakāne, a ua o'o nō 'o ia. Hele a hō'ili'ili i nā po'e a hui me ia. 'Ōlelo 'o ia iā lākou, "ua nele kākou ka hale a me nā pono a pau. Ua ho'opakele 'ia kākou mai ka 'ino a mai ka make. 'O ke Akua nui ma ka lani me Kona aloha nui loa iā kākou i ho'opakele iā kākou mai ka make. 'Akā, ua waiho 'ia kēia ke'ena hale, 'o ia ho'i, ka halepule.

Kūlou kākou a pau loa e mahalo kākou i ke Akua ma ka lani no ka ho'opakele iā kākou. 'O kēia wale nō ka hale i waiho 'ia. Pehea lā, he 'ailona paha kēia no kākou. E pule kākou.

> E ke Akua ma ka lani
>
> Ke kūlou ha'aha'a nei mākou iā 'oe.
>
> Ua ho'opakele 'oe iā mākou mai ka 'ino
>
> 'Akā, ua hana 'oe a ma'ema'e ka 'āina.
>
> No ka mea, nāu nō ka honua a me ka lani.
>
> Ke mahalo nei iā 'oe. Nāu nō e lako mai nā pono no mākou.
>
> Ke nonoi nei me ka ha'aha'a e ho'omaika'i iā mākou a pau loa, ke 'ākoakoa nei ma kēia ke'ena hale.
>
> Nāu nō kēia hale, 'akā ke komo nei mākou i loko no kēia pō. Ke nāpo'o nei ka lā. Nāu nō e pale i nā mea 'ino e hō'eha ai iā mākou. Mahalo nui e ka Mākua nui i loko o ka lani."

Me kēia pule komo ka poʻe i loko o ka hale. ʻAʻole hoʻokahi leo o ka poʻe. Ua hele lākou a makaʻu. I ka nāpoʻo ʻana o ka lā, ke nonoho nei ka poe me nā ʻohana. Nānā mai a nānā aku.

ʻO nā kamaliʻi, uē nei no ka pōloli a me ka makewai. ʻO nā makuahine, ke pāpā nei iā lākou e hoʻomanawanui a hiki ka ao ʻana o kahi lā.

I kēlā manawa nō, ʻike kēia kupunakāne i ke kukui ke iho nei mai ma uka. ʻŌlelo ʻo ia i nā poʻe kāne ma laila, "Auē he aha lā kēia?" Pehea lā, he mea ʻino paha?ʻ ʻOi nānā aku lākou a kokoke kēia kukui, a lohe lākou i ka ō mai o ka leo. Auē, ʻo ka ʻohana nō o uka. Ua lawe mai nei lākou i ʻai, wai inu, a me nā pono no ka poʻe ʻohana o kēia nei. Nui nō hoʻi ka hauʻoli. Kūhea kēia kupuna e hoʻomaikaʻi i kēia makana i lawe ʻia mai nei. Pau ka pule, hoʻomaka lākou e ʻai. Hānai mua ʻia nā kamaliʻi a nā mākua ka hope. A ʻo ia ka moʻolelo.

TRANSLATION: *In the olden days I lived here and I was young at that time. After a while I married a husband from Hoʻōpūloa. The right name is Kaumuloa. Later I will tell you the story of Kaumuloa. Now it is known as Hoʻōpūloa.*

We lived there in the year 1926 and lava came from the uplands. All the houses were burnt and covered with lava and then the lava entered into the sea. We ran to the other side where we would be safe from the fire. The lava went right down and entered the ocean. So much trouble and yet the land belongs to Pele. She made [the land] and she [can] take it away.

We moved to the other side, then the government came in and started to build houses for us. Some of the other families moved to the uplands. The other families, because they were so scared, moved to Honolulu and that's where they live. As for us, we're still living here and this is the story and the reason we came to Miloliʻi.

In the year 1898 on February 5, there was big trouble at this place and I was young at that time.

That's when a big tidal wave came up. You see that point outside there? We call that Laeloa, that's the name of that point. From that point there were all houses. Never had roads for cars to run on, only trails.

At the time of the tidal wave, all the people's houses, canoes, and fishing equipment were taken by the sea. The only thing that was left was the

Kalawina church. Those pine trees down there where the school is and below that, that's where the church was. One huge wave came up. It carried this church and placed it near that stone wall. Not one board was broken and windows were not shattered. Even the foundation was taken. The bell kept ringing until the sea calmed down.

All the places, when you looked at them, looked like they were scrubbed clean. There was an elderly man at that time. He gathered all the people with him and told them they were now without home, without everything they have. "It's all gone, but your lives were saved from death because there is a great God in heaven who loves you and protects you from death. And yet, this building is left which is the church. Let us all bow our heads and thank the great God in heaven for saving us because this is the only house that is left. I wonder if this is a sign for us. Let us pray.

Our Father in heaven

We are bowing with humble hearts to you.

You saved us from [evil] and yet you made the land clean

Because you own the earth and the heavens.

We thank you. You will provide us with [all we need].

We humbly ask you to bless all of us who are gathered here in this church.

This house belongs to you and we are staying in it for the night. The sun is going down. It's for you to take away all the bad and all the hurt from us. Thank you, oh great God in heaven."

With this prayer the people entered, and no one made a sound because they were so scared. The sun was now setting, and the people were sitting here with their families looking after each other. As for the children, they were crying because they were hungry and thirsty. Mothers and fathers tried to cool them down and told them to wait till the next day.

At that time this elderly man saw lights coming down from the uplands. He told the menfolks, "I wonder what this is, whether it's something dead or not." They watched the lights until they came near, and then they heard the call of voices. They kept looking and they said, "Alas! That's our family from the uplands!"

The family brought food and water for them and things to keep them warm. There was a lot of gladness. Later, this elderly man gathered the people all together and prayed to thank God for all the blessings. After the prayer, the people began to eat. First they fed the children, and the older people ate last. And this is the story.

This story was so touching that tears just streamed down my face. Even the other kūpuna who were sitting there had the same feelings I had.

The way she told this story, you almost could visualize what happened at that time. This date was kept as a reminder of what the sea can do. Anyway, Aunty Kapeka sang a song about that day; the words and tune were just beautiful.

The only thing this kupuna told me is that she hopes young people will enjoy what they have treasured all their lifetime. To me it was an honor that they shared their knowledge with me. I didn't dream that I would become one of the ʻohana.

The others also told me some stories and showed me some places of interest. As for the other stories, I have them all.

Good-bye and aloha.

JUNE 1946, MILOLIʻI

Dear Diary,

This morning looks real nice and I think I'll go nose around south of the schoolhouse. Anyway, I'll go make me some sandwiches, an orange, and a bottle of water to take along with me.

Today I am going to walk that trail along the beach and see the sights and how far I can go. Also, I'm taking my ʻopihi bag and knife. Maybe I can get some ʻopihi on the way. Well, got to go now and I'm taking you along so I can tell you what's on the way. So I'll see you on the trail…

Hello Diary,

I am now at some area where it is kind of far from the beach. Back some ways I passed the last house and some graves high above the cliff overlooking the sea below. I have a strange feeling that there is much more to know.

The trail now goes over the lava. Although it is now about nine o'clock in the morning, I can feel the heat while walking on the trail. Ahead I can see a grove of trees and what looks like a wooden step. Anyway, the trail seems to lead to that area.

Where I'm resting and writing to you is under this kiawe tree. It looks like a very old tree, and I think if it could talk I think it would have lots to talk about. It must have seen many feet, both old and young, passing or resting under here in the shade of this tree. What a secret. I wish it could talk and tell me all the wonderful things that I don't know about.

I'm looking down along the shoreline and the water is so calm and blue. I can see two canoes out there from the village. Oh well, I better start going or I'll never get back by sundown.

JUNE 11, 1946, MILOLIʻI

Dear Diary,

Today is a holiday and there is no school here in the village. My legs are so sore from that walk I did yesterday. I walked all the way to Kapuʻa Bay. I guess from climbing up and down those rocks to look at something unusual my knees and thighs are just really hurting. Anyway, I saw some interesting sights on the way. By studying and observing them, they must be some heiau or kūʻula and burial grounds. I'll try and ask some people I have known here. Perhaps they can tell me more. I came across a lot of graves on a hill overlooking the sea. It seems like a family graveyard because of the way the graves were set. I came across three sand bays. The second bay looks like it must have been a village. Lots of old house foundations around.

The third bay had only two houses standing there. The house on the Kohala side is about to fall. It seems like no one lived in it for a long time. On the Kaʻū side is a cattle pen, and next to it there's a little house and another little house on its side. It looks as though people still live in it. But what happened to them? Gee, I wish I knew how many miles it is from this village to the third bay. It was so beautiful there that I hated to leave the place. So quiet and peaceful. Only the waves splashing on the beach. I wish I could live there. Anyway, I stayed a while before I started back to Miloliʻi. The sun was going down pretty fast. I hope I get home before it gets dark…

Home at Miloli'i School, 8:15 p.m.

Aunty Sarah and family are all in bed, and I thought I'd sit a while and tell you all about my hike today. Boy, I wish I took my camera, but I forgot it here on the table. It was a nice walk, only wish I had someone who knows those places. Maybe they could tell me some interesting things that I don't know about. Oh well, next time.

Right now, I'm so tired that I think I could sleep twenty-four hours. Anyway, sitting there at that third bay, I kept thinking, I wonder how many feet have walked or played here on this sand?

I can't think of any other words to describe these areas I have seen today. So peaceful, and everything looks so real. You know what, I'm going back there again. But with someone who knows the place. Perhaps I can learn more and also the mysterious good feeling I experienced today.

Well Diary, I'm so tired so I'll close now and lay myself down to sleep. So till then, aloha.

September 25, 1946, Wednesday 8:40 a.m., Kapu'a*

Kapu'a, I love you. Yes, the very first time I visited Kapu'a, I fell in love with the place. This is the hometown of my husband, where he was raised. His place of birth was at Kaupō at least a quarter mile down the seacoast from this area. But his roots began here at Kapu'a.

I feel that everything at this place is just immaculate, or what I mean is, it is so peaceful and clean. The beach and water look so clean that you feel as though you're really wanted, and not a stranger.

The bay itself, so clean, with its sandbank so high. To get down into the bay, just roll yourself down and have all the fun you want. I have done it, and it is great fun. Only, I had some time getting the sand out of my long, long hair. Just digging my feet into the sand and letting the sand run between my toes makes me wonder how many tiny feet, small or large, had done the same thing I'm doing now.

It must have been a pretty picture gone into the past. I can almost visualize the years that have gone by. Yet it seems it was only yesterday that this all happened. Well, one can always dream about it and paint a lovely picture in one's mind of the days that have disappeared.

LATER

This morning, after an early breakfast, Abel and I went for a walk. He wanted to show me the hōlua slide, the ponds, the pōhaku kuʻihili, Mahana, Pākaʻalana, and another big pond in the back of their house, the healing pond Haleola.

He told me when they were sick or had a fever or some kind of illness, they were taken to this pond to be submerged there, and that helped to cure the sickness they had. It somehow reminded me of my village, as we do have a place like this called Kapahukapu. The only difference is, the tide has to be low before you can enter the water. Oh well, I guess every other place has its own custom.

To really get to know this place, I think I have to spend more time here, visiting all the areas.

We left there and started back to where we were camping. Guess what! Frank and Abbie Paulo came on the canoe to be with us. It was so nice to see them come over to join us. Lots of joking, laughing, and making remarks about our honeymoon. Anyway, it was fun to listen to all the silly jokes going back and forth with the two men and Abbie.

It is nearly lunch time so I better quit writing and go see what we are having. We got poi, rice, some fried fish, raw fish, and ʻopihi. Abbie brought some poi and dry ʻōpelu and a bowl of wana. Boy, we'll sure have a feast. Well, I'll see you later. So long!

Publisher's note: This camping trip was Mona and Abel's honeymoon.

SEPTEMBER 26, 1946, THURSDAY 9:27 A.M., KAPUʻA

Another morning and day and we're still here at Kapuʻa. Abel and Frank left camp and headed south with their cast nets. Be back by or after lunch. They went net-casting yesterday and came back with lots of fish. We roasted some for our lunch, fried some for dinner, and still had some more fried fish with our breakfast. ʻOno, ʻono! Abbie went for some more ʻopihi. When she gets back, she and I will go dive for some wana. Right now I just finished preparing some sandwiches and cooked rice and other food stuffs for lunch. However, I try to find time to get back to my diary. I have listened to the stories of the lifestyle, how my husband and his family lived here. The hardships, happy days, and the sad, gloomy times. The very first word that came into my mind was "compassion." Pity and tears would just well up in my eyes and overflow. Why? Because I can almost see the hardships that this family has endured all during their lifetime here in Kapuʻa. As I sit here on the sand writing this episode, I keep imagining all that took place here. I for one was raised almost similar to the lifestyle of this family. The only difference was my family were farmers and I was taught the lifestyle of a farmer, kula, or the beach. So I am not a stranger to this lifestyle.

Still, it does not compare. It can never be compared to what this family has suffered through their lifetime.

There are so many memories for this family about Kapuʻa and places all along the seacoast. They were fishing people and that was their livelihood. Their father died here in the water close to Kapuʻa and was never found. A good swimmer, as I was told, but no one knows what happened. Many other events, both good and bad, took place here.

Yesterday evening, my husband and I, and Frank and Abbie Paulo (the couple who came about lunchtime to join us on our honeymoon) sat on the sandbank to watch the sunset.

My husband and Frank disappeared for a while. They later came back with four green (or young coconuts) which they offered to Abbie and me, a coconut each. Then my husband broke one coconut and offered it to me and said, "Eat."

I looked at the coconut and I thought it was rather strange. Where was the shell and the water supposed to be? There was nothing, just the fleshy part of the husk. So I asked my husband, "What kind of coconut is this and are you both pulling tricks on us?" Abbie knew what it was and began to eat her coconut. I just held my coconut and looked at my husband, who had a wide grin.

Then he explained, "This is what we call the pulu ʻono coconut. There's only two trees in the Kapalilua district. One tree grows here on the Kaupiko land and the other at Miloliʻi (Kalihi)."

This coconut you can eat from the skin until the inside. So I said, "But that's funny, there's no shell or water like the other kind of regular coconuts."

Then he said, "Yeah, that's how this coconut is. Everybody who comes here like take the seed for plant, but it never grows. Even my mother. She tried to plant, but it never grew. When you break the dry ones, all you find is husk all the way. No shell, meat, or water. Somebody said it may have come from the South Pacific Islands. When I was stationed on Guam, Guadalcanal, and the other islands, I ask the natives about this kind of coconut.

Those who understand English said they never heard of it and don't have any such kind of coconut. Maybe Tahiti or Tonga Islands may have, but they were not sure."

The taste of this coconut was just like the regular young coconuts with spoon meat. I ate the whole coconut except the stem. But it left a stain on my teeth for two days. It took a vigorous brushing to get that reddish stain off. Really, it looked real weird to look in the mirror and see how your teeth look. Goofy! It was really sweet. Anyway, when I go back to Hilo I would like to take one back for my mother to taste and ask her if she knows or has heard anything of such a coconut. This is very new to me. I never in my life heard of such a coconut.

Perhaps someday, I may run into someone who might know more of this strange coconut. Imagine, pulu 'ono coconut.

What an experience, but it's a good one. Well, it is nearly 12:15 p.m. and my husband and Frank will be back to camp from fishing. Abbie went below to pound for 'opihi and I had the chore to fix us lunch.

I think I have to quit writing now because I can see Abel and Frank coming into our camp. My goodness, they are really loaded with fish and 'opihi. Anyway, lunch is ready, and Abbie is also coming back. Wow, looks like a lot of work. Clean fish and 'opihi. Aloha for now.

So I'll stop writing now, and continue perhaps later.

SEPTEMBER 27, 1946, FRIDAY 5:20 P.M., STILL AT KAPUʻA

Well, I think this will be our last night at Kapuʻa, as we're about running out of ice for our food and fish stuffs. Tomorrow morning we're breaking camp and starting back for Miloliʻi where we left our car.

Frank and Abbie live there. So nice for them to come over to join us. We really enjoyed ourselves being here at Kapuʻa. Borrowed my brother-in-law's boat and a small canoe that belongs to Abel's stepfather to get here. Abel and I will leave for Hilo about tomorrow evening. Abel is a fisherman on a large flag line boat; me, I'll go back to work at the pier.

It is now evening, we're through with dinner, and the men folks are with their beer. Abbie is digging in the sandbank for shells. I found a chunk of sponge. I'll save that. Maybe I will have a baby someday, I hope, and can use this chunk of sponge for its bath.

Well, we're sitting here on the sandbank watching the sunset. The colors are just out of this world. It's so magnificent and beautiful. Especially with the clouds that sail or drift by in every shape you can imagine. Abel showed me the Cock's Comb and Tail on the island in the bay (Lepeamoa Island). Where I come from (Nāpoʻopoʻo) we have a Lepeamoa too, and there's a legend connected with it. I wonder if this one has a story?

Many questions passed through my mind. Most of them are unanswered because there are no words to describe the feeling. I guess these will be only memories which always remain silent. Watching what God Almighty has created and set there for many to see and appreciate. Anyway, the couple of days we've been here, I've watched the clouds form as if someone is sweeping them. The sunsets are so beautiful with their red, orange, and golden colors. Even to see the bright blue flashes as the sun sets into the horizon, that was something.

The clouds and the colors, they really can fascinate anyone, even me. Funny thing, it sort of gave me the inspiration to write a song while watching them drift by, to put down on paper what I see, hear, or dream. So this is how I got the title of my diary and now a song which I just thought about.

"Clouds of Memories" is born. So before I forget that inspiration, I'd better hurry and get the feeling and words down on paper before it really gets dark.

Clouds of Memories

Drifting with the winds
On clouds of memories
The wind that blows
When my memories grow

My dreams are built
On clouds of memories
On a starlit night
With the moon so bright

The soft wind blows
A gentle breeze through the trees
My hopes and dreams
I give to you

Drifting with the wind
On clouds of memories
The wind that blows
And my memories grow
Drifting, drifting, drifting
On clouds of memories
Drifting, drifting, drifting

Finally completed and we're all going for a short walk across the bay and back to camp to turn in for the night. I have to close now and say aloha till my next entry. Aloha and it is now almost 7:45 p.m.

MAY 9, 1946–1957, 8:30 A.M., NAS HOUSING

Dear Diary,

Today is the happiest day of my life. We have a newborn baby son. I pick him up from the hospital first thing tomorrow morning. Kealoha called me to give me the good news. Charley and Kealoha are giving us this baby for our very own. I can't have any children of my own.

Abel has gone down to the dry docks because today the boat he will be running for flag line fishing will be christened and slid down into the water. Abel will be the skipper for this fishing vessel. However, since the baby was named Kaimana this boat is also being named *Kaimana* after our baby. It means "the power of the sea" or "diamond."

Abel has come a long way, fishing most of his lifetime. He started at the very early age of six. At age nine his father fell from a canoe and attempted to swim to shore. He did manage to get up on a high rock, but at that same moment a large wave came up and washed him away. A search party of families, friends, fishermen, and the police came to help, but no luck. His father was a good swimmer and the family could not understand why he didn't make it. Being drunk he may have drowned and washed in some cave where he got stuck. He was never found again. After a couple of years, Abel's mother got married again. His father's incident took place on May 29, 1929, near Moku Naiʻa almost to Kapuʻa Bay where they resided.

As for Abel, he fished to help out the family until he was in his twenties. During World War II he was drafted into the U.S. Army in 1940. He got an honorable discharge in November of 1945. He returned home, back to fishing, and we got married. We adopted a wonderful baby boy and he is my world of joy.

There were other fishing boats Abel skippered until he was transferred to this brand new fishing boat, the *Kaimana*. Sometimes when he was short of crew, I would have to fill in until his crew came back.

"Flag line" is deep-sea fishing where they travel many miles from shore and along the coastline. Catches are big, but money-wise it is not too keen. Anyway, Abel fished until the later part of 1957 when we decided to come back to Kona due to my health. I had to go to a warm climate. In a way, I was glad, because my mom was sick and there was no one to tend the coffee farm. My dad works for the Territorial Highway Department as a surveyor and highway inspector. My sisters and brother are married and have families of their own.

Anyway, all of them work and seldom have time to help at the coffee farm. The piggery had to be taken care of and so did the taro patch. Boy, so much to do, but I enjoy it as I like farming.

For a while Abel did a little fishing on the canoe at Nāpoʻopoʻo, but only to put fish on the table for home use or for sharing with other families.

He was then hired to work for Ideal Construction Company as a laborer. A year later, Sure Save hired him to work as a janitor. He worked at this job for nearly a year, when he was promoted to stock clerk. Later, a few years before retiring, he was promoted to assistant manager of the produce department. This position he held until he had to retire due to a heart condition. By this time, he had worked over nineteen years and eight months before he retired.

History of Abel Pepe Kaliliaku Kahele: Father's full name: John Halena Kahele; Mother: Maria Haleaka Nunuha Kahele; Brothers: John Haena, William Komaka, Peter Kahuakaʻe, Henry Nahinu; Sisters: Ellen Kalawaeʻa, Hannah Koanohano.

JUNE 12, 1971

It seems like we will be going back to Miloliʻi to live out our declining years. I am not too happy about it as I can't stand that terrible heat. Furthermore, there's nothing good growing in that lot. I know I'm going to have lots to do, the stones to be picked up and the yard to be put in order before I really can get something growing.

I love farming and if I have to live down here, I'll make those rocks and rocky land bloom. I know there's a lot of work involved, but that's the chance I've got to take.

The shack is already built and soon we will build another better house. Anyway, plans are now in process and we are only waiting for the plans from the contractor (Hicks). I already got the building permit and am just waiting for the contractor.

SEPTEMBER 26, 1980

Dear Diary,

Today is my first day teaching at this school, Hale O Ho'oponopono (House to do right). It is a school supported by Kamehameha Schools.

This is a school for kids from Konawaena who are dropouts, slow students, or wayward students. I am a teacher of Hawaiian language, history, and culture. Even though I have been told most of these high school kids are disrespectful, I found it quite different. They treated me with respect, as a friend and someone they could really look up to. I felt like I was a mother or grandmother to them.

There were times they would come to me with their problems, from home life to school activities. There were times that I got emotional, especially when they poured out how they were being treated at home and at school by some ornery teachers.

SEPTEMBER 28, 1980

Some of the students have problems, from sex abuse to whipping, and chores that have to be done almost all night. By the time they get to their homework, they are so tired they fall asleep and homework is never done and brought back to school. Some wanted to commit suicide, others got involved with stealing, smoking in school, fighting back with teachers and being suspended.

I can see the hurt, neglect, prejudice, and frustrations. Poor souls. I wish I could really do something better for them. The only advice I can give them is to walk with Jesus, because He is always there to lift you up. Another thing, even though things are tough with you, don't give up on school. Get that diploma no matter how hard it is. That diploma can renew you all your lifetime; I mean, good jobs and a good name for yourself. Build yourself a good future.

_ ꝰ_

OCTOBER 9, 1980

You know, Diary, two girls approached me with tears and so much tension. They needed to talk to someone they could trust. I felt so sorry and I told them let's wait until lunch time, then I could listen to them. They were there along with eight others. What they told me was sickening. I was angry, and oh boy, I just couldn't answer them right away. I sat quietly and just listened, filled with emotions. All I could do was stand up and look in their faces with eyes so searching and my mouth speechless. They waited for me to say something. I just couldn't say anything but tried to hug them and let them pour out the tears that needed to be poured out. I just couldn't shed any tears but was so angry about how these young people were treated.

_ ꝰ_

OCTOBER 22, 1980

Before school is over for the season or whatever, I'll try my best to help them. Oh, we have some real hardcore cases that none of the staff members want to put up with. So gardening, some carpentry work, and a lot of lectures. Out of five hard ones, only one made it. The other four were sent to Job Corps.

I'd better stop now because I have lessons to prepare for tomorrow, which is good old Friday. Next week is test time. So aloha and see you later.

_ ꝰ_

NOVEMBER 12, 1980

Dear Diary,

I really am hurt to see how these students are treated, even by some of our staff members. I don't have any problems with them. Even the hard ones the staff claim are out of hand, with me I don't see anything wrong. All they need is someone to share their hurt, misunderstanding, and the love they most need. Aloha.

_ ꝰ_

NOVEMBER 12, 1980

Dear Diary,

Today I am so uneasy with some of our staff members. I wish they would stop abusing these children. They come to school to learn but how will they learn if some of the staff members favor some and leave the others on the side? There's no love.

JANUARY 6, 1981

Dear Diary,

I have been hired by the Department of Education to teach at Hōnaunau Elementary School. I teach Hawaiian studies, history, and culture. It is a good outlet to share the language with all ethnic groups. My reasons are many. Most of all, I want right pronunciation of names of places and an understanding of their meanings. Fact is, here in the islands, Hawaiian names are in great use. The language is another thing.

Imagine: at one time the Hawaiian language was abolished from the schools. We couldn't even speak to each other. If caught, you were made to write on paper 100 times the words, "I must not speak Hawaiian in school." Only English. We had a hard time, and even some Japanese kids had a hard time learning English.

Today they want you to teach the language in the schools. Well that's another point the Hawaiians have won. I like it at this school, but some teachers resent the idea of our kind of studies. The principal is a nice, understanding man, and I get along with him and some of the other teachers. Well, I think I'm going to like working here. So wish me luck in my daily work. Aloha.

AUGUST 12–13, 1983, SATURDAY, CAMPING AT KAPUʻA

The kids really enjoyed the story time, but Daisy had so many questions. Abel didn't know about this story, and was so happy to hear it. He wondered where I got this story. I told him, "From your mother." Well, the kids are crawling into their blankets. Now they are looking up to the clear sky trying to count the stars. Abel is throwing some more logs on the fire. It seems like Pala, Daisy, and Bradley are fast asleep. Tracy is still up just about falling asleep. Randy is already sleeping. That leaves Abel and myself.

A well-spent afternoon and evening for the kids. While I'm trying to brush all the sand out from our hāli'i, Abel is getting us both cups of coffee. Well, we're just about settled for the night.

It is now 10:00 p.m. and all the mo'opuna are bedded down on the sand. Just Abel and myself, up sipping coffee. Boy, this is great, fire glowing so brightly and I'm trying to write by firelight. We're both talking of days gone by. This is what I want very much to jot down while Abel is reminiscing about the past.

ABEL: You know, honey, when I was a small boy, we never had much, yet we all was happy. My father, all he do was fish for our living. When I think of my mother, she don't know how to swim until she died. And yet when my father go out fishing my mother had to go out with him or else he beat her up. He was a real mean father. Sometimes when he hit her, boy we like hit his head with the stick. Outside when we go 'ōpelu, my mother throw the ka 'ai, me, I hold canoe, and my father look in the glass box. If my mother no throw the palu quick he turn around, grab the hoe from my hand and hit her. I jump on him, pound, pound his head with my hand. I cry, cry, cry for my mother. More worse he grab me and my mother and throw us in the water and say, "A na ka manō e 'ai mai iā 'ōlua." My mother grab the side of the canoe and hang on. He like hit her with the hoe. But we hang on and every time I have to dodge when he swing the hoe. Sometimes when I think about that, just like I still can see what he do to us. But that's our living. No matter how hard.

My father was so mean that's why my older brother wen run away and he never come back to Kapu'a until he make. Even Peter and William, same thing, they take off because my father mean, mean. Only Kalawae'a the one who stay home take care us when my mother gotta go fishing with my father.

You know that's why she no can read and write. Poor thing. Even the time she hānau to Kepani. My father tie my sister with the rope and hang her up. She scream, scream, my father slap her mouth. My mother go near for help, he grab my mother, throw her outside the house. My sister hang up and that's how Kepani went born. Dirty old man. But that's still my father. As for Hano, my aunty from Waipi'o wen take her for hānai. But she was big already. So only us stay.

The worst time, when the Japanese boat come over here, he know them. He go drink up sake with them. When he come home drunk, my mother put the poi and the fish for him to eat. He stand up lick my mother for nothing. Sometimes we cry, cry. Kaluahalawa them come over for help, he like lick them. He was something [sniffles]. Well, that's those days. Gee, if this sand can talk maybe can tell you all the story over here.

MONA: All during that time, Abel, when you folks lived, how did you folks get what you need? I mean like food and other things?

ABEL: Well, you see, those days we only fish 'ōpelu from Kaulanamauna to Miloli'i. Every place we go, maybe we stay about two weeks or sometimes more. The 'ōpelu we kaha, salt, and dry. That's all we do, day in and day out, till we dizzy only look at the 'ōpelu. Then when we get so many ka'au, we pack 'em in the barrel, then my father and my brothers load 'em on the canoe and take to Ho'ōpūloa wharf. When the ship come in, then take our fish. Used to get the Pākē store Honolulu.

MONA: Do you still remember their names? Those Pākē you folks send your fish?

ABEL: Yeah, Wing Hong Young and C.Q. Yee Hop. My father order flour, poi, sugar, cracker by the case. But the most he order is the salt, by the bags, big load. When the ship come back that's when bring all our ukana. That's how the old man Ka'ana'ana went give or lend my father one small place Ho'ōpūloa for build one hale ukana. Because we get too much ukana, so we gotta wait till mālie the kai then can haul the ukana. You know, today when I think back, really I pity my brothers, Mama, and my father. They sure work hard for our living. Poor thing. That's why today I cry, because today I can give my parents all the help, and they no need work hard. But they no more today. Maybe over here would get good house. Who knows. Anyway that's how we live.

MONA: Daddy, what kind of games did you folks play, or did you play at all?

ABEL: Yeah, when my father in the mood we used to go get the lau niu and pull each other down the sandbank. All this place the sandbank high. That's the only time my father play with us. Most of the time we swim. Only when we went to school we learn how to play ball, play kinikini, and play master. Otherwise we gotta go fishing whether we like it or not.

But when my father wen make, we was stranded. But my mother and my brothers still go 'ōpelu until was coming more hard then Peter wen go work on the boat. And William, because he kolohe, wen take i'a, him. That's when he went Nāpo'opo'o, he used to go with Naha family, fishing. By and by we hear he get wahine.

Kalaluhi them was still staying with us. Aki was fishing, too. Kalawae'a went marry John David and stay Ke'ei. Hano married Filipino and stay Ka'ū. So leave only us. By that time Mama already going with the old man Kalani.

Me and Nahinu went Ka'ū. From Miloli'i School then Hano wen take me Ka'ū. We stay way up Kilea and I come down go Nā'ālehu School till seventh grade I quit school. That's the time the NRA WPA job wen come up. So we stay Wai'ōhinu old school and we go work on the road. Mama and the old man came Ka'ū stay. By that time they had Kepani, Taketu, Kaihe, and Kamakakoa. Then I wen get drafted and went in the army. Nahinu, he volunteer and follow me. Most of the boys Miloli'i was working Ka'ū. Antone them, too.

The old folks then came back over here to stay for a while then they wen move to Miloli'i because Uncle Kukulu told them they better move near Miloli'i because the war was getting more hot. When Peter came back that's when he brought Becky and Peter Boy. Becky, I pity her. I think she wen stay longer over here than Maria. That's another one who wen suffer, too, with the hard life. Walk to Miloli'i and come home. Some too Peter for lick and hana 'ino his wife. You know, how many time she and Peter Boy ran hide behind here on the a'ā. Really, my brother was something. Anyway they wen move to Miloli'i more first than the old folks.

Most of the time we go Miloli'i fishing and holoholo.

You know, the old man Kaluahawa and Kaliliaku when they see Franklino, they call him 'o kūkae.' Why, I don't know. Well that was those days. But when I think back, really, how the hell we came through.

MONA: I think that's quite a hell of a lot that you went through during your growing up days. Yes, we have so much to not take for granted. You have come a long way.

ABEL: Yeah, Honey, that's why I said to myself: if I ever get wife, I'll never, never lay my hands on her. I see how my father do to my mother, and my brothers how they lick their wives and all the kids screaming, that was the end. So you see us two, we stay together over thirty-five years, little more forty years, I never do that to you. Anyway I get no reason to do that to you. I know I do many wrongs behind your back. Every time I think about that I like kick my own ass. Really.

You made me a decent man. Made me rich in money, love, home, partner, and all what I get today. Although us two no more our own kids, God was so good to us. I know all the trouble you went through, doctor after doctor, only for get baby, but no luck. If not for Charley and Kealoha, us two no more baby. But we lucky we get our own son. Now we get Dolly, a lawa loa. Although us wen take care plenty kamaliʻi. Sometimes I think I wonder if they know how much we love them. Me, I don't know how to pay you back. Because if you was somebody else, I don't think you would care for my family. But you took them to your heart like your own. That's why I love you too much. Nobody knows how much we love all the family, maybe someday they will understand.

MONA: Daddy, in a way I am glad I could do what I can for them. Only I wish that I could do more. Being brought up alone and not knowing what it was to have a big family in the same house, to me that was something new. As my tūtū always said, "If you love everybody and help them, God will love you the more. Like how you live Him and serve Him, the same He will do for you."

Maybe that is why we could never have children of our own. Because there were others who needed our love too. I didn't come from a rich tūtū. Our living was weaving hats to trade for food and clothing. That's how I got my education, from weaving. Another thing, we raised pia and sold it for five dollars a bag. The pumpkin we sold to the ʻōpelu fishermen for two dollars a bag. Sometimes we traded the pumpkin for ʻōpelu, and that's the way we got our fish.

When we go down the beach from kula, my tūtū used to make four or five hīnaʻi to catch hinalea. This type of fishing, we do when the wana is fat, because we use the niho and shells as bait for the hīnaʻi. Sometimes if the puhi don't go in the trap, by the time we get to go home we have about one kaʻau or more. My tūtū would share some fish with the other tūtū at the beach.

Well, come to think about it, we did not pick ourselves for mates, but God Almighty put you and I together. That's why we have a good life and a happy one. We both shared our ups and downs but we still came out in our best. We have always put God in all our doings or ahead of us. Today, you and I are still as one. As for children, we have moʻopuna of every kind and we're still with kamaliʻi regardless.

ABEL: By the way, Ma, you never talked about your family much.

MONA: I never spoke too much about my family because I never lived with them much. Only when I married you and my tūtū died that I got someone to go to: my mother, whom I love so much, and my father, whom I didn't know was not my own father. Put two and two together, that's why I went from hand to hand. To think the one who showed me love and care was his own mother Lokalia. My own mother could not care for me because my father could not see me in the same house.

When I was young my tūtū used to always say to me, "Even though aloha 'ole kou pāpā iā 'oe, aia nō kou makuahine. He aloha 'eha'eha 'o ia iā 'oe. 'Ā, 'o wau nō ho'i, mai 'oe ha'alele ia'u a hiki ku'u make 'ana. Makemake nō 'oe e ho'i me kou makuahine, aia 'oe. Hele 'oe ke kula, ho'ona'auao. 'A'ole like me a'u, 'ike 'ole i ke kākau a me ka heluhelu. 'O ia ka'u mea make-make au iā 'oe, mai 'oe, noho mai ke kula. 'Ike nō 'oe nā lima hana na'u i hō'ike'ike iā 'oe. A ho'omau aku nō 'oe. Aloha nui ka'u iā 'oe.

You know, sometimes I almost can hear her telling me these very words. There's so much hurt that I just don't want to talk about it. I know what it was to be hated. And that's what is hurting me today. But with God's love, I'm happy to have you, my children, mo'opuna, nephews, and nieces. Most of all, God Almighty.

ABEL: Well, you and I learned the hard way. I guess that's why, no matter what, we still can face the living and live our way.

MONA: You, your lifestyle was much harder than mine. Even though we didn't have much, we were happy. Just like you, same thing. The funniest thing is, when it came to our children, we just couldn't see them go through life like how we did. We tried to give them all we could. But yet, when you look, just like it's not enough. I guess this modern lifestyle has lots to do with it.

ABEL: You know, Ma, I give my sister-in-law credit for taking her children away from Miloli'i. I think that's the best thing Becky wen do. The kids wen get education. Today they all right. You look at these kids at Miloli'i, man, terrific. Just like what you said, you never going raise our kids at Miloli'i. Today, I see what you mean. I look at the village today, gee, little more they going marry brother and sister. Hoowee-u!

Well, looks like we are having company tonight as we can see the lights shining at the top of the coconut tree. Abel went for another cup of cof-fee, and I'll light another cigarette. What a peaceful night. Only the waves below us that are crashing on the shore, and of course the crickets. Haven't seen any kanapī tonight. I hope we don't have any around us.

Those car lights finally arrived at the entrance to the sand bay. Abel went to help guide them over the sand to a camping spot near his grandfather's grave. Wow, one truck and three Blazers. One of them is coming over to our camp. Anyway it's nice to have company, but for a while we were really enjoying the quiet and peace.

Perhaps if the sea is shaky we may have to head home for Miloli'i. By and by, if the water gets a little more rough, we won't be able to board the boat. Right now the boat is anchored outside the entrance of the bay. We'll see how it is. I guess we have to turn in for the night. So till my next episode, aloha.

Hello again. We're home. We had to leave Kapu'a early as it was getting rough. We just made it out of the bay. Had we stayed longer, maybe we wouldn't have made it. Abel and I were more worried for our mo'opuna because some of them are not good swimmers.

On our way home, I pointed out some places of interest, like Moku Nai'a, an island separated from the land. Showed them the 'ahi ko'a and explained to them what a ko'a meant. Daisy had one million questions to ask. In a way, when she does ask questions it means that she does have interest in what we're talking about. Abel pointed out where his father fell into the water and was never seen again. Again the questions bombarded us. Then we headed out to sea to catch aku. Caught one and the mo'opuna had fun watching it being pulled in. We had that aku for poke and soup. They sure ate all of it as if they never ate fish before. They felt as if they caught the fish.

We headed back to Okoe Bay and all along the coastline, at the same time telling the names of each place we passed until we got to the ramp. Daisy and Pala were more interested in Okoe and Omoka'a because they know the legend of why these places were so named.

Now we're finally at home, and the short camping trip is over. So much to talk about. They really enjoyed their trip, so much that they can't stop talking about it. Perhaps maybe someday we can go again and maybe spend more time at Kapela and walk down to the slide. Time will tell. The kids are left to go swimming and I guess that about filled their dreams and questions. So till then, aloha.

FEBRUARY 1985

Dear Diary,

Much as I miss teaching, I now have to stop and retire. My health is a problem, especially my right leg which is giving me such a problem. I really miss the kids at school, the teachers, and of course, the principal and all who are on the staff. They really treated me like I was their real grandmother. I was made to feel at ease and I love them so much. To them all my love and more:

Miss J. Tomono, Miss Sandra Yoshioka, Mrs. Helen Ikeda,
Mrs. Kimura, Mrs. Elaine Harai, Mrs. Nakano, Mrs. Kasumi,
Miss J. Rocha, Mrs. Elaine Regodor, Miss Thelma Ushiroda (Secretary),
Mr. Yoshiki, Mr. Imai, Mr. Ken Sugiyama, Mrs. Kadota, Mr. Kadota
Mrs. Masunaga, Mrs. Navas, Mrs. Brandt, Mr. Walter Kahiwa, Jr.
Mr. Kaneko, Mrs. Mitchell, Mr. Glen Matsumoto, Mr. Clinton Miller,
and Mr. Walter Kimura (Principal).

All these people made and played an important part in all the years I was at Hōnaunau School. So all these people, whoever helped me—and especially Thelma, who tried to get equipment I needed for my classes—to all of you all my aloha and I wish you all the best in this new future.

NOVEMBER 12, 1987

Dear Diary,

The crimes that we now have are countless. Crimes vary from domestic problems, firearms, murder, theft, and now an introduced crime which is from pot (marijuana), to drugs of all kinds. Many of these drugs were never heard of or known in the Islands before, but now we have them.

Well, to make things short, I am being made a consultant or counselor for our Hawaiian people who are in trouble. In other terms, a kupuna for the ho'oponopono system. To make right and create harmony. Truth and facts of intelligence are the main factors in the lifestyle of our people.

I have clients that I used to sometimes wonder about. Will they really adjust themselves as they have stated and promised? Oh, I hope and pray these clients will really abide by their words.

What's becoming of this world and the human race? Really, I don't understand. What more can be done? To me, I think greed, power, and money is the root of the stench of mankind.

Well, who knows? For myself, I know God the Heavenly Father is the only one who knows, gives, and takes away.

JANUARY 5, 1989

Dear Diary,

It has been a real thrill to be able to cope with things that have helped me along in my lifetime, working with people from all walks of life. You know, you get to learn many things and share the experiences of my lifestyle. I do have so much to offer. I hope my son and daughter and their children will grasp all the knowledge and wisdom I have to offer. Perhaps their lifestyle will be different when they get to be my age. Anyway, I hope they do, because this is their heritage and culture, and there is much they can gain by going over my notes that are left collecting dust.

JANUARY 26, 1989, 7:18 P.M.

Dear Diary,

Just got home from an all-day hearing on the Kapuʻa issue. Many individuals gave their testimony. Listening to them and their testimonies was kind of draining on my temper to a point that it nearly exploded. Especially with the statements made by an archaeologist who said that all his findings of the historic past seemed to be the same as found on all the island sites. I wonder: how can he claim the findings are the same, when the beach people were mostly fishing people and of different clans? The people from the upper lands are farmers and are of a different culture and also belong to clans. They are not the same. They have different habits as to how and whom they worship. I think the statement he made really stinks. Well, it is just now break time and I need to go to the bathroom so I'll talk to you later. (Ten minute break.)

Well, we're back again and still listening to all these non-meaning fools. I think all this is malarkey. But that's it, and much dirty politics is involved. Well, we'll see what the outcome will amount to. (Ten minute break.)

This break business is going to drag on. Looks like we won't be out of this hearing until after four. Nuts and lots of nuts.

Guess what? This hearing is finally over and we can now go home. Hurrah!

Gilbert* is taking Abel, me, and our friend Jonathan home. Really tired and hungry.

I guess when I get home maybe I have to do the cooking as usual. Oh well, this is it. I'll say good-bye for now as another day is passing by.

Well, I'm home now. While Gil and Jonathan are on the phone, I'll start dinner. I'll have some fried fish, oh, and Dolly has some buns and I'll go warm up the chili. Gil went to take Jonathan to meet his wife. So we'll wait till he gets back, then we'll eat. Kukuna and Luhi went with Gil for a ride.

Gil came back with some Chinese food. Well, we're all pau eat, and we're sitting around talking. Gil is leaving to go back to Kailua and everybody is heading for bed. Looks like another cold night. So good night and see you next time.

Publisher's note: Gilbert Kahele is Mona and Abel's hānai son.

FEBRUARY 25, 1989

Dear Diary,

This is another day. The countless chores around the house are just endless. Well, anyway, today I decided to straighten up and clean the front room. It was in such an upside-down sight.

Abel fixed the ceiling. He had taken part of it out to see where the leak was coming from as water was leaking so bad that we couldn't sleep in the room. Bedding got all wet. Anyway, the roof over that room was rotten and the holes had to be covered. Abel had it fixed. Hope it doesn't leak anymore.

Tonight I will sleep in that room. Sitting here on the back steps, gazing down below at the ocean. Thoughts of my childhood come floating before me. My family and school days and of course the endless farm work. From soybeans, coffee, taro, sweet potatoes, pia or starch, and for home use, chickens, pigs and vegetables for our table. All that hard work to survive in the world.

Now just me (the eldest) and my youngest sister are on this planet. As for our family, they all departed to be with the Great Maker up there in heaven. I guess we were left behind because we are still needed here to do the Lord's work.

So much has crossed my mind, and it is very sad.

Trends have changed so much that it is a pity. It made me think of what happened to Sodom and Gomorrah. I know the time is getting closer and closer, but we will be ready. It really sends chills up and down my back thinking of how much abuse has been caused in this world.

Oh well, I'd better get back and finish what I was doing. So I'll be with you perhaps tomorrow when I get home from church. Aloha.

MARCH 11, 1989, SATURDAY EVENING

Dear Diary,

Today is the longest day I've had for a long time. I am so mixed up, and oh, you name it, I've got it. I know the trials I'm going through, and it is not an easy street. So much is on my mind that sometimes I just want to scream my heart out.

I am full of worries, frustrations, and remorse over all that I could ever feel. The reasons are many.

I know my health is declining with the pains I'm having in my right leg, stomach, and chest. Sometimes I almost want to give up because when the pains come on, the only thing I can do is try not to think about it and keep myself busy by doing anything I can get my hands on to do. My fingers and right arm are giving me a bad time. At times, I almost cannot feel the objects in my hands or even write. My eyes are going bad, I know, because certain words I can't even read, or see, even with my glasses on.

I've spent many a sleepless night because I just can't find any comfort. So, what can I do, but think how much I am concealing from my family. I don't want to complain about any of my problems to them, for fear they might think I am useless. I know I am getting old, but I still have a mind all to myself.

So many times I've spent all my spare emptiness talking and complaining to our Father in heaven. I know He loves me because when I feel I want to do things, I know He is listening and helping me. But when I get so involved with my work, I let Him slip through me. It really is unthinkable sometimes.

Every time I hear my husband complain of his condition, I get so irritated that I just want to hurt him more with my biting words. The more he complains, the more I get disgusted. To me, I feel that he has all this self pity, and I get so frustrated just listening to him.

Many times I cannot reason with him, even when I speak our own language. He can never understand. Instead we always end up in arguments. With him not being able to read well or write, and being hard of hearing, I have a hard time making him understand. It is always the same old thing over and over. Even though he is my husband and I love him, at times he makes me feel he is only my friend. We have been married for forty-four years, but in all those years, say about the first twenty years, I was never happy. Having my baby son was all the happiness I had, and I built my life around him until he grew up. In all the years we've been married, I was never slapped or beaten by my husband. We argued, but that was it. He was a good supporter, but at times I know he maybe wished he was free. Although, after nearly twenty years, he stopped his liquor drinking. That is the best part of it, because that's what made us go broke. Besides, I got sick and spent so many months in the hospital, that was it. Oh well, it is done and past. Now is now.

Today my son has a family of his own. Six children, and he works so hard. I wish I could give him more to make things easier for him and his family. I now have a daughter who has a family of her own, too. She has two children and I wish I could do more for her, too.

I love them so much. I wish they had more than what they have now.

Someday, perhaps with God's help, things will be better for them. I try to share whatever I have, and that's the most I can do for them. But love is all I have for my son Danford and daughter Dolly and their families. Oh Lord, grant them their needs, and provide for them in all their daily needs. Food, money, home, and happiness, and most of all, Father, they must remember You. Likewise, me and Abel, too. See you later when I'm back with you. Aloha.

APRIL 9, 1989, SUNDAY AFTERNOON

Aloha Diary,

I am happy today. I spent time with God in his house this morning because Abel and I went to church this morning. Every time I walk into Kahikolu Church, I feel I am at home. Lots of strange faces and some of the 'ohana were there. It was so nice to see Howard and Harriet in church.

Nui nō ke aloha no kēia wahi. 'O kekahi o ko'u 'ohana a pau loa ke moe nei ma loko o kēia pā halepule 'o Kahikolu. He nui nā mana'o maika'i akā 'a'ole i hiki ke kākau 'ia no ka mea, nui nā 'eha'eha a ho'omana'o nō ho'i o ku'u mau mākua. 'O ia ho'i, ke moe nei lāua ma ka lihi o ke alanui. 'A'ole hiki ke pa'a nā waimaka. Nui nā ho'omana'o. Aloha 'ino. Ua pau nō kēia, a hui hou kāua no kekahi manawa. 'O wau nō. M.K.K.K.

TRANSLATION: *The love for this place is great. Some of my family are lying in this cemetery at Kahikolu. I am filled with good feelings and yet I don't know how to write them down as it hurts so much when I think of my parents. They are lying here by the edge of the road. You can't stop your tears. You're thinking so much. Oh, the love is great. This is all for now, we'll meet again another time.*

APRIL 22, 1989, FRIDAY 9:43 A.M.

Dear Diary,

You know, every time I think of Miloli'i I get so upset that I really can't think what else I can do to make things right.

What is happening to these people? It seems like the village is divided into two parts: the opposers and the nonopposers. What is the cause of all this ruckus? Is it for power and glory, or greed? Which is it? Such an inferior feeling. The air is not the one I knew and found when I first went to the village. At that time, the warm understanding and respect, all there.

The respect for the kūpuna in the area was just marvelous. They meant the world to the young people. Even the young were held in high esteem by the kūpuna. Visitors were treated as one of the 'ohana. I wish all this was being maintained for the next generation to come. Not like today where the picture of Miloli'i is painted with hate, greed, power, glory, and dirt, and where the news media swallows every bad profile of the village and its people.

However, there are some respectable people in the village. But when there's an uprising, the respectable people are also hurt. But they maintain their pride and their educated minds and are themselves. Culture is there, but the outside influence is damaging.

I've learned also the attitudes of the young people or adults and how they conduct themselves. I mean, when most of the kūpuna or old-timers were still around, everything they related was obeyed. But today, the young try to rule. There is a feeling where some want glory or to be heard by the entire village.

What is the entire background of this situation? Oh well, see you later when I have some more news. Aloha.

LATER.

I still think and feel this is the last fishing village in the whole state of Hawai'i.

Reasons:

1. The name Miloli'i. Milo is to braid or weave. Li'i is very fine. Other definitions are the small, swerving currents.

2. I believe Miloli'i was always a thriving fishing village, even before the Ho'ōpūloa flow of 1926.

3. Facts:

    a) Olonā was famous here.

    b) Cords for fishing were made here and shared or traded with other fishermen along the coastline both south and north of Miloli'i.

    c) The best fishing cords were made at Miloli'i. My grandfather and uncles had these cords that were made by the people of Miloli'i.

    d) For that reason I believe that Miloli'i was always a fishing village from hundreds of years ago up to now. Reef fish, shellfish, or crabs are safe to eat, even the limu. There are other places where reef fish are a hazard and cannot be eaten. I wish these ho'opili mea'ai will leave Miloli'i as it is and not choke it with pollution or their "Johnny come lately." Well, I hope and pray God will help us with these problems. Especially these money chasers with greed and power in their hearts. I pray that they are punished. Aloha and see you later.

Gilbert called me this morning to notify me that the state has selected me to be the representative for the Miloli'i community. However, I wonder what the people will say or feel when they hear about this. Really, there is so much to be done within the community itself.

Rubbish along the road and junk are real eyesores. Perhaps before the groundbreaking we may try to clean up.

This can be a beautiful and serene village if only our young people would realize what they have instead of fighting all the time.

See you later and aloha.

APRIL 26, 1989, TUESDAY 5:30 P.M. TO 9:00 P.M.

Dear Diary,

I just reached home from the meeting with the fishing committee. That meeting was something. The thoughts they talked about were just and neutral, but the air was hostile. To stop that marina* is a big issue. If only these higher-ups would leave the village people and their fishing grounds alone, I think the issue would be all right. We know the ocean is changing. The water has a changeable temperature, and fish are migrating. To make things worse, the bait or chum that is being used is something else. I know that a long time ago, ʻōpelu was rubbish along the coastline and koʻa. People here only used taro or pumpkin for chum. During a certain period of the year they would only feed the fish until they knew it was time to catch them, then all the fishermen would go out to net them. Today all these new methods, big boats, and using fish for chum has really spoiled the ʻōpelu, the ʻūʻū, and other fishing grounds. Before, they had to use shovels to take the fish out of the canoes and sampans. Today, lucky if you can fill up a big cooler or fish box. So much changes.

The people have only a little to live on and to get by on from day to day. But some individuals cannot see the fishing people get ahead and they create a drastic issue like so much tonnage of fish going from the village where no quota was met from 1986 up to now. Furthermore, only three people in Miloliʻi have fishing licenses. As for the rest, they sell some of their catch to markets, or trade it, put it on tables to eat. What they are getting to is that they don't see the other picture but want to hurt the fishing people by claiming they don't pay taxes. I think this is the big issue. What these bad individuals don't understand is that I am pretty sure when you file your taxes there are other expenses to be filed also. Too bad it becomes such a controversy.

There is a split between families now in the village, and that is a pity. Welfare was good in the village, but some of the people took advantage of that help. Others really need it, if they use it wisely. Anyway, so much was said. I made a remark that if the fishermen weren't careful, always fighting, conservation might happen here. This is just what happened at Nāpoʻopoʻo where I was involved, too. The main idea is that these developers who are with the Riviera Resort don't choke the fishermen. Those were my remarks. Abel stood his ground and told all, "No fighting." All must live happy. So I'm sleepy. See you by and by. Aloha, me.

Publisher's note: The marina issue began in the mid-1980s with the proposed Hawaiian Riviera Resort, a condominium-marina-resort complex and golf course in Manuka. Miloli'i residents were united in their opposition to this development at Pōhue just south of Miloli'i. The project was eventually abandoned by its developer Charles Chidiac.

MAY 5, 1989, FRIDAY 10:25 P.M., WAIPĀ, KAUA'I

Dear Diary,

I didn't dream that I really came to Kaua'i. We're at a place called Waipā at a home of our lapa'au 'ohana. Such a nice family. This is a place I would call the Garden of Eden. Nui nō nā po'e i hele mai no kēia 'oihana. Mai Honolulu kekahi, no Maui mai, a 'o Moloka'i nō ho'i a me nā poe o kēia 'āina 'o Waipā, Kaua'i. Nui nō nā mea i kūkā a mo'olelo e pili ana i kēia wahi.

'Ekolu lā ana mākou ma kēia wahi. Kēia ka lā mua. Maika'i ka launa pū me nā po'e. 'O wau nō e ha'i ana no ka ho'oponopono mai ka wā kahiko a hiki nō i kēia wā hou. A 'o Kahu Kāwika Ka'alakahi no ka lā'au. Nui nō nā mea hō'ike'ike maiā mākou. A he aha lā ka hana i ka lā 'āpōpō? E nānā aku. He aha lā? Kēia manawa ua pau ka hola 'umi i kēia ahiahi. Nui ka hu'ihu'i o kēia wahi. Like me kō mākou 'āina 'o Kona. He 'eleu nō. Laki ua lawe mai au nā kuka mahana e pakele mai i ka hu'ihu'i o kēia wahi.

Ke makahiamoe nei a lawa paha kēia mau mo'olelo i ha'i nei iā 'oe. Aloha, a hui hou nō kāua i ka lā 'āpōpō. Aloha, 'o wau nō.

TRANSLATION: *Lots of people came for this gathering from Honolulu. Some came from Maui, some from Moloka'i, and all were met at Waipā, Kaua'i. Many things were in discussion, stories about that area where we were, Waipā.*

We will spend three days at this place; today is the first day. It is so good to meet the people. For me, I have to talk about ho'oponopono from the past and of today, the difference. I wonder what kind of work we're going to have tomorrow. Oh well, let's see what it is. It's now ten in the evening. This place is so cold. It's just like Kona. Oh, too good! It was a good thing that I brought a warm coat; it has saved me from the coldness of this place.

Well, I'm getting sleepy and I think this is enough, this story I'm telling you, so good-bye, and you and I will meet tomorrow. Aloha, just me.

MAY 6, 1989, 11:46 P.M.

Dear Diary,

Well, this is the second day of our workshop. La France [Kapaka-Arboleda] is so generous. I mean, the hospitality she offers us, plus she makes sure that we are comfortable in her home. She and her husband are so wonderful. The people here and the Niʻihau people are just tremendous; they went all out to see to it that we really enjoy our stay here.

Today is Harry Mitchell, and the next session is Kupuna [Henry] Auwae and Sabina Mahelona of Hilo, Hawaiʻi. They will be presenting their arts of healing with herbs. Tom Solomon will present his banana healing also. Lomilomi by Aunty Margaret [Machado].

Pretty soon it will be lunch time then back again for workshops. All went well today. At least we will have a little rest before the next session this evening. Boy, this place is so cold. Lucky I brought lots of warm clothes and socks. I'll see if I can get some pictures before I go home.

MAY 7, 1989, 7:00 A.M.

Dear Diary,

Today is our last day here. I don't think we can make it to church, as we have a business meeting before we leave for home. That is around twelve o'clock. Hate to leave so soon, as there is so much to see here.

The meeting was terrible and disgusting. Anyway, I wonder if the committees who stayed back made progress. Anyway, the next session will be in Honolulu.

I took some pictures of the loʻi kalo. Boy, acres and acres of loʻi, and all water, too. What a sight. I met many nice people, and hope to see them again.

Now I'm at the airport and waiting for our plane. No wonder they call this the Garden Isle. It really is, because everywhere you look is green with lots of streams. There is hardly a dry area. All the shades of green.

MAY 31, 1989, WEDNESDAY 12:23 P.M., KAPUKAWAʻA, MILOLIʻI

Dear Diary,

It is now so hot that I can't do any more work outside. The sun is so hot down here. It seems like I'm coming down with a cold, and we are in the process of moving out from this shack. We have to pack up all our things. Abel took some things over to Peter's house (Hoʻōpūloa). The rest of these boxes have to go up to the ma uka house. I will keep only what we need down here. Looks like we may have to live in the boat garage until our new home is built and we move into it.

Right now, the boat garage will be our temporary home if it is not in the way of the new house. Anyway, we'll see how things turn out. We already moved our beds and kitchen things, and tonight is our first night in here. If it ever rains, I think we're in for trouble because I'm sure the roof will leak. The sides are all open due to the fact that Abel is so smart with his rotten ideas. Really, he is something. Tell him that and he thinks his ideas are great. Anyway, we'll see when the rains do come. Be with you again when I have time.

JUNE 2, 1989

Hello again,

I never dreamed I'd have so much to do. The lot needs to be cleaned up, although not trash, but plants that were around the shack had to be removed. Most of them I planted at the ma kai end where there was nothing. As for the rest, they were just piled in one corner to grow again or not. But the rocks had to be cleared. I hope I can finish by tomorrow. The sun is so hot, and boy, how I got through today I don't know. I guess God Almighty was there to give me the strength.

Tomorrow we'll do the foundation for the water tank. We did a little this evening. Boy, the big rocks we took out! The next step is to pack ʻiliʻili and sand for the cushion. Oh, I'm so tired and I got to do our dinner. Gee, by the time I'm finished with dinner I'll be ready to flop down in a deep sleep. I wish my kids could come and help us. Danford works, and Dolly is ready to have a new baby.

JUNE 21, 1989

Aloha Friend,

Gil came to visit today. What he had to tell me made me feel sorry for the applicants of Phase Three.* The way things are going, we might not have that phase due to one individual who tried to take the show. She made some insinuating remarks that do not seem good to the state or developers.

When our club Pa'a Pono was working hard for Phase One and Two, she really kicked up a ruckus. She claimed they tried for twenty-five years but never got anywhere. Well our club did it in three years with the governor even flying to Miloli'i on his chopper. We are proud to say someone big did listen to us, and he has the last word. Everything was done. Now, there are new homes for all the people who have a lot, yet the same person is still there to upset the works. Well, we'll see how far [she gets].

Publisher's note: Phases One, Two, and Three refer to state-sponsored housing development plans in Miloli'i.

⟶

JUNE 26, 1989, 4:20 P.M.

Aloha,

Ke kākau nei au i kēia mau mana'o e pili ana nā mea i kuni 'ia ma loko o ka nūpepa o Kona.

'Ano 'ē nō ka no'ono'o o kekahi po'e. He hana 'e'epa nō me ka kū'ē 'ana o nā 'ohana.

Pehea lā kēia hana? Inā no'ono'o lākou, 'a'ole ka honua no ke kanaka. Ke kanaka no ka honua. Ua hana 'ia nā mea a pau ma kēia honua, 'akā hana nō ke kanaka ka mea 'ino. No laila, nui nō nā pilikia.

Ua kākau 'ia kekahi leka ma loko o ka nūpepa e pekapeka kekahi i kekahi. Kēia 'ano hō'eha'eha wale nō i ka po'e 'a'ole i pili ana i kēia mau māhele.

Ma mua, i ka manawa i hele mai au i kēia wahi 'o ia ho'i 'o Miloli'i, kēlā manawa, hiki 'oe ke 'ike i ka aloha me ka hui pū mau o nā po'e 'ōpiopio, nā po'e keiki, me ka po'e kūpuna. Inā noho 'oe ma waena o lākou, hiki nō 'oe ke 'ike i ke aloha nui a me ka launa pū me nā 'ohana, a kekahi hoaloha. 'O wau he malihini au. 'Akā lawe nō kēia po'e ia'u i 'ohana, 'a'ole mea 'ōko'a.

Inā pēia ka po'e o kēia manawa, 'a'ole nō pilikia. 'Eha'eha nō ka pu'uwai inā e nānā a ho'olohe i nā 'ōlelo puniwale, i ka lapuwale no ka hana a kekahi ho'ohakakā.

Noho au ma kēia ʻāina i nā makahiki he nui. Ua ʻike au i ka noho ʻana o kēia poʻe o ia manawa. Kēia manawa, nui nā hoʻokano a me ka ʻino a ka ipukea ma kēia wahi. Aloha ʻino.

Ua huli nā ʻōpiopio a me nā mākua i nā hana o ka ipukea. ʻAʻole hiki ke alo aʻe, no ka mea, kēia manawa ua huli i nā mea hou o na poʻe ma waho o kēia ʻāina. Pehea lā? "E nānā aku." Aloha kāua.

TRANSLATION: *Well, here I am writing again all that I'm thinking of about what was printed in the Kona newspaper. Some people have a funny way of feeling or thinking. They do foolish things, and they try to stay away or separate from their family.*

I wonder what kind of work this is. If only they would think. The earth is not for man, but man is earth. He was made from the earth and yet he did all these bad things. That's why there is so much trouble.

Someone wrote a letter to the newspaper, and they just gossiped about one another. This is not good; it'll only hurt. People hurt those who are not familiar with these kinds of incidents.

If the people had good thinking, there wouldn't be trouble. There's a lot of hurt in the heart when you look and listen to the words that are being said, but I believe the bad will only cause fights. Too bad.

I've lived on this land for quite some years. I have observed the way the people lived now and before. Today they are so sarcastic, and they try to imitate the white man of this place. Too bad. The young and some of the older people have tried to search for work of the white man. They can't help it because now everything is new, from outside of this land. I wonder how it will be. We'll wait and see.

JULY 5 – 6, 1989

Aloha,

Today was a busy day for me. I had to rush and see that food is prepared for Abel before I go up ma uka to meet Susan and Gail of the CPS office, then we'll go to see the clients I have to counsel.

Well, it is almost 9:30 and I got to go. They came after 10:00 a.m. but we made it. After the session, I rode with them to go to my ma uka house. This evening I will be giving a lecture at Puʻuhonua O Hōnaunau National Park.

Well, it's all done. Pretty good crowd. Tomorrow I have another lecture at the Board of Health clinic with some nurses and doctors. It's a lecture on Hawaiian medicine and what different herbs are used by the beach people. I even showed the diagrams on basics.

JULY 7, 1989

Aloha iā 'oe,

Today, I can finally see we are progressing in the building of our home. Concrete was finally poured for the four corners. Tomorrow will be the removal of the molds. After that, I don't know what else. Well, we'll see. Aloha.

JULY 8, 1989

Tried to call Dan, but that line is so busy. I guess I'll call later. Last night the line was busy too, so we gave up. Dolly called to say hello and check how we are this morning. So far, so good.

John Aiken, the contractor, brought our house plan this morning. Abel went to help Raymond put his wall up. They are still working. Pretty soon it will be lunch time, so I got to quit talking to you till later on.

Guess what? Our house will be thirty-four feet high. I think that is a good height. I may have to build a ramp in place of the steps. Anyway, we'll see what the outcome will be. Until then, we'll just have to wait and see what the builders see fit.

There has been so much controversy over who is to have a new home built. Anyway, I'll just let the executive see who qualifies. What more? To have an investigator is just the worst. Well, see you later.

FEBRUARY 19, 1990, MONDAY 10:21 A.M.

Aloha,

Today the wind is really blowing and I can see the white caps on the sea. Waves are very high and cause huge splashes on the cliffs below our house where the lighthouse is stationed. It is beginning to get cold, and the ocean looks so dark.

Abel has left to go up ma uka. He has a bad cold, and probably his blood sugar is up. He has been so finicky, unpredictable, and fussy. Sometimes I just don't know how to handle him. It seems as though with all the help I give him he is just not satisfied at all. Anyway, he needs to see the doctor.

Although I miss seeing his long face around the house, I feel so relaxed, and now I can think of what I must do to keep myself occupied.

With the house still being built there is so much to do, from cleaning up to the unfinished jobs in the back and front yards. Sometimes I wonder what more can I do. Uh-oh, I have to stop now as the health department nurses are here to give me my monthly checkup. Wish me luck that nothing is wrong. Aloha.

SAME DAY 7:48 P.M.

Well, here I am again. Just finished doing my dinner dishes and am having a cup of coffee. It is very cold, and I'm dressed warm. The wind is still blowing but no rain. I'm down here at Miloli'i alone. Abel won't be coming home until he is better. Dolly called me to tell me all about how Daddy is. I think it is better he stays up there for a while until he is better.

For once, I like this being alone and having some peace without bickering and hard words. Sharon came back with me for a visit. She had lots to talk about. I just listened. After about an hour or so, she left to go home. I lay down on the bed and turned the radio on. I kept thinking of what Sharon had told me, plus thinking about Abel's condition. So much was going through my mind. Oh Lord, take all these impurities out of my mind and make me think of something more pleasant than all these evil things.

This talk show on the radio is kind of interesting but I'm sleepy. So off goes the radio, then prayer, and to bed. So good night and see you another time.

FEBRUARY 28, 1990, 10:17 P.M.

Aloha my friend,

These past two days have caused me to wonder what is really going on with our club Pa'a Pono and its members. I just got home from the meeting and my mind is not at ease. So much was said, with no discrimination. All because of this resort [Hawaiian Riviera Resort]. Tonight's meeting was based mostly on the interveners and the letter that was submitted to the commissioners by our president Gil for the removal of the club and himself from the hearing on the resort. What I can't understand is why did he urge Shirley, Willie, and others to attend these hearings, when he didn't show up at four of the hearings where he was the intervener? In the end, he submitted a letter to have the club removed from the hearing without knowledge or reason given to the members of the club.

Anyway, to make things good for the club, the majority voted for Willie and Shirley to be the interveners for the club at the hearings. They were made aware that no matter what goes on, they are to report all issues to the club, whether they are good or not. The only new nominee was a recorder who was voted in. She is to attend all sessions with the secretary and interveners.

I think this will make things better and less controversial.

Gil is to remain in his position as president of the club until he himself relinquishes that position. Majority overrules, and there's nothing I can say.

New members will be accepted to the club this Sunday. Well, that's that for the night, and I'm home. Goodnight, and see what news there is tomorrow.

Similarities and Differences Between Hawaiians and Inca Indians

HAWAIIANS

Farming

Fishing

Handcrafts, etc.

Wood, stones

Bones and shells

Cords from various tree barks
and leaves

Building - wood, leaves, grass, and
stones

HAWAIIAN STAPLES

Taro

'Ulu

Potatoes (Yams)

Bananas

HAWAIIAN SYMBOLS

Sun, moon, stars, ocean, and earth

INCA INDIANS

Farming

Fishing (scanty)

Handcrafts, etc.

Wool weaving

Building – mud, reeds, bricks,
stones, and skins

INCA INDIAN STAPLES

Corn

Potatoes

INCA INDIAN SYMBOLS

Sun, moon, water, and earth

<u>Memories</u>   Aug. 8, 1987

<u>Entry</u>: Notes From May to July 1931

Notes I have kept all
through the years I was
growing up. Now, I am
trying to compile all these
notes into one place where
I can reach them when ever
it is needed.

To me, it is very import-
ant as it served a very good
impact during my early years
as a youngster. Sometimes
I wish that if only my
paternal Grandmother could
only read or write, maybe
I would have gained more
than what she had shared,
and made me understand
that to love, listen, share and
help is the most important
things in the entire life time.
As I grew older and learned

Page from Aunty Mona's diary

Early Years

Lokalia

There were times while working in the pia patch or potato patch when my tūtū was not close by that I would smooth out the dirt. With my fingers I would write words like "ball," "girl," "boy," "mother," "father," or "brother," and "sister." These are words I learned to write in English. I felt I was big because I could write and read a little English. I was proud of myself, but to my tūtū it was a big *No* to learn the haole language.

Whenever I had homework to do, my tūtū would ask me if I was writing in Hawaiian. This hurt me so much because I had to lie to her, one whom I loved so much. Sometimes she wanted to know what I was writing about and I had to translate it into Hawaiian, or I had to tell her it was our language I was writing, yet I felt so guilty.

I remember one incident, the day I learned to write the word "ball." I was so tickled that I wanted the world to know about it. I asked the teacher for a piece of chalk. She gave me a whole chalk and I took it home. With the chalk, I wrote that word on the walls of our house. Wherever I could reach, or on empty walls, I would write the word "ball." I also wrote it on the walls of the toilet house and on the toilet seat. Tūtū asked me, "What kind of picture is that?" I told her, "Since our walls have new paint I thought I would make a nice design." She just smiled and said, "It looks nice." I turned away and grinned but I knew I did a big sin by lying to her. Well, it stayed there on the wall. Every day she looked at it, and I still can remember how she would size it up and smile.

Nearly two weeks went by and my father came to visit us. He didn't say hello to us because he was so angry. He got off his horse and walked around the house looking at the walls and grumbling at the same time. He knew I was the culprit who had made all those scratches. The fact was that I led my tūtū on a great lie. In the end I got the nī'au broom, that famous "stick of knowledge," plus a bucket of water and rags to clean up the walls. My father didn't leave our house until I had really cleaned the walls good.

My father made my tūtū understand that there was a law where every child must learn to read and write English whether you liked it or not. The schools did not teach Hawaiian anymore, but at home I had to speak Hawaiian so

I wouldn't forget my own language. My tūtū agreed but still she couldn't understand the law. All she told my father was, "I hate haoles. They took our customs, our culture, and our lands. Now it is our language. What next? Our life?" By the time my father left for his home, up ma uka, my tūtū was so confused that she told me everybody was crazy.

Well, someday we might have back what they took away from us. Come to think about it, she was so right. Today we are trying to keep what rightfully belongs to us—culture, language, and land, if possible.

At times when we went to visit my parents, I used to envy my family and how they spoke English, even my brother and sisters. Sometimes when they spoke to me in English, I would just stare at them because half of what they were saying I didn't understand. At times I had to look at my mother for help. By using gestures and Hawaiian, I knew what they were talking about. Little by little my mother would teach me English words for objects in the house and to spell the words so that I would be able to recognize them whenever I read a book. I was called "stupid" by my cousins and some of the other relatives. It made me cry and wished I could hide from everybody. My tūtū was no help at all. It took her a long time to give in. Sometimes I could hear her argue with my mother about teaching me the haole language. My mother would tell her, "Your moʻopuna is my daughter and she is going to learn English whether you like it or not. Nobody's going to call my daughter 'a stupid.'" My tūtū did come around and I was free to read and write English, but I could not speak it in our house. Yet my tūtū was the very one who pushed me to learn all I could. That I did, and I still speak, read, and write my own language, Hawaiian. Tūtū died before I finished high school and two years of college.

I think of the countless lauhala hats and mats she wove so my tuition at school could be paid and we could have extra money for our support. When I think of the constant nagging to keep going to school, I just can't forget her.

One day, Tūtū asked me to teach her how to write her name. I wanted to fall over because she detested every time she had to pick up my pencils off the floor. She would always say, "Ka hana o ka poʻe ipukea" meaning, "the works of the white people are good for nothing."

The reason she wanted to learn to write her name was so that when she died and went to heaven, she could tell the Great Father there that she could write her name. Well, she did learn to write her name: Lokalia. She was so proud about it that she had to tell my parents and her daughter, mostly to taunt her daughters who didn't want to teach her. When my father saw her write her name, he hugged her and told her no more signing her name with an "X." She said, "That name is too short and ugly." Every time she was told to make an "X" she always thought that was her name.

She died at the age of eighty-five or eighty-seven. It was only three years since she had learned to write her name. There are so many things I learned from her and my other kūpuna. Today when I get to thinking about them, the values and the knowledge and the wisdom they tried to instill into the young ones during my time paid off. Today when culture and the Hawaiian language are taught in the public schools, I am glad I am in that line. We are thankful to our leaders for bringing these things to life again. And yet, why did the government banish all these treasures from the people? I sometimes wonder and it really hurts.

I guess in our way of thinking, we are a sensitive race. Whenever we are turned away in some kind of situation, the feeling is shame. But now that most of our people are educated, we are not afraid anymore. We will try and try until we reach a goal. So we as Hawaiians should be proud and hold our heads up.

Many of our race are active, whether in government or in the community. I for one am involved in some community activities. It is good to see and hear what our race is trying to accomplish, after so many years of hurt.

Growing Up

[AS TAKEN FROM DIARIES CIRCA 1930S]

I recall lots of things that took place while I was growing up, the never-ending reminders of who you are. Always remember you're Hawai'i and nothing else, and you are not to ask questions unless you've been told to do so. There are countless rules that must be obeyed. Some are easy, some are hard, and some I think are just silly. You must observe almost everything that is done, or take all the scoldings that come after every lecture.

These are some of the rules I can remember so vividly that sometimes I almost can hear the voices of the past:

1. Remember God and prayers.

2. Respect your elders and kūpuna.

3. Always listen and watch how things are done.

4. Always speak your language, never mind the haole.

5. When kūpuna speak, you shut up, no questions asked.

6. At all times you must learn your culture whether you like it or not.

7. Watch and learn by observing.

8. Make sure you finish what you start.

9. Work is the main thing in life.

There's an old saying in our household that goes like this: "Inā kaula'i ka lima i luna, pōloli ka 'ōpū" meaning, "If your hands are always kept clean, hunger of the stomach is always there." In other words, if you are lazy, you end up with nothing. Sometimes when you hear this saying over and over, it gets so tiresome that at times you want to scream or tell them "shut up," yet who are we to tell our elders "shut up?" Today I am old and think of my elders. I wish they were still alive so I could really thank them for what

I have learned from them. To me they were a real treasure. I used to get stubborn with my tūtū and her constant nagging about going to school and yet I was forbidden to speak English in the household. At that time I could not understand why she was so insistent, but later I understood.

One day, I was about to turn thirteen years old and she said, "I have something to tell you. I am nearly seventy years old and don't know how to write my name." She had never gone to school and never learned to write her name or read her Bible, which she treasured so much. Yet, all that time I thought she could read because she always quoted some verses from the Bible. I asked her, "How do you know where certain verses are found?" She said, "When I hear the minister say where that particular verse is found, I memorize it until I remember it well."

She used to think that maybe when I grew up and went to school, I might be able to teach her. To read and write was what she wanted most of all. Every time she would ask my aunts to teach her, they would always tell her they did not have any time. Many a time she wanted to ask my father or my mother to teach her, but she was ashamed that maybe they would tell her the same thing that my aunts told her. I told my parents about this and they were not too happy to hear what my aunts did.

My father told me his mother was too proud to ask anything from him, so I would have to do the job. At first I asked him, "Why has to be me?" He said, "If you love your tūtū very much, do it!" I tried but the response was not too good as she had no patience for writing her name over and over. Sometimes she would throw the pencil on the floor. After some days of trying, she gave up and told me I would have to be the one to learn. I told her that I would try to do my best. And that's what I did.

There is so much that I could tell about my tūtū, yet on paper it is so hard to do. The values you gain from your tūtū are so precious that it is hard to just throw them on the side as our generation of today is doing. If people or kūpuna like us today just keep the culture moving ahead, it will never be lost.

My Life Story

Moana means horizon and it was my legal name. It was Dr. Dickson who changed it to Mona on my birth certificate. Many a time I wanted to write about my life story, but I just could not find the words to express my feelings: the love, hurt, sense of loss, and the happiness that took a long time to grow and heal. Well, I guess I have to start this way: I was born into a family of six children of which I am the eldest. As part of tradition, the firstborn of a family is always raised by the parents of the father. My father was raised by another family, which became his adopted parents. I was taken and raised first by my father's adopted parents at the age of three. In this household were my grandparents, their daughter and her husband, and eight children who were all my cousins and older than me. Why was I to be raised by these grandparents? I didn't have the slightest idea. Years later, my grandfather said that I cried so much that at times he would saddle his horse and take me for a ride to quiet me. They knew that I cried for my mother.

Grandfather was a cowboy and worked for a cattle owner who first settled in areas of Kona. Horses were his pride and glory, and he owned several of them. My father and mother were good riders and had their own horses for transportation. All Grandmother did was tend the kids in the home and make lauhala hats and mats to sell to help support the family in the house. My aunt did the same thing, too. But when coffee was in season, she worked in the mill as a coffee sorter. Young as I was, I was taught to sort the good hala leaves from the bad ones. All these types of work I had to learn.

The only time I got to see my mother and father was on Sundays at church. Every time they would get on their horse to leave for home up ma uka I would hide behind the kukui tree and cry for them until my grandma Mele would come and try to wipe my tears away. Eventually, I somehow got over the idea of crying for them when they headed home. Sometimes when I got to crying over them, my mother would turn back and get down from her horse to soothe me. I often asked her, "Why must I stay with my grandparents and not with you?" She told me, "When you are old enough to know the difference in life, then maybe you will come home with us. For now, be patient and wait." Then she would get back on her horse and ride away, even looking back and waving at me. I could see the tears rolling down her face. When I think back, that was not a rosy time. It was just a reminder of how life's pattern starts. I know at times it hurt inside, but I did learn things that I don't think youngsters of today could ever cope with or put up with.

Mo'olelo o Ku'u Wā 'Ōpiopio

My father's name was Isaac Kapioanuenue Kapule. He was an engineer and inspector for the Highways Department under the Territory of Hawai'i before Hawai'i became a state. He retired and later died. My mother's name was Daisy Kaehamalaole Kaolulo. She was a part-time teacher and then devoted her life to raising children. She had also been a farmer of coffee, soybean, and taro. Both of my parents were born at Nāpo'opo'o, South Kona, Hawai'i. I had four sisters and one brother. Four of them died of the same kind of sickness, leukemia.

As was the custom of the Hawaiian people, the makahiapo or firstborn was always given to the grandparents to be raised according to the lifestyle of the family. Whether the grandparents were farmers or fishing people, the child learned their lifestyle. Usually the firstborn, if it was a boy, would be given to the parents of the father. If it was a girl, it was given to the parents of the mother. However, I was raised and taught the lifestyle of my father's mother. My kupunawahine, Lokalia, lived alone and was a farmer as well as a fisher.

There were certain rules and beliefs that I would have to obey and abide by. But as I grew older and understood these things, I rebelled against my grandmother. I kept trying to make her understand that she was wrong, because it was a Christian era and she should leave the past behind. She would get furious at times but never made an issue of it.

I grew up in a circle she built around me. I couldn't play with other children. Even though she kept telling me, "You know, someday you're going to sit high up and your brains will put food in your mouth," I used to wonder what she meant. Now I know.

However, the greatest demand Grandma made was that I go to school so I could read and write for her. The one handicap she possessed was that she couldn't read or write. But you couldn't fool her with paper money. She could distinguish a dollar bill from the larger amounts by studying the portraits on the money. She spoke fluent Hawaiian, and this was the only language I knew due to the fact that the haole language was forbidden in our household. She took me to school and demanded that the teacher teach me, but no haole. Many a time I wished I knew that language.

I went to Nāpoʻopoʻo School and after a few months the Hawaiian language was forbidden in the schools. This was hard because my homework could never be done at home. Many times I would wait until my grandmother was not around, then I would practice my ABCs. The very first word I learned was "ball." I wrote this word all over the place; on dirt, smooth rocks, sides of the house, and at the beach in the sand. All my cousins used to tease me, but I never gave up.

However, when I reached the sixth grade, the teacher decided I should be transferred to Konawaena Intermediate School because of the good grades I had. She spoke to my grandmother who didn't like the idea because Konawaena was too far for me to walk. At that time there were only seven students sent to Konawaena and I was the only Hawaiian. The others were five Japanese and one Filipino boy. My grandmother used to walk with me up the trail from Nāpoʻopoʻo Beach until Government Road, then she would go back home. She would do this every day until school vacation. As for the cousins who used to tease me, they were still in the fourth grade while I was in the ninth grade. They got too old for that grade, so they quit school. By the ninth grade I was real good with English, reading and writing. I was already writing things like stories and legends that I had heard around the village, even from both of my grandmothers. I learned the different names of areas in the village and names and events of certain areas and why they were so named.

I my days, paper or writing tablets were very hard to get due to the fact there was not enough money to spend on those things. We earned our living by weaving hats and trading them for food and clothing and whatever was needed. Coffee season meant jobs and my grandma worked in the mill sorting coffee beans. We used to order our crackers, flour, sugar, and other goods from Honolulu. My grandma saved the paper that was used to wrap these things and ironed it flat until no wrinkles were in them. That was my writing paper. Sometimes when I went to school and saw the other students with their fancy store-bought tablets, I used to envy them. They used to make fun of my writing papers and tears would just fill my eyes. But when I thought of my grandmother, the tears would just dry up and I would think twice about how hard she worked just so I could go to school.

I remember one Christmas my parents asked me what I wanted the most. All I said was, "A fancy tablet." Instead, they gave me four tablets. I was so happy that I just wanted to look at the tablets and not use them. In fact, I didn't use them until I was a ninth-grader.

I attended Konawaena until I was supposed to be an eleventh-grader, then we had to move to Hilo. My grandmother was sick and old and we couldn't walk to see the doctor anymore. During those times we only had one doctor by the name of Dickson.

I had to go to Hilo High School and that is where I finished up. A year later a private business school opened. I registered and was accepted and I was one of the first eight students. Besides going to school, I worked at a laundry at night just to support my grandma and myself, working for fifteen cents an hour. That business school later became Commercial College. I attended less than two years, then I couldn't continue anymore as I didn't have enough money. The teacher there got me a better job working at Pier 1 at Hilo Harbor as a clerk and it paid better than the laundry. My grandmother was getting worse and had to be put into the hospital. There went my earnings to pay medical bills. I had to put school out of my mind because I didn't have enough money.

That is when I finally gave up and wanted to get married. Abel, my boy-friend, was already drafted into the Army. He had been stationed on O'ahu when it was attacked in 1941. By the latter part of 1945, I had only seen Abel once when he came home. Before I knew it, he had been transferred to the South Pacific while I kept working. There were times that this was hard for me: my kōko'olua away and my grandmother still in the hospital. The war was bad in the South Pacific and I still didn't know where Abel was since I didn't hear from him for nearly a year. The agony I went through was endless.

I never missed one day visiting my grandmother in the hospital. The war was just about ending, and my grandmother died. It left me one burden less, but I had a pile of hospital bills, funeral bills, and worry about my future husband. I kept on working until Abel returned in 1945. He was discharged from the Army and I was so happy: no more loneliness. We got married, adopted a baby boy, and I left my job to be a full-time mother. Abel went back to fishing. From 1947 until 1959 we raised twenty-three children from all walks of life and educated them. Today some are parents and some are not. Most of the boys are retired from the service and hold good jobs and the girls all have good jobs.

My grandchildren are the offspring of the children we raised. Altogether with the grandchildren, my husband and I raised thirty-nine children. Many people call us crazy, but to us if we can offer all the love and attention our children need, that is all the satisfaction we need. We raised all these children with no help from any agency, only with what we could afford. None of the twenty-three children ever did anything wrong, whether at school or in public.

All I can say, is thank the Good Lord above who helped us through life. I come from a family of six children of which only two live today: myself who is the eldest and a sister who is the baby and the youngest. Perhaps if we had more parents doing what we did, this generation would not be involved in things that corrupt their lives and communities. Sad, sad, sad.

Some of the work I have done, in addition to being an active mother and grandmother, includes helping people with their genealogies, doing ho'oponopono when asked by individuals or the courts, and being an active historian. I was a kupuna and teacher at Hōnaunau Elementary School, taught Hawaiian Studies for adult education, and was a teacher for drop-out teens at Hale O Ho'oponopono School in Hōnaunau. I have been a member of Kahikolu Church (and was the moderator for twenty-three years), a board member for the South Kona Educational Center, a board member of the Pa'a Pono Club, and a board member of the Hawai'i County Economic Opportunity Council.

All the children we raised are always scolding us and ask when am I going to stop helping people: The only answer I can give them is: "When I die."

These are just a few stories that tell of my life.

Kealakekua

PATHWAY OF KUA

[TOLD BY MY UNCLE HENRY LESLIE I]

Many people translate Kealakekua as the "Pathway of the Gods." A question frequently asked is, "the pathway to what god?" It is correctly pronounced "Ke-ala-ke-Kua" and not as it has been pronounced by some people as "Ke-a-la-ke-a-kua." There are quite a number of stories that were written about Kealakekua, but this is the story I heard from one of my uncles who lived in the village when he was a young man. He heard this story from one of the kūpuna of that village.

Long, long ago, the Hawaiians had many gods. The earth, heavens, stars, moon, land, sea, birds, hours, canoes, and men—in fact, everything of nature—had a god. The most important of all gods were Kane, Kū, Lono, and Kanaloa. Today, they are known as the four major gods in tradition and culture.

However, the people had another god—"Kua," the Great God of the Sharks. He was an ancestor to the people of Ka'ū and Kona. Kua had the secret ability to become a man without anyone suspecting it. He did not bear any marks of any kind. Kua traveled the water from Ka'ū to Kona, around Hawai'i Island, and to the other islands. On his return trip to Ka'ū, he usually stopped at Kapukapu, Kona, for a nice rest.

On one of his trips, Kua decided to mingle with the people of Kapukapu. He changed himself completely into a man. The people received him with much aloha. He lived among the farmers as a commoner and, from them, he learned how to do planting, fishing, and canoe building. He had never done these tasks before, but he was doing them now.

The fishermen loved him the most because he was good at catching fish. He was very cooperative and gave his aloha to the people. Likewise, the people expressed their gratitude toward Kua. They didn't treat Kua as a visitor, but as one of them.

Kealakekua

Finally, the time came for him to tell these wonderful people that he had to return to his own people. They were so sad and heartbroken, for they felt that they were losing a member of their 'ohana.

They begged him to stay with them, but he just thanked them and said, "I have enjoyed my stay here. You have treated me as a relative and not as a visitor. I will come and visit you again someday. Until then, let me leave you with these words: When the sun is bright and the horizon is red and gold, I will be here. Even when I am not, you will always be safe in these waters, or wherever you travel. This will also be true for your generations to come."

The people couldn't quite understand this, for they didn't realize that Kua was the king of sharks. Kua stepped into the water, bent down, cupped his hand over his mouth, and chanted with a booming voice a chant that only his lips knew. Suddenly, there were two dark lines on the sea which formed from the horizon to the shore. Kua stood still and watched this formation.

The people whispered, "What kind of man is this? He chanted over the water and now there are two dark lines coming toward the shore. He must be an ali'i, and those lines his approaching canoes!" But as the dark lines touched the shore, the people's voices sounded, "'Auē! This must be a god!"

Kua stood in the center of the dark lines. He turned around and waved to the people on shore. By this time, the bottom half of his body had changed. Without saying a word, Kua turned and dove into the water. He reappeared as a big shark swimming between two rows of sharks, whose fins had formed the black lines earlier. They all swam toward the horizon as the sun was setting in the ocean.

Now the people were certain that Kua was none other than the great king of sharks. They were so happy that they had treated Kua with kindness and love. For all the good deeds Kua did for them, the people named that spot "Kai-a-ke-Kua" (Water of Kua), and that's where the wharf stands at Nāpo'opo'o today. The trails or pathways where he had walked were named "Ke-ala-ke-Kua" (Pathway of Kua). As Kua had promised, there were never reports of anyone being bitten by sharks at Nāpo'opo'o.

This is how Kealakekua came about. Today, we have a post office by that name. Banks, stores, medical centers, flower shops, and other buildings are also located in Kealakekua.

Paliomanuahi

The Legend of Paliomanuahi

CLIFF OF THE FIRE BIRD

[TOLD BY MY MATERNAL GRANDMOTHER KAHIKIKALA AUKOʻO KAOLULO] 1936

Long ago fire was not known to the people of the beach, so foods were eaten raw or dried. A boy lived here with his family at the bottom of a cliff. His name was Manu.

One day, Manu was looking up the cliff when he saw smoke and wondered what it could be. For several days, he saw this thing called "smoke." He could not stop thinking about what he saw above the cliff, so he made up his mind and began to climb up the pali to see what was really there.

When Manu reached the top of the pali, he looked around. There was a fire pit, but no smoke nearby. As he neared the fire pit, he saw two sweet potatoes on the hot coals. He reached for the potatoes but drew back his hands very quickly, for the potatoes were hot and hurt his fingers.

Manu thought to himself, "What is this? Why can't I touch the potatoes?" He looked around but nobody was there, so he turned again to look at the potatoes.

Just then, he heard a voice calling to him saying, "There are two sticks by the fire pit near the stones. Pick the sticks up and rub them together, and you will have a fire."

Manu looked around to see where the voice was coming from, but all he saw were two white birds. There were no humans around. He said to himself, "I wonder where that voice came from?" Becoming frightened, he turned slowly to look at the two sticks.

Again he heard his name being called, and this time when he turned, he saw two beautiful girls standing nearby. Instead of standing still, he backed away from them slowly.

One of the girls said, "Don't be afraid, we will show you how to light a fire."

Manu was so stunned, he couldn't even say a word. He just stood there dumb-founded. One of the girls took some dry grass and made a pile. The other girl took the sticks and began to rub and rub until Manu saw the smoke. Then she blew on it until fire began to burn the pile of dry grass. Next, they added some twigs and then bigger sticks. Soon they had a nice fire going. Finally, they placed the potatoes on the hot coals. When the potatoes were done, the girls shared them with Manu. He was so amazed with what was going on that he was not afraid of the girls anymore. In fact, he liked the cooked potatoes better than eating them raw or dried. Manu thought to himself, "Now we can eat cooked food. When I get home, I will teach my family and the others how to light a fire."

The girls and Manu became good friends and enjoyed each other's company. Manu had so much more to ask them. They told him all they could answer, except when Manu asked them where they came from. They said that was one thing they could never tell him.

"But when you need us," they said, "Just call out 'Manu ahi,' and we will come to you."

Soon it was time for Manu to return down the pali to the seashore where he lived with his family. He had to leave his newfound friends who taught him how to light the fire. He thanked the girls for teaching him how to cook the potatoes. They told him he would cook other foods the same way. As he started to walk toward the drop of the pali, the girls went after him and gave him the two sticks. One stick was light in weight, but the other was heavy. "Use the heavy stick to rub on the light stick. Do it as we taught you," said the girls.

Manu thanked them again, told them how much he enjoyed their friendship, and how he hoped to see them again. But in his mind he kept wondering, "Where did these girls come from? I wonder why they didn't want to tell me. There is nothing on the top of the pali to show whether there is a village or people living up here."

He turned and waved goodbye to them, then started down the pali.

The girls called to him to wait, for they had something to tell him. When they got close to Manu they said, "You are the first human of your village to learn about fire. From this day on, this pali will be known as Paliomanuahi."

Then, as he turned to wave to them, they changed themselves into white birds and sat on his shoulders until he arrived safely at the bottom of the pali.

There they bid him farewell by fluttering their wings. Then they flew away, never to be seen again. Paliomanuahi still stands at Kapukapu Bay today.

Keaopuka (Today called "Keopuka")
PATHWAY OF THE RAIN CLOUDS

[TOLD BY MY MATERNAL GRANDMOTHER KAHIKIKALA AUKOʻO KAOLULO] 1938

R ain clouds from way out on the ocean sometimes form into water-spouts that spin their way to land. These spouts usually occur during the summertime or late springtime, especially during dry weather. As these spouts head for land, they usually pick up speed at their mouths, or openings. They often drop heavy loads of water they gathered on the way to land. As they pick up speed, they twist upward toward land, and in their paths they cause destruction to houses, land, or anything in their way. Damage is not too bad, however, when they rise above ground. Objects that are devoured by the mouths of the spouts can suddenly seem to disappear or disperse as the spouts move over flat and open land, as well as hillsides. When they disappear into the forest or mountains, floods and heavy rains are sure to follow. In Hawaiian, the waterspout is called waikōʻihi, waipuʻilani, or ʻōpua.

I got this information from my maternal grandmother who was very familiar with this area. She told me this story because she always heard people say "Keopuka," which she claimed had been shortened or slurred by people's laziness to say the right name. She got very angry when she heard the name mispronounced. She always said, "By and by, the real or true name and meaning of every area's existence will be lost."

She also remembered the many times they had these spouts, and often worried about future ones. Whenever her family saw waterspouts heading toward them they would worry because spouts were always followed by floods in their area. Their taro patches were washed out and so were parts of their coffee farms. The relatives and neighbors who owned land faced great losses because of the floods and heavy downpours.

In 1929, when I was a young girl, I remember watching three spouts out on the ocean. One of those spouts turned toward the land at Keaopuka, and then it headed upland. About an hour after it disappeared we heard a loud crash above our taro patch. Before we knew what was going on, the neighbors who lived above us called to us to evacuate our house because a big flood was coming down the hill. By the time we got out of the way, we saw part of the neighbor's coffee house coming down with the water. The next thing we saw was part of our house being ripped away, as if it were torn apart by someone. Half of our coffee farm and the coffee house—where all the dry coffee was stored until shipping time—were swept away by the floods. There was so much commotion with everyone trying to help one another. The flood had not subsided when we started to feel earthquakes. This was a terrible year for most of the farmers; like us, they really suffered. This is what Keaopuka, the coming or opening of the clouds, can cause.

The floods did stop after a couple of days, but the earthquakes lasted through-out the entire year. While our house was being torn down and moved to a new location, we had to live in tents for the rest of the year. Even though the new house was completed in a month, we still couldn't move into it because the quakes kept on coming one after another. All our neighbors, who were mostly Japanese, Filipino, and Hawaiian, gathered to rebuild each other's homes that were damaged by the floods. All the young people like myself, and all of my neighborhood friends, got together to help care for the farms while our parents were busy helping each other. Today, you don't see that kind of selfless teamwork anymore. It seems that monetary gain is all that people are interested in.

Kalepeamoa

COCK'S COMB

[TOLD BY MY FATHER'S ADOPTED MOTHER, MELE K. KAPULE]

When the islands were young, the menehune were the first people to come here to Hawai'i. Upon their arrival to the islands, all they saw were steep pali. Looking at all the pali, they decided this would be a good place to live. At one particular pali, they began making plans to build a pathway from the water's edge to get up the side of the cliff to see what was on the top side. Perhaps they could find an area where they could do farming. "We must have food if we are to stay here," said the king of the menehune. They tied their canoes under a ledge, and when the pathway was finished they could then carry their canoes to new homes. It was getting dark, so they began to gather rocks to build a pathway up the cliffs and over to the other side.

Now during that time, the god Kāne had two roosters. One rooster was a guardian for the forest. The second rooster, who was named Moa Kani Hewa, was always crowing at the wrong time, so that's how he inherited his name.

The menehune had just begun to work when they heard a rooster crow. All work stopped, for the crowing meant daybreak; according to the law of the menehune work was allowed only at night. This went on for three nights, and the menehune grew frustrated and angry. "Why must the rooster crow so early, as if he doesn't want us to finish our work?" the king of the menehune said. "We have to catch that rooster and do away with him."

So they began making plans for how to catch Moa Kani Hewa. The king of the menehune called all the menehune together and said, "We must catch this rooster, or we will never finish our work. First we need a volunteer."

One of the menehune who was a chanter answered, "O King, I will do anything should you need me."

The king asked the chanter, "Can you cluck like a hen?"

"If I try, maybe I can," answered the chanter.

"Then let me hear how you do it," said the king.

The chanter began to cluck, and he really did sound like a hen.

"That is good," said the King. "Now, we will catch this 'āpiki chicken. He interrupted our work for nothing, and he must die."

The king of the menehune told the men how to go about with the plans. As soon as darkness fell, the chanter started for the highest area and stayed hidden. Some of the other men had their nets ready and were in an assigned area close to the chanter. As for the rest of the menehune, they pretended to work by throwing stones to create noise that sounded like they were hard at work.

At the sound of the rocks being thrown in place, Moa Kani Hewa thought to himself, "I will not let those menehune finish their pathway because if they finish what they have started, I will have to work more. So I will put a stop to their work."

Just at that moment, he thought he heard a sound like a hen. He began to follow the sound while at the same time crowing, because he could hear the rocks being thrown by the menehune. To be sure he heard a hen, he crowed again. This time the clucking seemed so near, and he was growing very happy at the thought of having a mate. But little did he know he had walked right into the trap of the menehune! Moa Kani Hewa was tied up good.

They carried Moa Kani Hewa to where the chanter was hidden. When the chanter saw the rooster, he began to cluck like the hen. Moa Kani Hewa was all excited even though he was tied up. Moa Kani Hewa became so enraged that his body bounced up and down and pounded into the ground until only his head was left with the comb sticking out of the ground. Menehune can do supernatural things and so turned Moa Kani Hewa to stone. His comb, which was above the ground, became a landmark. The path the menehune intended to build was never finished.

During certain times, lights were seen by the people of Nāpoʻopoʻo beginning from the water's edge and going up the steep cliff, disappearing on the other side. It sometimes looked like a torch parade. When these lights were seen, the old people of the village would say, "Ah, the menehune are heading for safety as danger is approaching. It is either a storm or a tidal wave." Likewise, the people of the village would head for higher ground.

The last time these lights were seen by the people of the village was in 1960, when the tidal wave hit, destroying eight homes, one of which was mine. We lost everything we owned. That was the first and the last time I have ever seen such lights. I never did believe what the old people said until I saw it for myself.

_epeamoa Island at Kapu'a Bay

Waiolekaikaulumāhiehie

Waiolekaikaulumāhiehie

[TOLD BY LOKALIA KIKAHAKUPUNAWAHINE] AUGUST 1937

I n the olden times of long ago, there lived a couple in the uplands of Kona. The husband's name was Kahau and the wife's name was Loa. This couple were farmers. All they did was plant taro, banana, pumpkin, sweet potatoes, fern shoots, and other plants that were good to eat. As for fish, they didn't have all the time.

If the fishermen or others who lived at the beach needed taro and other things to eat, they would go to the uplands and trade their fish with the farmers. Before the fishermen would go to visit Kahau and Loa, they would catch lots of fish. They salted and dried the fish. When there were enough fish, they would go up ma uka to visit Kahau and Loa.

Upon arriving up ma uka, so much happiness took place with these families. They even took their children along as Kahau and Loa enjoyed having them. But, when it was time for the fishermen and their families to go home, the couple became sad because the children left to go home, too. The couple didn't have any children to love, the one thing they wanted so much.

One day Loa told Kahau, "If only we had a child, we would not be so lonely."

Kahau never said a word. The next day they went up into the taro patch to pull the new weeds that had appeared. Loa was busy weeding when she came across an odd plant she had never seen before. It grew close to the ground. The leaves were round like hau leaves and they were on long stems. The flowers had a fragrant smell and were dark purple in color. She thought to herself, "Well, I will take this plant home and plant it near our house so we can always smell these flowers."

When they were ready to go, she took the plant home. She planted it on the left side of their hut with other flowers. She watered the plant and it looked as fresh as ever.

The next morning, she went out to look at the new plant. She was amazed to see it had grown with more and more flowers. Loa called Kahau to come and look at the new plant and told him where she had found it.

Kahau told her it was beautiful and smelled nice. They both admired the plant. Then Kahau said, "Maybe it is a good omen. Let us wait and see!"

That very morning, all around their taro patch and hut a fine, misty, feathery rain came down. Loa said, "This rain is good for all things, especially the plants that are growing."

So they decided to stay indoors because it was too wet to do any weeding that day. Kahau repaired their tools while Loa tidied up their hut and prepared their food. After their evening meal, they talked a while, then they retired for the night.

That night, Loa had a dream. The next morning when she awoke she told Kahau about her dream. She said she saw a beautiful lady in a green pāʻū who came to tell her that when the moon becomes full in the sky nine times and the flowers outside her door bloom profusely, the leaves will drop because the plant is heavy with flowers. Their household will be full of happiness yet they must bear all burdens and pains with patience. As the lady was about to go away, she turned and smiled at Loa. Loa asked her, "What is your name?"

"My name is Waioleka and I come from nearby. I will come again when the ninth full moon is in the sky."

With these last words, the lady disappeared. Loa could not identify the scent she had smelled when the lady was near her in the dream.

All day she kept thinking about the dream, so much that she didn't go to the loʻi kalo to help Kahau with the weeding. Instead, she stayed around the hut to do some minor chores and pour some water on her plants.

She finally recognized the scent of the lady in her dreams. She thought to herself, "So, this is that plant, waioleka." As she watched the flowers, it seemed as if they could read her thoughts and mind, and began nodding their blooms in respect. Loa thought, "This is very strange."

Just at that moment she heard Kahau coming home. Loa revealed to him what she had discovered. Her husband sat silent for a while, then he answered his wife, "Let us go to see the kahuna. Perhaps he can explain to us about the dream and the new plant."

Loa agreed. After their evening meal, they both started out for Hōnaunau where the kahuna lived. Before they reached the kahuna's place, he already knew that they were coming and waited for them. When they reached his house he invited them in to sit and rest. Then he asked them, "What is on your mind that you came all the way to see me?"

Kahau answered, "We came to ask you if you can tell us the meaning of the dream my wife Loa had about the new plant we have at home."

Kahau started to tell the kahuna about the dream. The kahuna listened. After Kahau was through telling him, he remained silent for a moment. Then he burst out laughing. The couple glanced at one another and wondered, "Why is this kahuna laughing?"

Loa whispered to Kahau, "Is he making fun of my dream?" Kahau didn't answer her.

When the kahuna regained control of himself, he finally spoke and began to explain what the dream was all about. "It is a good dream, that is why I laughed. Now, first, the 'nine times full moon' are the nine months. That means, Loa, you will have a baby. The lady of your dream told you her name. You will have a baby girl and her name will be Waioleka. As for that new plant, it is a good omen. Take good care of that plant for it will bring both of you happiness."

At this explanation, the couple thanked the kahuna and said their aloha. The walk home was shorter than when they started out. It was already dark, but the sky was full of stars. That night Loa went to sleep full of happy thoughts.

As days and months went by, Loa found herself heavier with child at every full moon. She was getting bigger and bigger around the waist. Finally, the last full moon was growing full and it was almost time for the baby to be born. The woman in the green pāʻū came to Loa in a dream again. This time she told her it was time for the baby to be born. "It will be a girl. Call her by the name of 'Waiolekaikaulumahiehie' after me, for I belong to the plant's 'ohana. Raise her in a most fitting way and you will never be sorry. For this is the happiness I promised you."

With these last words, she disappeared.

All that was foretold came to pass. Kahau and Loa were so happy that it made them light up. Waioleka grew to be a most kind, beautiful, and loving daughter. As she grew to womanhood, many chiefs sought Waioleka as their wife, but they never won her charms.

One day Waioleka told her parents that she wanted to go up into the forest to look for maile vines to make some lei. Her parents told her not to stay too long, for, "If the dark mist or fog comes down, you will not be able to find your way home."

Waioleka promised and then left. As she entered the forest, she was so entranced with its beauty that she lost track of time. All of a sudden the forest became so dark she couldn't see in front of her or find the way home. The dark fog was all around her. She sat down to rest and wondered, "Now how will I get home? Am I ever to see my parents again?"

At this she began to cry bitter tears, blaming herself for being disobedient to her parents.

The forest was awfully quiet and misty. It held an eerie feeling. She thought to herself, "Perhaps if I sing or hum a tune, it will cheer me up."

But before she could sing or hum, she heard a strange and lovely song. She listened and it sounded like a young woman singing. Waioleka stood up because she heard her name being mentioned in the song. She tried to follow the voice, but every time she got close, the voice moved further and further away. Before she knew what was going on, she found herself in her parents' lo'i kalo and she could see the hut below. As she got nearer to home, the voice and song seemed to end and there was no more voice to be heard.

She called out to her parents and they came out to meet her with tears, laughter, and scoldings. They were so worried about Waioleka. They hugged her and took her into the hut to eat the food that was prepared for her.

When Waioleka finished her meal, she began to tell her parents what had happened, how she had found her way home. It was the sound of the voice that led her out of the forest.

The song was so pretty she began to sing it to them. They liked it so much that they made her sing it over and over. It went like this:

> Ho'ohihi kahi mana'o
> 'O Waiolekaikaulumāhiehie
> He pua nō 'oe na'u
> I ke anu o ke ahiahi
> Ke wela nei ku'u aloha
> Ke lawe nei iā 'oe
> Kou kino i ke ao nei
> Aloha nō kāua

Mine, my one and only admiration,
O Waiolekaikaulumāhiehie;
You are a child of mine,
Out in the cold of evening,
My love is burning so much for you
I am taking you
Your body from the cold darkness
For I love you so much

Her parents were so entranced by this melody that they kept encouraging Waioleka to sing the song. A sweet aroma drifted into their hut. It was a nice smell and it came from the plant outside, full of blooming flowers.

Waioleka grew up to be a beautiful woman. Many chiefs tried to win her heart, even as far as threatening to have her killed. She told them no matter what they did, "I will never be your wife." Her heart belonged to someone whom she loved dearly. No one could take his place. She married the man she loved and was very happy. They had children one of whom she named after her father, Kahauloa. She lived a happy and wonderful life with her husband, parents, children, and grandchildren.

One day, Waioleka told her family it was almost time for her to leave them for a while. A rainbow would come and stand at the doorway and she would go away into the sky.

Waioleka held her mother's hands together and told her, "Remember you both wanted children? I was sent to you by my real mother who lives up there in the sky. Now it is my turn to help you and other people. I belong to the king and queen of the rainbow. I will come to you when my work is finished. Do not be sad, for you now have grandchildren, great grand-children, and a son. Be happy and I will always be happy when I see you, always. Most of all, treat my husband well. He is also your son and I love him so much."

One day it began to rain. It rained so hard that Kahau became very worried because it could ruin their taro and banana plants. Waioleka sensed what Kahau was thinking and said, "Father do not worry, the rains will slow down and become light. That is the time I will leave all of you."

Her family gathered around her. Before they could say anything to Waiole-ka, a rainbow stood in the doorway. A voice called out from the rainbow. "Waioleka, it is time to go." It was the voice of the king, her real father.

Waioleka stood up from her mat to bid her family aloha. She walked to the rainbow and turned and told her family, "When that plant is full of flowers and no leaves, that means I will come home." With these last words, she stepped into the rainbow. The rainbow and Waioleka disappeared.

For days and days the sun shined hard. But the plant kept blooming and blooming. It was filled with blossoms. Then one day it began to get cloudy and it seemed like it was going to rain. Kahau and Loa watched the sky as if hoping to see someone. All of a sudden a rainbow began to arch in the sky. One end sat in the lowlands and the other end in their doorway. Kahau was so happy because he knew that meant Waioleka was coming home. Her husband and children were waiting also.

The rainbow began to settle and glowed more brilliant than ever. Out of the colors stepped Waioleka. She was now more beautiful and radiant than ever. Her family just gazed and gazed at her.

Waioleka reached out for her husband and parents. With kisses, hugs, and tears she greeted her children and grandchildren. Out of the rainbow came a deep tone of voice saying, "Aloha my Waioleka, a hui hou nō i ka wā hiki mai. A lo—ha!"

The rainbow began to move away from the doorway and disappeared into the sky.

For days, months, and years Waioleka lived happily with her family. Her parents, husband, and children were growing older. But as for Waioleka, she still looked young and more beautiful than ever.

One day, Waioleka told her mother her time was coming near and soon she would leave them again. Loa looked at her beautiful daughter and said, "We know you will be leaving us again. For we saw that faraway look in your eyes. We have learned to live with love for you, as your own mother loved us very much. She shared you with us, and perhaps some day we will all be together again forever."

Waioleka was so happy to hear what Loa had to say. "Now I know it will not be too hard when I go away."

Her eyes filled with tears as she hugged Loa. "Well, my time is very near. Let us call all our family together. They will hear me out and meet my father and mother of the rainbow."

Loa stepped outside the door to call Kahau and the grandchildren. There appeared in the sky a brilliant rainbow. All the family looked up knowing

Waioleka would leave them again. They hurried into the house to tell Waioleka, but she knew what they were going to tell her. She called forth the son she named Kahauloa. "From today on, this place will be named Kahauloa after you and my parents on this earth. Trees and plants for food and medicine will grow here, and the soil and climate will be the best. Take care and you will never be hungry. As for water, I will bring the rains so the sun will not scorch the forest or the taro and other plant life. As for that plant outside, it is a waioleka. I am named after it. My mother in the sky is the queen of all rainbows and the waioleka plant."

She turned to Loa and said, "Find a wife that is suitable for my husband so he will not be lonely when I go away."

To the grandchildren and children she said, "Love your kupunakāne and kupunawahine."

Her family just cried and cried. Finally, one end of the rainbow stood at the doorway and they heard voices coming out to greet them, "Aloha e nā 'ohana."

Waioleka's family returned their greetings. Then out stepped a beautiful woman with a green pā'ū and a tall handsome man with a malo of many colors.

Waioleka bowed down and said, "These are my parents of the rainbow. So you see, I am a rainbow child."

Her family all bowed down to the floor. Waioleka lay down on her mat, tears streaming down her cheeks. She bid aloha to her family, closed her eyes, and died.

Loa was so stunned she couldn't say a word. The woman in the green pā'ū was the woman in her dream. The woman moved closer to Loa and reached for her hands saying, "Loa, you and Kahau took good care of Waioleka. You both gave her love and care. Do not be sad. She will be with you always when you see the rainbow. Someday you will all be together again forever."

The father of the rainbow kneeled down where Waioleka lay and lifted her gently. He turned to the family and bid them a tender aloha. The woman moved near the man who held Waioleka and they stepped into the rainbow which moved slowly upward. As it moved they heard the woman singing the song Waioleka had sung to them. Soon, the song ended and the rainbow was gone.

The family lived for a long time together. One by one they died until none were left. Waioleka met every one of them, and now, as she had told them, they are all together again.

Today Kahauloa is on the map and located in South Kona. So ends this story.

Legend of Nāpoʻopoʻo

[TOLD BY MY PATERNAL GRANDMOTHER, MARY K. KAPULE, AND MY FATHER ISAAC KAPIOANUENUE KAPULE, SR.] 1937

Kaiakekua had two great ponds. These ponds were wide and filled with fresh pure water. One pond was at Keʻei and was shallow. The other was shaped like a bowl or basin and was at Kaiakekua.

The people who lived there never went without water. They had more water than they could use. Life was very good. There was much to eat and lots of good water to drink, and the people were happy.

One day, however, trouble began to brew between the people and the aliʻi. Whenever a new aliʻi became the head of the people, he wanted the ponds for himself, and this enraged the people immensely. All of their lives the people depended on these ponds for their uses, and so did the aliʻi.

This new chief was mean and treated the people so badly that they cried out to their gods for help. Before the people knew what was happening to them, the chief ordered his guards to watch over the ponds. The guards were never to allow the people to have any water from these ponds because the water belonged to the aliʻi.

The people suffered very much. They had to drink brackish sea water from the beach, and no fresh water could be obtained for miles and miles. Death was the penalty if they were caught taking water from the ponds! The trouble went on and on. More people were killed for taking the water and the kapu system became more restrictive. If one child was caught drinking from the pond, the entire family was put to death. How gruesome could these aliʻi be?

One morning when the people and the aliʻi woke up, there were no ponds of water to be seen in the area. In their place stood rocks that were dry as could be. There was no sign of water anywhere! It didn't seem like there had been ponds there at all the evening before. It was strange.

The legend of Nāpoʻopoʻo

The ali'i summoned the kahuna and asked if he could tell him what had happened to the ponds.

The kahuna answered, "The ponds have gone away forever because you have treated the people badly and made them go without water. Now you must go without water and suffer like the people you have made suffer. You were mean and greedy. Where the ponds have gone, I cannot tell you."

Strange as it seems, the pond at Ke'ei had moved up to higher slopes and became Wailapa, as it is known today. The other pond went to the ocean and became Waihapakai. However, the story is that these ponds were actually brother and sister and they had come from the Hidden Island. They traveled and traveled until they landed at Kaiakekua. They looked for water to drink, but there was no fresh water around, only brackish sea water. All they could see was barren land, a'ā lava rock for miles and miles. No trees or grass, not even birds, could be seen on land. So, being children of kahuna, they changed themselves to ponds of fresh water.

The birds began to arrive. Trees and grass began to grow. Soon all the land was green with all kinds of plants. People began to come and settle in the area. They had lots of water to use and lived with happiness and contentment until the mean chief was made ruler over them all. That's when the trouble started. Thus, in the place of each pond was left a great dent, or a hollow, like a bowl. This is how Nāpo'opo'o was named, for Nāpo'opo'o means "the great dents."

Mo'olelo Ho'omana'o

HOW NĀPO'OPO'O GOT ITS NAME

[TOLD BY MY TŪTŪ MELE KUALAU KAPULE]

In the south part of Kona at Nāpo'opo'o a very long time ago, there were two wells of spring water. One well was at Ke'ei and the other was at Nāpo'opo'o. The well at Ke'ei was wide and shallow, while the other at Nāpo'opo'o was wide and deep. The water tasted so good and pure.

The people had more water than they could use. Finally, trouble started among them due to the royals claiming ownership of these wells. The people continued to use this water to drink and bathe but the trouble did not stop. It went on and on.

One morning, when the people woke up and went for water, the wells were nowhere to be found. Nothing was there, just clear, dry land.

The people began to wonder where all that water disappeared to. So strange! They searched and searched but could not find any wells nearby.

The well at Ke'ei moved up to higher slopes and became Wailapa (playing water). The other moved to the ocean and became Hapakai (brackish water). That's why the brackish water is near the shoreline. Wailapa sits up on the higher slopes and sends down pure water. When it reaches the sea, it turns to brackish water.

The people, especially the royals, were so greedy that they went without pure water and they had to drink the brackish water to quench their thirst.

As the story goes, these wells were actually brother and sister. When they were in human form, they couldn't find any fresh water to drink. All they found was sea water that was too salty. So they changed themselves into two wells of fresh, pure water and never went thirsty again. By doing this, they also helped the people. But the people became so greedy they needed to be taught a lesson.

Where Hapakai was sitting and then disappeared, a great hollow place was left. Nāpoʻopoʻo means dents or hollows.

This is how Nāpoʻopoʻo got its name and so ends this story.

Note: If you should ride up along Palipoko, try stopping your car and looking down toward the wharf and toward the bay. You can notice the hollow area there. This story is a slightly different version of the legend of Nāpoʻopoʻo and has been included for interest's sake

Kepulu

WHERE KAHIKOLU CHURCH STANDS TODAY

[TOLD BY MY UNCLE HARRY KAOLULO]

One time, my cousins, my grandmother, and I were cleaning weeds and chopping down the ʻopiuma trees that grow around the graves and the back of the church building. It was almost lunchtime, and the day was so hot we stopped working and went to sit in the shade of the kukui trees. While my grandmother was getting our lunch ready, I asked her, "Why was this place called Kepulu (to wet, or the wettest area)? There is no spring water here and it doesn't rain all the time. This place is so hot and dry. We have to bring the water from home to water the plants up here at the cemetery." Before she could answer me, my uncle spoke up and said he would be very happy to tell us the story. So here is the story and why the place was named Kepulu.

During Kalaniʻōpuʻu's time, an event took place in this area; in other words, a war. King Alapaʻi had a son by the name of Keaweopala. On his death bed, he called this son a coward because during a war with the commoners of Kohala, Keaweopala ran away from the battle.

When Kalaniʻōpuʻu heard Alapaʻi was dead, he left Kaʻū to come to Kona. On his trip to Kona, he stopped at Kamaohe to rest. He sent his scouts ahead to see if anything was going on while he was away from Kaʻawaloa. The next place he stopped to rest was at Kapuʻa. He spent a few days there before continuing on his trip. He stopped at Miloliʻi in order for his scouts to report back if there was a war going on near Kona. His scouts did not return until he had reached Waiʻea almost to Kalahiki, Kona. When Kalaniʻōpuʻu heard the news, he hurried home to Kona.

Keaweopala was at Kawaihae when he heard that Kalaniʻōpuʻu was returning to Kona. He raised a multitude of men and marched to Kauluwai, the upper land of Kealakekua. They camped there and waited for some news of Kalaniʻōpuʻu.

While Keaweopala was still at Kauluwai, Kalaniʻōpuʻu and his men moved on to Hōnaunau, then to Mokuokae (the old name of the place we call Mokuʻōhai today). Next, he moved on to Koʻopapa, Keʻei. From there he moved up to the kula (center) of Kahauloa, and this is where Keaweopala and Kalaniʻōpuʻu's armies clashed.

Keaweopala came away the winner of this war. Kalaniʻōpuʻu lost. Lots of tears, blood, and sweat flowed in this area. So much that even the ʻaʻā was wet all around the place.

Kahikolu Church and its cemetery stand on this very place. They named it Kepulu, not for real water which is not found here, but for the wetness that came from the human beings in battle. They gave their life for the sake of their king and the people left behind. People like you and me. Maybe I wouldn't be here to tell you this story if our ancestors were among those that were killed here. So like this church that has a history all its own, so does the name of this place. This ends the story of Kepulu.

By the time the story ended, our faces were all wet with tears, and none of us wanted to go back to clean up. Instead, we packed our tools and went on home with that story still fresh in our minds.

Kahikolu Church

The Legend of the Pōhuehue

[TOLD BY MY MOTHER DAISY KAEHAMALAOLE KAOLULO KAPULE] JULY 18, 1936

One day long ago, a chiefess went to the beach for a swim. After a while, she climbed upon a flat rock to rest. She ran her hands through her long hair and spread it out so the water could drip out. She thought to herself, "If only I could ride the waves like they do on land. The men can ride their sleds down the hōlua slides. I wish I could ride a surfboard on water. Oh well, perhaps someday I can ride too."

As the chiefess sat there on the rock gazing out to sea, wild thoughts entered her mind. Thinking she was seeing things, she spotted a strange-looking plant in the distance. What was unusual was that it was composed entirely of vines covered with purple flowers in full bloom, and it was floating on the sea.

The plant floated until it reached the rock where the chiefess was sitting. She reached out for the vines and thought, "My, this is strange. How could this plant be blooming while floating on the sea? I wonder where it came from? Maybe it is from our 'aumakua." Questions kept going through her mind.

She took the vines home and planted them under a shady tree. That night she fell asleep and dreamed that the vines she planted were calling and crying for help. The plant was begging her to please take it to the beach and place it on the sand. "If you will help me," it said, "I will be able to help you someday. But if you leave me here under this shady tree I will die and won't be able to help you. I must have sea water and sea breeze to continue growing."

The chiefess woke up with a chill. "My goodness, what kind of dream is this?" she thought.

She ran out to check on the plant. What she saw filled her heart with sadness, for the leaves of the plant were yellow and dry and lay flat on the ground. It was such a pity to see this plant looking so dried up. The chiefess thought, "It's strange, when I planted this it was so fresh, but now it looks dead."

The legend of Pōhuehue

As soon as it was daylight, the chiefess got up and took the plant to the beach where she laid it on the sand as she had been told to do in her dream. She then went for a short swim. When she returned to the place where she had left the plant, she shook with fear. The yellow leaves that she had placed on the sand a short time ago were now green, and the stems were standing straight up! The flowers were as fresh as if they had just bloomed!

The chiefess returned home more shaken than before. She stayed at home all day, for she was too afraid to look at the plant again. Soon, evening came and it was almost time to go to sleep. Falling asleep eventually, she again had visions about the same plant. This time, however, the plant was thanking the chiefess for saving its life, and now it wanted to help her.

According to the kapu system, as a chiefess, she was not allowed to care for her own baby. She also could not nurse her baby because she had no milk. Instead, the baby had to be nursed by another woman of the household. The chiefess wanted so much to care for her own child and to feed the child milk from her own breast.

Finally, she thought of the plant. "I wonder if that plant can really help me, as it has promised in my dreams? My greatest desire is to be able to nurse my own child. Perhaps if I talk to the plant, it will help me. Who knows?"

She went to the plant and began telling it of her greatest desire. Later, after thinking about it, she thought how foolish she was for talking to a plant. After all, it was only a plant. What could it do for her?

Her thoughts that day were so heavy that the chiefess did not realize that it was evening already. Again she began to question whether the plant really had the power to help her. "Perhaps tonight the plant will talk to me in my dreams."

No sooner was she asleep then the plant reappeared in her dream saying, "I know of your desires, and now it is my turn to help you."

The plant began to tell her what she must do. "First, since you like to go surfing, take my vines and whip the waves, especially the small ones. In no time, the waves will grow and you will be able to surf on those rollers. Now, take one of my vines and slap it on both your breasts, and you will have enough milk to nurse your child until it is weaned. With your right hand, pick five shoots from my plant and with your left hand pick five more. Eat all these shoots, and it will make delivery much easier when you have your next child. Crush the leaves, and they will heal bruises. Finally, crush the seeds into a powder and drink it with water for a laxative."

Everything the plant revealed to the chiefess was true. The chiefess was happy and the plant became her very best friend. Because she followed all the instructions by huehue, or instinct, and the instructions were given at pō, she named this vine "pōhuehue." In later years, some native mothers tried these same instructions and found that they indeed worked.

The pōhuehue can be found growing near seawater, so when you go to the beach, you will see the plant growing near the seashore. Remember this story, and about taking the vines and whipping the waves to cause big rollers, for it is true. When we were young we did it, and our grandfolks would scold us when we got home. They warned us time and time again to stop using the pōhuehue, for they feared that we'd anger the ocean. After all, the sea has feelings, too.

Nā Pali Kapu o Keoua

THE FORBIDDEN CLIFFS OF KEOUA

According to the many conversations and stories from the old-timers of Nāpoʻopoʻo, I learned that the pali was named after an aliʻi nui by the name of Keouakupuapaeikalaninui and not by King Kalaniʻōpuʻu's sons as some people have stated in their written stories.

Much has been told of this pali. Many caves face the ocean and there is another cave that runs the length of the pali; the entrance used to be at the ma uka end of the bay and the outlet comes to the sea. Numerous earthquakes caused landslides to seal the entrance to the cave.

I remember my kupunakāne telling us how he used to take some ipukea people in that cave. Almost in the center, you have to stoop down because the cave becomes low. There are many remains there. Some look like an entire family or perhaps an aliʻi with all his retinue. The caves have some pools with water that tastes almost fresh. If the tide is low, the outlet near the ocean can be reached. It is impossible to reach the outside if the tide is high because the sea washes into the cave entrance.

This pali holds many unspoken mysteries. Some of the caves facing the ocean were burial grounds for the aliʻi. However, this is the information I could get from the people of Nāpoʻopoʻo. I know they do not like to reveal too much as it has something to do with their religious beliefs, cultural reasons, or because certain cults are involved, and it's best to respect that.

Some of these names are never heard anymore. Only old-timers of Nāpoʻopoʻo knew these names and their meanings. Some places were named after famous people or a chief; some names are for events that took place within the area; and some names come from legends or stories connected with a certain area or village.

KAAWALOA

mamo

awe Kaheka

Awili

NA pali 'Kapu o Keōua

anapuka

Hali:lua

lights .R Arizona - 1960

Pukaana

Lepe-a-moa

Keala-ke-kua
Kapu-kapu

Nā pali kapu o Keōua

Keawekāheka

Keawekekahialiʻionamoku was a king in early times. The tide pools were close to the place where he lived. This is the secret story of Keawekekahialiʻionamoku, the king who was first put in Hale o Keawe, a place named after him and where his bones were placed.

The secret was that in the early days, fish were so numerous that every type of fish the king wanted was in these pools. There were all the kinds of fish he wanted to eat.

Now, during those days, the women folk were forbidden from eating certain fish caught in the deep waters. Fish in tide pools, seaweed, shellfish, and reef fish were the only things the women could eat.

As for Keawe, he preferred to go to the tide pools or reefs to catch his own fish to eat. Because of his desires and habits, the tide pools and reefs near the area where he lived were forbidden to anyone. Any man, woman, or child caught in these areas was put to death. So the women folks called this place Keawekāheka or "Keawe's tide pool." This was the secret of Keawe. He only caught his fish at night.

Kalaemamo

The cape of many races—called Kalaemamo—was a point where canoes entering Kaʻawaloa or the bay would have to watch for. It is a sharp turn with dangerous rocks hidden under water. Navigators from all different islands or countries would watch carefully as they came past this point. The mamo fish are plentiful here, and there were large ones in this area, not those little ones we see among the corals or reefs. Kalaemamo, however, was not named literally after the mamo, although these fish are here. It is a poetic allusion to these fish because the mamo is a fish of many colors. The cape therefore refers to the many different races of people who came aboard the foreign ships that would anchor here.

In later years, the Kaʻawaloa lighthouse was erected here, and it is still there to this day.

Maunaloia

A cliff above of Ka'awaloa

During troubles or wars, the people would hide in this area. There used to be a cave there.

When the trouble started with Captain James Cook, the other chiefs and warriors took Kalani'ōpu'u to Maunaloia and hid him there for a while. He watched all the action that was taking place on the beach. He remained there until the troubles were over, Captain Cook was killed, and his remains were taken care of.

'Āwili

Mixed currents

'Āwili was so named because this is where the currents met and mixed. The inner currents from the pali, the bay, and the other surrounding areas all joined up together. In fact, one of my uncles told me this is the place where the big waves form or meet and start the tidal wave action. That is why in the old times, the people would always look this way when the sea gets extra rough for signs of a tidal wave coming. This is also the place where King Kalani'ōpu'u composed this saying:

Mai kēia lā aku, e 'āwili nā koko o ka 'āina

From this day forth, various bloods of the land will mix

Ua inu ka wai 'awa'awa a ha'i

For the bitter water of strangers has been drunk

What the king composed came after observing what was happening to the people, especially the women folk who were enticed and taken aboard ship by Captain Cook's men where they were raped and beaten. Some of the women were beaten badly because they wouldn't do what the sailors wanted them to do. Some of them died and were thrown overboard into the water. Those who got away reached land and told what happened to them. Some of these women became pregnant. Others became very sick, could not be cured, and died from the sickness they had contracted from those men on the ship. Some of these women were ancestors of the people who told me these stories. This is what the king meant: blood of other countries mixed with the Hawaiian race.

The "bitter water" was the fighting with Captain Cook and the sickness that was imposed on the people. It was just like a plague. The situation got to the stage where the king, the other ali'i, and the people did not trust Captain Cook and his men. The foreigners had made the people believe they were gods. It took the women to find out the truth, resulting in 'Āwili being so named and Kalani'ōpu'u's words ringing true. Today, almost every race in the islands has a tint of Hawaiian blood.

Captain James Cook, 1778–1779

Captain James Cook arrived as the first Westerner to "discover" the Hawaiian Islands. Natives thought he was their god Lono returning to them. Captain Cook was given a big welcome and treated well.

Cook and his men needed food and water. The people supplied him with hundreds of pounds of pork, dogs, and water by order of the ali'i. The natives were made to believe that these strangers were gods. Some of the sailors stuck their hands in their pockets and brought out objects, leading the people to believe that they had hollows in their bodies where they could put and take out things. They smoked in front of the natives and blew out the smoke through their mouths and noses. Their skin was white and god-like, not like theirs, which was brown. The natives called them "hā 'ole" meaning they had no breath of life.

On Captain Cook's third trip to Hawai'i, bad weather hampered his departure and he was forced to return to Kealakekua Bay. The natives did not welcome him as they had done before. Instead, the natives were restless and suspicious. They must have known the truth about these foreigners. The natives stole a small boat for its nails. They had learned what they could do with metal.

Some of the native chiefs had gone onboard Cook's ship to explore, and a couple of them were mistreated. It was embarrassing for a chief to be treated like an ordinary person, and they fought back. However, these chiefs were killed and their bodies were hung in the front of the ship as a warning to the other natives of what would happen if they did the same. This didn't stop Kamehameha from going aboard to study their guns without the knowledge of the foreign men on the ship.

Some young girls were stolen by the crew and taken aboard, raped, and held captive. Those who were strong fought back and got away by swimming back to land. Some of the girls who were stolen and got away related that when they scratched the men, they hollered in pain and blood began to flow. This is how the people found out these foreigners were just as human as they were.

After the incident of the stolen boat, Kalani'ōpu'u was to be held hostage by Cook's men until the boat was returned. The pleading of Queen Kalola and Kalani'ōpu'u's chiefs and warriors almost never worked, and the king was ready should he be taken. Some of his warriors could not be restrained. They attacked the men with Captain Cook, and Cook was killed by one of the natives. Perhaps if they had been honest and tried to show the natives the right thing, Cook would not have been killed.

From that time on, the natives started to get sick and die because of the diseases that were brought to the islands. Captain Cook's body was taken to the heiau of Puhina o Lono. As was customary, his body was burned and the flesh was stripped off the bones. Some of the bones were given to his men to take back to their country, and the rest were buried here. His hands were used as fly swatters, and his intestines were used as a marker for his grave to warn other ipukea what could happen to them.

Quite a few years later, the missionaries came.

Hāli'ilua

Hāli'ilua is a little pool with a flat rock on the inside. The pool is shaped like a bathtub, and it is where the women of the ali'i clan took their baths. The water in the pool is cold and used to be very clean. A family that used to live nearby kept this pool very clean. I remember when I was a young girl about ten or eleven years old, my father took me to this place. He told me not to go into the pool because Uncle Lanui Kaneao kept it very clean. He thinks his family used it for domestic purposes. He told me to respect the area. But when he died and the rest of the family moved away, nobody took care of the area and it became neglected. After many years, I got married, had a son, and went back there to see what the place looked like. I cannot explain how I felt. It was such a sad sight. It was so dirty that you could not see the bottom with rubbish, leaves, and branches from the kiawe trees that had grown wild and covered the pool. Even empty beer bottles had been broken and thrown into the pool. The whole area was littered and looked so ugly. That was the last time I went back there, sometime in the 1950s. Aloha 'ino kēia wahi.

Puhina o Lono

This heiau is inland a little way from the beach and is where Captain Cook was taken after he was killed. The body was burned and the flesh was stripped from the bones. Later, some of the bones were taken aboard Cook's ship for the crew to take back to their country. The rest of the bones were buried there on Kaʻawaloa where Cook's monument is located.

The first Kahikolu Church (or Kaʻawaloa Church)

The first Kahikolu Church was erected here when the first mission people came to the islands. It was later moved across the bay to Kepulu overlooking the village below.

Anapuka

Anapuka is a cave a little way above Hāliʻilua, on the ma kai side of the ridge of Lepeamoa.

I remember when I was a young girl, my tūtūkāne took me and two other cousins to this cave at Kaʻawaloa. The going up was not so bad, but coming down we slid on our backsides most of the way. Before entering the cave, Tūtūkāne did some chanting and mumbling as a pardon and for our safety. Some of the words I understood, but the rest of the chant I couldn't make out.

He turned to us with a warning: that we could look at what was in there but we could not touch anything because the things in there belonged to the dead. Being young, we were afraid of the dead. I made sure I held on to Tūtūkāne's hand whenever he moved. He showed us a kāhili with the handle made of human bone. It looked like a knee bone.

There was a canoe that was cut in half or not completed. I asked my tūtū, "Why is that canoe in half?"

His answer was, "Kulikuli." So I never did learn the reason for the half canoe. There were poi stones, tapa things, dye sticks with faded colors on them, poi boards, and fishing hooks made from bones. Tūtū pointed out balls of fishing cord, which I later learned were made from coconut fibers and olonā bark. There were some idols that were real ugly. Us kids, we called it "obake." We even saw two baskets that were woven of some kind of fiber and had a human skull by the opening. We were told they were dead ali'i. There was a bead lei that looked like it was made of clay. Perhaps it had come from the foreigners who came here. In one of the calabashes was something all covered with feathers. Tūtū said, "That's the 'a'ahu the ali'i used."

There were many things made from stone, wood, shell, and bone. My tūtū lighted one of the stone torches because it still had something dark like kukui nuts in it. It did burn, but the smell was so terrible that Tūtū put the light out. In fact, most of the things were scattered around as if someone had gone through them. My tūtū said, "There are some things missing." He kept grumbling, "Whoever came in here was nasty and a stealer."

He said someday he was coming back to tidy up the place so when the ancestors looked, they would have a clean house. But Tūtū never had a chance to go back there to Anapuka, because a ship once came and anchored outside of the monument. He got into his canoe and paddled across to where the ship was anchored and watched the men going up toward the cave. They entered the cave and later came out carrying bags and boxes, but Tūtū could not see what they had in those containers. They carried all these things and put them in a small boat that was tied up to a rock. This time he saw one of the men carrying the kāhili that had been in the cave. He didn't say anything, but was so angry he paddled for home.

When the ship left, my tūtūkāne and one of my uncles went up to see what was taken from the cave. All that was left was the half canoe, a few stone things, and one broken poi board. The calabash with the capes in it was missing; so was the kāhili, which he saw them take. Almost all of the fishing things were taken. As for the other things, they were smashed and scattered all over the place. They came back and told the people in the village. They were so angry that another uncle went there and sealed the cave with cement, and today that cave is still completely sealed. Mother nature has helped. Landslides caused by numerous earthquakes covered it completely. Where the cave was located can never be found.

Lepeamoa

Lepeamoa, or "cock's comb," is a ridge that reaches down to the sea. When the tide is low, walking from the bay along the shore you can walk all the way to Ka'awaloa, but if the tide is high, as soon you reach Lepeamoa, you will have to swim around the area or point to get on the other side.

Whenever the people of the village would go for shellfish or seaweed, they would try to go back before the tide rose.

There is a story about this ridge and about a rooster who always fooled the menehune, so in turn the rooster became the biggest fool. (See page 73.) There is an omen about this ridge, too. Whenever the people of the village saw lights going up the ridge and disappearing over the other side of the ridge, that meant bad weather was approaching. Sometimes it's high wind or tidal waves or twisters, and this is when the people head for higher ground.

Puka'ana Caves

There are many caves in this area on the cliffs above the sea or shore. Some of these caves were used as burial grounds for some ali'i of the past. According to the stories, when an ali'i died, the corpse was let down from the top of the pali. His trusted men or retinue—usually two or four of them—would descend with the corpse to a cave. At the same time, the kahuna, who was usually the executioner, would descend after these men. When they entered the cave, the kahuna would remain outside the opening. He would make sure that none of these men returned to the top of the pali or to their people. The ali'i's trusted men would then be killed and the cave would be sealed so that no one else would find it.

Many years later when my cousin and I were teenagers and had gone along the beach below the pali to gather 'opihi and seaweed, we came across some bones we thought were animal bones. Another time we came across half a skull. Being inquisitive, we turned it over with our knife to see what kind of bone it was. One part looked like where the eye should be, and part looked like the mouth. My cousin then said, "You know, it looks almost like part of a human skull."

Still being nosey, we began to prod it with our knife. It was very yellow and fell apart like powder. It scared us so bad that we scrambled up those rocks like someone was after us. We headed straight home. We never told anyone about it for nearly a year. One day my cousin and I got into an argument, and she threatened to tell our grandmother our secret and why we didn't want to go along to the pali anymore. I felt guilty and afraid, and before she had a chance to tell Grandma, I beat her to it. My grandma was not too happy about what we did. Although we both got scoldings, it made me feel good. No more nightmares. She told us maybe the bones belonged to one of our ancestors. She told us, "Maybe it must have fallen from one of the caves above?"

We had no business doing what we did. We should have left it alone and let nature do its job.

We never went back there again until today. The pali is now so steep from all the earthquakes that the slightest sound can cause a landslide. Sometimes we don't feel the earth tremors, but we see the landslides. Now only the birds fly or nest along the pali.

Paliomanuahi

There is a story about Paliomanuahi, or "cliff of the firebird." (See page 69.) It tells of a boy who used to see smoke and thought to himself that he would climb up to the pali to find out what it was. He found out what fire was and to make it with two sticks. In turn he went back to his people and taught them how to make fire and eat cooked foods. This pali was named after Paliomanuahi because his name was Manu and he made fire.

Kapukapu (now Kealakekua Bay)

In the old days, it was kapu for the maka'ainana or the kauā to swim or surf on the waves at this bay. Only royalty could swim or surf at this bay. The real name is Kapukapu, because it is forbidden to anyone else. For many years it was a sandy bay. Today, many people come here from all over the world to swim or sunbathe. This is also where the canoe races were held yearly.

Some of the boys and men go out bodysurfing when the waves are high. Even some of the girls do this kind of sport too. They would challenge the boys. Most of the old-timers would gather on the sand and watch. They seemed to have lots of fun watching, especially when the girls went upside down, because the girls would swim in their mu'umu'u. (Their legs would go up, the mu'umu'u would go down, and everyone could see bloomers made of rice bags, sewn to read "100 lbs." on the rear.) My son used to do this kind of surfing until he got into an accident. He had trouble with his neck and never went surfing again.

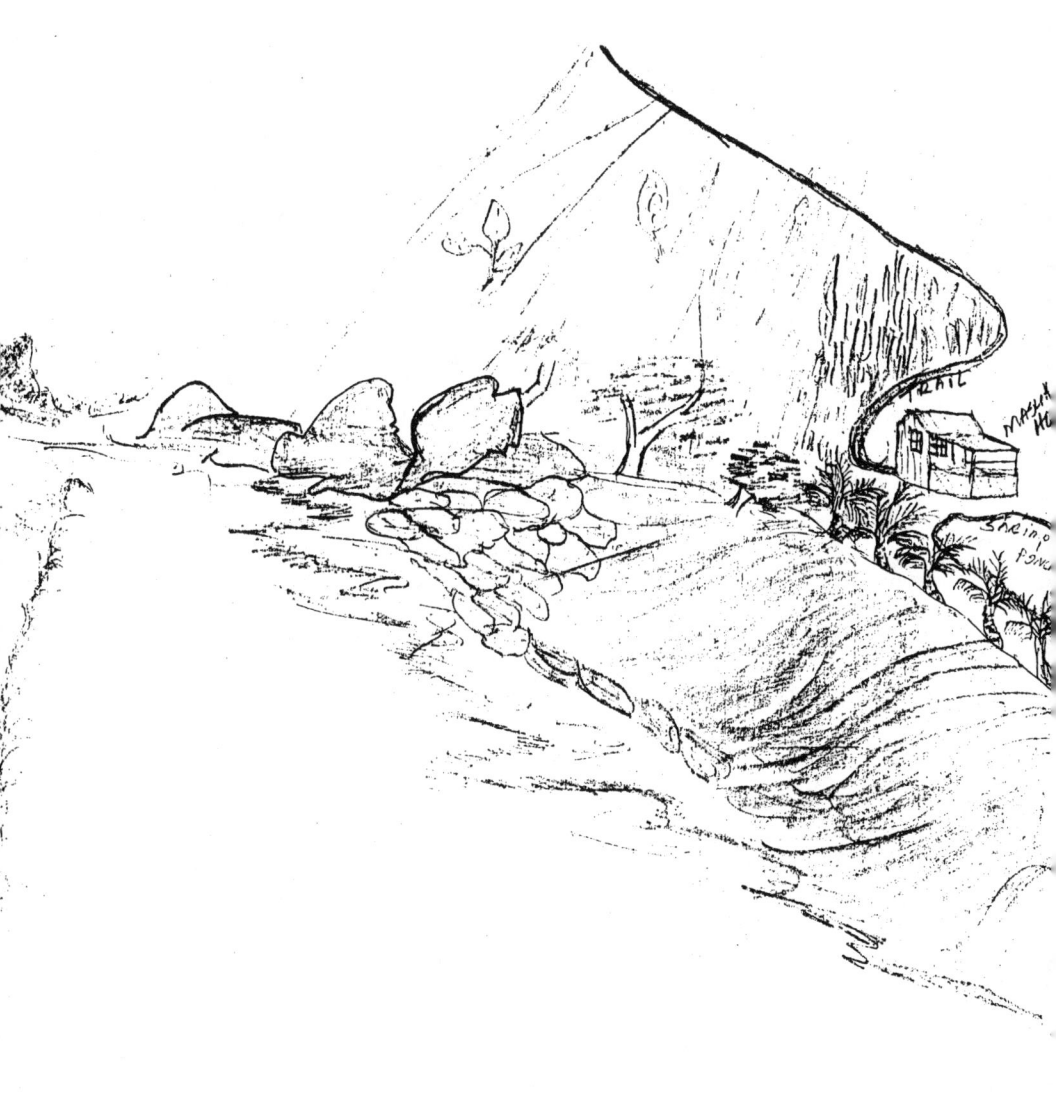

View of Kapukapu Bay

The sand used to be deep. No matter how deep you would dig, it was only sand. Suddenly, in the 1950s, we had a freak hurricane named "Nina." Within three days the sand all disappeared and in its place, banks of rocks were strewn and left where the sand used to be. It was hard to believe that all the sand had disappeared. Most of the rocks that were washed up on land were so odd. Some were shaped like a baby's head with eyes, noses and mouths—even had ears too. There were others that were shaped like the feet of men. Some were like the body of a human with no head, hands, or legs. People were picking up all these odd-shaped rocks for their rock garden or their collection.

A few feet back from the bay was a large fishpond that was built for Kalani'ōpu'u, according to bits of stories I learned from the old-timers. Some of the old-timers had ancestors who helped build this pond. This fishpond was built a certain way.

During the time when Kalani'ōpu'u was in the process of building the Hiki-au heiau, he asked Hewahewa the kahuna to build him a fishpond. Hewa-hewa gathered certain men of the ali'i class to help him build this fishpond. The rocks were gathered from across the bay. Every rock was set in place and fitted in a certain way until it was completed. Then it was filled with fish for only the ali'i to eat.

However, as time went by and the past died away, a Japanese family came and lived on the north side of the pond. That pond had been so neglected. This family cleaned it up and raised shrimp. I remember when I was young, the lady used to come with her basket to sell shrimp. Ten cents' worth would fill a large bowl. My grandmother used to buy and dry the shrimps to eat only when there was no fish in the house. When this old couple died, the pond was neglected again. For many years it stayed that way. Nobody seemed to care whether the pond was there or not. Sand began to fill the pond. Every time when the sea got rough and the tide extra high sand, rocks, and debris would just wash into the pond. Mud washed down from the hillside when it rained.

A few years ago, somebody tried to clean the pond, but the big machine got stuck in there and had to be pulled out by another machine. Up above the bay there is another heiau named Pahu. The fishpond was named Kilou and Lokoli'iloa after the palaoa of Kalani'ōpu'u. Today the name is Kalua'ōpae. I wish they would put the right name and not names because of what was done there.

Pahu

This place was used as a warning place for the people. Whenever canoes were sighted at sea, the drums would sound from this area to warn the people. When they sounded a certain way it was a friendly group, if they sounded a different way, then it meant enemies. That's about all the story I got from the old kūpuna.

Kealakekua Bay

There's a story about how Kealakekua came about. (See page 65.) Perhaps this is where the name came into use. Sometimes I wonder why they say it is the pathway of the gods. Is it named for the belief of the people and their gods of the past and where they worshipped, or was it named only for a particular god as the story states? Only the people of the past know.

Hikiau Heiau

This heiau was known as the "temple of the priest" and was ordered to be built by King Kalani'ōpu'u in the 1700s. This is where the kāhuna and sons of kāhuna trained. It was also used as a pu'uhonua.

This is a little story I heard from the elders of the village. I don't know if they were telling me the truth or they just wanted to spice up this story but here it is, the story of how the heiau was built:

When the heiau was started, four ali'i of lesser rank were chosen as well as four kauā. The kauā were to dig the holes for the four corners after the foundation was laid out. When the holes were almost complete, the four ali'i were told to do the last digging. While they were busy, the kahuna or the executioner took a stake that was cut and sharpened to a point, then the stake was driven through the men without warning. After this was done, the kauā covered it up, and the kauā were killed and thrown to the sharks. This is also the way the women folks were treated; some were thrown in deep pits.

The main building was started after some rites were done. The other buildings that made up the heiau followed. Every rock, pebble, and thatching material had been consecrated. The huts and everything else were treated the same way. The ancients prayed to gods and idols. Human sacrifice was held during the completion of the heiau.

Opiuma

Opukahaia's Monument.

This tree is not here now).

Hikiau Heiau, Above

Part of Kapukapu Bay. This tree was our favorite resting place.

This is how I heard this heiau was built. However, some archaeologists claim it was not done that way. The fact remains, only the builders and God in Heaven know exactly what really took place during those days.

Sometimes I wonder what really did happen long ago. Our people had their own customs and beliefs which today are traditions of the past and a culture to know. We do not have to practice the traditions but knowing their life-style, one wonders how they accomplished so much, including navigation, astronomy, agriculture, and much more.

The heiau was erected in an area where one can see far out to sea. This is where young boys were trained and taught to become the next priests or kāhuna. They lived there and learned everything that was taught to them. It also served as a place of refuge. Here is another story that is considered to be true:

In the Ka'ū district there was a war going on. Some of the men took their families and ran to the mountains or to another district to hide. The father of a certain family was forced into the army. The mother, fearing that they would all be killed, took her baby and son and tried to get away. She started out for Kona where she thought she would be safe with her children. She also had some relatives there who would look after her. The mother and her son and her baby ran and ran until it was dark. They rested for a little while and then continued on. Somehow some of the warriors found out she was running away from Ka'ū and they gave chase. This time she didn't stop to rest. They were only a few miles away from the pu'uhonua of Hōnaunau when one of the warriors threw a spear and killed the baby. She laid her baby in a hollow along the trail and covered it up with rocks. Taking the hand of her son, they ran and cried all the way as the warriors pursued them.

When they reached the pu'uhonua of Hōnaunau, the place was so well guarded that there was no way for them to get in without being caught. She then told her son there was only one more place for their safety, and that was to go to his uncle at Hikiau who was the kahuna there. As she looked back, the warriors were getting very close. Only a few feet from the compound at Hikiau, one of the warriors threw his spear and hit the mother. As she fell, she urged her son to keep going. Crying for his mother, the boy ran the last few feet. Just as he entered the compound, he tripped and fell down. Part of his body was inside the heiau grounds when a warrior caught up with him. The warrior was about to kill the boy when the kahuna raised his hands and proclaimed the boy safe.

The boy was spared and he asked to be taken to his uncle who was there. This uncle was the main kahuna of the heiau.

This boy was none other than Henry ʻŌpūkahaʻia. He was kept in the heiau and was taught to become a priest, but his heart was not set on what he would become.

Many times he thought of his father who may have been killed, of his baby brother who was killed and left in a hollow along a trail where he would never be found, and of his mother who was also killed when they had almost reached safety. His heart would cry out, but no tears would flow down his face. The hurt was too much to bear. ʻŌpūkahaʻia became so angry with the aliʻi and their greed and selfish powers, the ravage of wars, the violence, and the killing of men, women, and children. The laws and rules that must be obeyed were just too much to bear. All these thoughts of rebellion against the aliʻi he kept within himself. He could not voice them for fear he would be killed. He hoped that someday there would be changes for his people.

Little did ʻŌpūkahaʻia realize that his ambition would be realized, and that he was the one who would make it possible.

One day, a ship anchored in the bay at Kealakekua. By this time, ʻŌpūkahaʻia was a teenager and had begun to have wild thoughts of running away from all the animosity and the idiotic laws and customs. Without being seen, he would climb up the pali and sit watching the ship below. On this ship were some native boys who worked with the crew. He made friends with them and asked them many questions about what they saw and learned. These boys told him of the God Almighty they had learned to love and trust more than the gods that their people worshipped. They told him of the many good things they had learned from the haole and of many other things they had seen and done.

ʻŌpūkahaʻia asked them, "Does this god you said you love and trust teach you to kill or teach the kind of laws or kapu like our people have to obey?"

The boys answered, "No, our kāpena tells us not to worship idols because they cannot do anything or talk to you. There are kapu laws, but not what our people have or have taught us to obey. The kapu of the haole is better."

"Do I have to wear clothes like what you have on?"

"Yes," answered the boys. "The land that we must sail to is very cold. We must wear heavy ʻahu to keep us warm. ʻAʻole hiki iā ʻoe ke komo ka malo no ka mea he ʻāina anuanu. [You cannot wear the malo because it is a cold land.]"

Again ʻŌpūkahaʻia asked them, "How do I learn all these things you are telling me?"

They answered, "Mai ka poʻe ipukea. [From the white people.] ʻAkā, he Makua Nui i loko o ka lani. Hiki iā ia ke ʻike ma loko o kou puʻuwai, a ʻike nō ʻo ia kou manaʻo. He Makua i aloha nui loa iā kākou. No ka mea, nāna i hana ka honua a me ka lani. Like me kākou a pau loa ma kēia honua. [There is a Father who is much greater in heaven. He can see into your heart and also knows what your thoughts are. He is a Father who loves us greatly for He made the world and everything on the earth.]"

By now, ʻŌpūkahaʻia was ready to follow them. He thought to himself, "I am getting away from this lifestyle of my people."

He waited until the ship was to sail away. While it was dark he swam out and stole aboard the ship. The ship was far from the islands when he was discovered. He was then taken to the captain of the ship. He begged the captain to take him wherever the ship was going. He had heard that in the other land there is a god much greater than the gods of his people. The captain could not understand what the boy was telling him, and sent for the Hawaiian boys aboard the ship to come to his cabin. At first the boys were afraid they had done something wrong but when they reached the captain's cabin, they were so surprised and happy to see ʻŌpūkahaʻia, for this was the boy who had asked them so many questions.

The captain asked the boys to translate what ʻŌpūkahaʻia was trying to tell him. The Hawaiian boys told the captain about this boy and what he was trying to tell them. Because ʻŌpūkahaʻia was in his teens, the captain agreed to take him along.

When there was nothing to do on the ship, ʻŌpūkahaʻia would ask the boys to tell him more of that god, the Great Father they loved. Each time he listened, he felt as though his whole life was changing. They showed him the Holy Bible, and told him this is how the Great God talks to them. They said soon He would also talk to him, too, but that he must learn to read.

They taught him to say the Lord's Prayer. By the time they arrived at Boston, after many days sailing, he knew the prayer by heart. The captain took him to a mission home. It was now winter in Boston. Standing outside the door, cold and hungry and crying, he hoped he would be taken inside the house. A minister did take him in, asking, "Why did you come to this land?"

'Ōpūkaha'ia began to tell the minister his story with the help of the other boys as translators. He told of the Great God the boys told him about, how He loves all people. 'Ōpūkaha'ia said he would go back and tell his people all about that Great God. With compassion the minister received him.

Here in the mission home, 'Ōpūkaha'ia learned about snow and the coldness he felt standing outside the door waiting for someone to come for him. He remembered how warm it was at home. Here in this strange land, it was so cold. He was given warm clothes and shoes to wear. The food was strange to him although he had eaten some of these foods while on the ship so it didn't take him long to get adjusted to the food given to him.

The customs and lifestyle of the ipukea were also very strange. He no longer felt that he was being watched like how his people were watched. The other boys became his interpreters. Most of all, he begged to know more of the god they told him about.

Now his work began. He was taught to read and write. Next was to read the Holy Bible, where he learned about this loving Great God in Heaven and His Holy Son Jesus Christ. Finally, his studies were over and he was ready to go out and preach. All that time he was studying, he kept thinking of his people on the island he had left behind with their dark lifestyle.

The Mission Board asked him why he wanted to become a preacher. He answered, "Someday I would like to go back to my people and take this wonderful light of love."

'Ōpūkaha'ia was sent to Connecticut for his first mission work. It was during the wintertime and it was so cold. He met a girl there and married her. They lived in an old farmhouse that looked like a barn for animals. The floor was dirt but they managed to live and keep themselves warm.

All that time he spent doing mission work he was writing about his life in that strange land. It was almost time for him to go back to his people in the islands when he contracted the flu and became very sick. Because of him the first company of missionaries were ready to set sail for Hawai'i. He and the other Hawaiian boys were to go with them.

The missionaries went to bid him good-bye. 'Ōpūkaha'ia begged them to take the light to his people. "Tell them of our loving Father in Heaven and his Holy Son. Also tell them they must change their ways and customs before it is too late."

"Don't worry, we will do as you bid us to do. May the Good Lord take good care of you and someday take you back to your people and island."

Instead, 'Ōpūkaha'ia got worse and died. He was buried in a tomb in Connecticut. After his funeral, the missionaries made a promise to fulfill this wonderful man's desire.

The missionaries did come to the islands and they did bring the light. It was a hard struggle for them. When they found that the natives could not read or write, they took advantage of them. To get to the people, the missionaries had to work first with the ali'i, especially the chiefess Ka'ahumanu who was the kuhina nui, or dowager Queen, at that time. They managed to spread the good news, but also went beyond what was in the Holy Bible. Greed, lies, and trouble became their targets. Being afraid of this Great God they preached about, the natives became less and less hostile. Instead, they had to obey their ali'i and do what the missionaries wanted them to do. So much had happened in the islands. Some of the natives learned to read and write and in turn taught the young people.

Much later, power was in the hands of the "Big Five," corporations that were started by families of the first missionaries. Before the people knew what was going on, constitutions were adopted, the monarchy was overthrown, the Republic of Hawai'i was formed, a new constitution and more laws were established, sugar plantations and pineapple began, immigrants were brought in for labor, and the Territory of Hawai'i was formed and remained for many years until Statehood brought more, but maybe better, laws.

Today we are citizens of the United States of America and the Fiftieth State. All of this came from Hikiau heiau because of this one boy who ran away from his native land to search for new ideas and good answers for his people who were heathens. Little did 'Ōpūkaha'ia know what great changes would occur. His hopes were carried out—much more than he had anticipated.

Today some see the Hawaiian race as second class among all others in the Islands. The biggest question is "Why?" What the Hawaiian race had was taken from them. They were cheated because they did not understand how to read and write. Is it because of the crime rate where most of the prisons have more Hawaiians than any other races? Or is it that Hawaiians were so accepting and easy to dominate? Many questions arise from these situations. Hawaiians are a sensitive race and easily hurt. Yet, the love and kindness to receive others with open hands and hearts is there. But somehow, all these means have been taken for granted. Now being an American means freedom from the kapu system that the people had to obey. No more kapu laws of the past, human sacrifice, things from the past. We have the freedom to vote for who we want in office, to worship any denomination we want and freedom of the press. We can travel wherever we want to go, and can gain more education from whatever school or college we choose.

To me, freedom means everything in our lifetime. Crime of all kinds was introduced into the islands and must be stamped out. This is where Christianity came and established itself in the heart of every ethnic group in the islands.

We in Hawai'i have a state motto that says—and each Hawaiian knows it to their last day—"Ua mau ke ea o ka 'āina i ka pono."

Hikiau played a role in Hawaiians gaining knowledge of the modern age, taking them from paganism, idol worship, sacrifice, the teaching of future kāhuna, and refuge. 'Ōpūkaha'ia's wishes were fulfilled, bringing Christianity and lifestyle changes. Christianity almost destroyed the knowledge of Hawaiian culture, traditions, customs and what they were all about. Hawaiians' history was made to sound like something of stupidity. Anyway, thus ends the story of Hikiau heiau, built on orders of King Kalani'ōpu'u at Nāpo'opo'o, South Kona, Hawai'i.

During the early years, after the missionaries established themselves, schools were started. With the new laws that were being made and used, eventually the Hawaiian language was cast out and the children were made to learn to read and write the English language whether they liked it or not. Most of the children studied English and some of them forgot how to speak their own language. For those parents who didn't want their children to forget their mother tongue, the kūpuna made sure they didn't forget their language. I know because I was one of those who was drilled and reminded day in and day out. When I was at home, English was forbidden in our household. Today when I think about those times, I am very glad I can speak, understand, and even read and write my own language. Now they are teaching the Hawaiian language in schools and at the University of Hawai'i.

Piele

Piele, which means "to trade, or an eruption of the skin that causes sores," is an area is above Hikiau heiau. Here the natives used to plant sweet potatoes for their own use and to supply the ali'i. Sugar cane and ipu were also planted up there. The ipu were used as utensils for hauling water, storing food, for drums, or for storing fishlines and hooks. Other things were also stored in these containers for transporting or traveling.

There was a war that took place around Ka'awaloa, so the people ran up toward this area to hide. When the war was over and everything was back to normal, the people all came back to their homes. The chief was surprised to see the people so well fed. He expected them to be weak and listless. He asked them, "How come none of you look weak?"

The people answered and said, "We are not weak because we had something to live on which kept us well fed."

The place where they were hiding had lots of sweet potatoes growing. They could not pound the potatoes to make poi for fear the enemies would find them, so they had to mash them with their hands and between two flat rocks as best they could.

The chief asked them, "How did you cook the potatoes?"

"We cooked them in a hollow during the night. We made sure that no fire or smoke could be seen from the outside."

Because they couldn't make the sweet potato poi smooth, it was filled with lumps so they called it piele, whereas now we call it pālau. To them it looked like sores on the skin, and they traded the potatoes for other things. This is how the name Piele came into use.

Kīloa

In the area of Kīloa, which means "safekeeping," was a spring used for the sweet potato fields and other plants. It was also used for drinking when it hadn't rained for a long time.

Not far from here a prison was built at the request of the missionaries. When the ships used to stop here, the sailors would get drunk, and fights between the people and sailors would take place. The only way to control the sailors and the men of the village was to throw them in prison.

A sea captain used to make his regular stops here, and his family used to live in this area too. When this family moved away, the place became overgrown with mango, 'opiuma and ēkoa trees. The house was later torn down because it was falling apart.

I remember when we were kids, our grandmothers would gather the dirty laundry, buckets, and soap, and we would go to this place to do the washing. We only went there to do the laundry when the mangoes were in season. Us kids picked up the ripe mangoes and took them home to be cleaned and dried in the hot sun. The only time we could eat the mangoes was when we were under the trees. The only time we got to eat the dried mangoes was on Sunday afternoons when watching the older men and the young men play baseball. The older women would bring their baskets of goodies to eat, and this is where we had a chance to get to those dried mangoes.

Today, those mango trees are all gone, and in their place is the Nāpoʻopoʻo Beach Park. A pavilion is there too. As for the well or spring, it is not there anymore. Instead, there is a parking area and a playground in that area. Generations of the Gaspar, Leslie, Pakiko, and newer families live in that area.

Ke Koʻa

In the old days, the old men of the village who were fishermen had a shrine in this area for their fishing grounds. There used to be a rock in the tide pool. When the kids used to swim and then sit on this rock the old men would say, "Nui ka iʻa i loko [Lots of fish inside]." What they really meant I don't know. But if a woman sat on that rock or even a girl, they would get very angry and do a lot of cussing.

This area has a little cove that is difficult to paddle a canoe through without hitting the rocks that are sticking out of the water. Only people who use this cove all the time will not have any trouble with their canoes. The trick is, you have to wait until the tide is high before you can bring your canoe in without trouble. Even with all the hardship of getting their canoes to safety, the fishermen never gave up.

Kaiakekua

The wharf stands at Kaiakekua, which means "sea of the shark god Kua." Ships come here and anchor outside the bay. Freight is unloaded on launch boats and transported to the wharf to be unloaded for whomever owns the freight. Sometimes on the return trip, passengers will ride the ship in like manner. This ship comes in once a week. Cattle are shipped to Honolulu from here at Nāpoʻopoʻo by some of the ranchers in Kona.

The ranchers would drive their cattle through the village to the bay. The cattle were tied alongside the launch boats and taken to the ship anchored in the bay, then hoisted aboard the ship. There would be much activity when the ship came in. The only road to the village became busy with trucks hauling coffee. The farmers made contracts with the truck owners to haul their coffee to the mills or to the wharf. On the return trip of the ship, money and supply orders were brought back.

I remember my relatives ordering crackers, sugar, cream, flour, farm equipment, fertilizer, poison, burlap bags, spools of string, material for clothing, and sometimes canned goods or kerosene oil, which came in five-gallon cans. During Christmastime, my mother and her sisters would order ice, which came in cases packed in sawdust. There was no electricity during those days, and this was the only time we got to see or taste ice. To us young folks, it was great fun on ship days.

Rough days were more fun. The launch boats would capsize with the loads of freight from the ship and the young folks would swim out to help the sailors retrieve whatever they could from the sea. Ropes were tied to the freight so it could be saved and pulled up on land. Sometimes it was barrels of salt salmon. The stores who owned those barrels would give us kids some salmon to take home or give us a few cents for helping. So much happened in the village during those years between the 1920s and 1930s. These were happy and bad years, the bad years being when no ships came to Nāpoʻopoʻo wharf anymore.

Hackfeld

Hackfeld was like a trading post, according to the old-timers, owned by a man named Hackfeld. Where he had come from nobody seems to remember. They only knew that he was a German and came from a strange ship. They said when he first came here the people could not understand him. Later he learned their language and they could talk to him. Before then it was only gestures and showing him an object to explain what they were talking about.

Hackfeld later opened a little store where he traded with the people and sold their goods to other stores in Honolulu. In this way, he managed to get money to pay people for their products such as coffee, soybeans, and even koa lumber from the upper slopes.

Later, Hackfeld became American Factors. A big two-story building was built in this area. Living quarters were on the top floor with a warehouse and a post office below. The family members who lived upstairs were the bookkeepers.

During the 1930s, the porch used to be a place to play for all the kids of Nāpoʻopoʻo. Every steamer day almost all the people would sit out on the porch to wait for their freight.

Coffee was the main industry for Kona. There was a mill not very far from the Hackfeld building. Coffee was brought to the mill to be ground, husked, washed, and dried. The women folks sorted the coffee and the men operated the machines in the mill. After the beans had been separated from the yellow husks they were poured onto the conveyor belts and sent to the sorting room where the women did the sorting. From there, the beans were packed in bags and sent to Honolulu for roasting and sale.

The women were paid based on the number of bags they filled. They made more money if they were fast in sorting the coffee. The next few years were happy times. Around 1940, American Factors closed its doors and moved to Kailua. Even the mill closed down. The farmers were hit hard, too. Only the post office was left in that building. In the 1940s, the post office was moved across the road; my aunt was then the postmaster. When World War II came to an end, the post office closed its doors for good there in the village. Mail came by rural route delivery and people had to put out mailboxes near their homes. So much has happened in this village, but now all of these things are gone and only the memories of days gone by are left.

Waiʻawaʻawa

On the Kaʻū side of the wharf is the area called Waiʻawaʻawa, meaning "bitter or sour water," because the water is so salty. My grandfolks owned this place, so they dug a well for water. They did get water, but it was very salty. No matter how deep they dug, the water was still salty so they could only use it for domestic uses. Not far from this lot, another family lived and they also dug a well for themselves. Their well was not too deep but the water was not too salty, brackish water you could drink. My grandfather just couldn't understand why his well was salty. Anyway, that well is still there today.

Waipunaʻula

In the area called Waipunaʻula, which means "red spring water," a type of red seaweed was found. The seaweed made the water look as if it was stained red. At certain times of the year, people would pluck the seaweed from the rocks at low tide. My grandmother said it was good to eat, and crunchy, but I never tried it. There was an unusual thing about how this seaweed used to grow. If it got real dark red that meant the volcano was about to erupt; it made the rocks in the water look like little islands.

Somehow, through the years, this seaweed just disappeared without people noticing it, but the name still remains. The brackish water is good in this area. You can drink it when the tide is low.

Nearby stands the Kahikolu meeting house and the parsonage. The side facing the sea used to be tide pools. The area was filled to make it level with the back side and built high so the sea would not wash inland. After the war, all meetings were held in this building, as well as in the clinic. For many years, the meeting house remained standing. The people had done all the work by hand. To get materials to build the meeting house and water tank, some of the church members talented in playing music, singing, and dancing held a concert to raise money. Then in 1960, a tidal wave hit the islands. It lifted the meeting house off its foundation and moved it halfway to the road running through the village. About eight houses were damaged beyond repair. The house I was living in was also destroyed. We lost almost everything we had. Friends, church people, relatives, and the Red Cross helped us get back on our feet again. Although the tidal wave did a lot of damage at Nāpoʻopoʻo, no lives were lost, and only one person was injured.

Our church services were held in the meeting house every Sunday for quite a long time. The main church on the hill was damaged by earthquakes, so it was dangerous to enter the building. With the tidal wave destroying the meeting house, we held our services outside for nearly one year and ten months. Every Sunday the same members and children came for the service. Finally, the members got together and decided to build a chapel. When word got out, other relatives, friends, and people we didn't even know all pitched in to give a hand. Plans were drawn up and the work began. Even members from the other churches came to help. The children helped by gathering rocks and clearing rubbish around the area. The women folks prepared food to feed all the working people. The building supervision was done by one of the old time members. He was an inspector for the State Highway Department and did surveying when Hawaiʻi was a territory. He also knew about building houses. His name was Isaac Kapioanuenue Kapule, Sr. and he was my father. With plenty of manpower to do the job, they started the building in the early part of February 1961, and the chapel was ready to be dedicated and open its doors on September 10, 1961. All services were held in the chapel for many years. The parsonage located on the side has since been renovated for the minister who serves in the church.

This became our house of worship for several years. At the same time, plans were being made to repair the old church up at Kepulu. Money was the problem. Members collected recipes of all kinds from the past and present and from all different walks of life and put them together to publish as cookbooks. The proceeds from the books went to the building fund. Many donations came in from members, organizations, visitors, and friends.

It took many months to complete the repair work and to restore the old church to how it used to be. Lots of hard work was put in by many people, both members of the church and friends. Today it is serving its purpose. As for the meeting house or chapel at the seashore, it will become a meeting house after all.

Hōlualoa

A family used to live here in the area named Hōlualoa or "long slide." My grandfather Kalokuokamaile said, "This family lived more to themselves." They seldom ever mingled with other people in the village, but on Sundays they never missed going to church, and they always occupied the same seats. They were known as an unusual family but caused no troubles of any kind. When the flu epidemic began, this family dwindled to nothing.

There is a little cove here used by some of the fishermen in the area as a place to beach their canoes. Even my grandfather used it. There is a rock island outside of this cove called Moku Nui. Little rocks like islands are there too.

My grandfather and some of the other kūpuna used to sit on the high rocks above the cove and watch Moku Nui to see how the tide rises and drops. If the sea is rough and the waves wash over the moku, that means it is not safe to go out fishing. But if the waves do not wash over the moku, then the fishermen can go out to catch fish. In fact, my grandfather hardly ever got out to fish. He was a teacher at the Hawaiian schools where he taught only the Hawaiian language. When the language was abolished, he never went back to teach again. Instead he became the deacon of the church, a scholar of the village. He also was very much involved with the Bishop Museum in Honolulu, interested in genealogies more than anything else. He could quote any family's genealogy by memory, but come to his own, he had it all mixed up with other people's genealogies. This got relatives all angry, especially my grandmothers. It was hard to get along with him. Even my grandmother could not stand him, so she took me and left him at the beach house alone, and we moved up to kula or halfway up the hill from the beach.

We were much happier not listening to his endless nagging and complaining. We could do many things like plant things to eat or weave lauhala which he objected to so much. He used to get after my grandmother for not letting me do the things he did, like reading and writing. It just so happened that every time I had chores to do, he wanted me to get to the books and papers he had set out for me to study. Things were not too happy around the house when we left him alone with all the stories he had plus the histories and other things. At that time, I wished I knew how to read his books and papers. After a few years, when I was in high school, I managed to read all that he had stacked on the floor in the corner of his room. He told me, "You know, Ka'alo, the more you read and write, the more you gain knowledge. Don't be like your kupunawahine who doesn't want to learn to read or write. Be like your parents who are smart, and be like me. Someday when you can do these things, you will thank me."

Little did I realize that I would be doing the same things he used to do. I wish he was still here so I could hug him with all my might. As for my grandmother, everything was work and culture, which I am not sorry about today. When Kupunakāne died, all that he had in that room disappeared. We have a good idea who has all these things. Maybe they are happy, and that's okay. However, my cousin inherited the land and house. The house was torn down and the land is now covered with bushes and trees of ēkoa. My cousin is older than I am, so she got the bulk of the property. I have no hard feelings because I have what my mother had left for us kids.

On the Kohala side of my grandfather's place was a great big colonial-style home belonging to relatives of 'Iolani Luahine's family. The owner was G.P. Kamauoha, the only attorney for the people of the village. Queen Lili'uokalani spent her vacations in this home when she came to Kona. That house is now gone and in its place stands a big, beautiful beach home belonging to someone else.

Back to Moku Nui, anyone who swims from another cove across to the wharf is a newcomer to the village. But if someone swims across and climbs up on Moku Nui to rest, then stands up and looks around, that is an old-timer who belongs to the village. Only people who belong to the village will rest on this rock.

Waiʻamaʻu

People who live close to Waiʻamaʻu—which means "water to keep cool"—
say whenever they feel hot from the sun or the heat of the day, they get
into this pond and cool off by submerging themselves. The water is brackish,
but when the tide is low, you can drink the water. Most of the time, certain
areas of this pond are shady perhaps because of the huge rocks around the
pond. When the sun is overhead and the tide is high, seawater comes rush-
ing into the pond from three sides where there are openings. It makes the
water in the pond warm.

Here in Waiʻamaʻu, all the children of the village learn to swim. It is a pro-
tected area where the children cannot be pulled out to deeper water. There
is a flat rock almost at the end of the pond and it gets deep as a child swims
toward this rock. If the child can float and paddle to keep afloat, then they
are allowed to swim toward that rock. As soon as you can really master the
swimming arts, then you are thrown outside the pond into the deep water,
and from here the older people will test you. If you can't keep yourself
floating, you will not be allowed to swim in deep water until you really can
swim. I was taught in this pond the same way as all the children.

Above this pond, there is a well that was dug by the old people. It was kept
very clean because it was used for drinking and all domestic uses, especially
when it did not rain for a long time or when dry weather was taking over.

Tea and coffee made with brackish water does not taste good because of the
slightly salty taste, but the older folks like it for their coffee. When you are
forced to drink whatever they give you, who are you to complain? No child
answers back their kūpuna, and that is the rule in our household. They say
a little salt is good for you. In fact, when they would go upland to visit my
parents, my kūpuna would tell my mother to add a little salt to the coffee
to drink. They would say, "It takes the bitterness out of the coffee." My
mother roasted and ground their coffee for drinking and for sharing with the
kūpuna down the beach.

When it rained, water from this pond was boiled and used only for drinking,
to give to young babies, to give to the sick, and to give to visitors who
came to visit. Rainwater was very valuable to the beach people. Brackish
water was used for feeding the animals, doing laundry, bathing, or watering
the plants. Water in containers for the animals was changed many times
each day. It would get a little salty and the cattle would not drink much of
this water.

Pōhaku Pa'akai

Salt bowls

Now, in this time period, the lifestyle has changed. It is entirely different from when I was growing up. We now have running water where you need only turn the faucet on and you have all the water you need. Electricity came in the 1930s. Telephones were already operating, but just a few people had them. Now we have many modern things, and much more is involved.

Drug abuse was never known or heard about. Liquor was there but not the kinds that are on our store shelves today. Tobacco was the kind that came in bags. One was named Durham and another came in a red bag. The people used to plant tobacco, which they used for smoking or for medicine. There was no radio or TV but most people owned a phonograph that was cranked by hand. In fact, I can truly say that all these modern ideas have led to more criminal acts and violence.

Continuing down the road along the coastline, we come to an area where the Desha home used to be. Prince Kūhiō, whenever he came to Kona to visit Nāpo'opo'o, always spent his vacation in this area and at this very home.

The Kekumano family comes from this area, as well as other important people. Four ministers came from this area: Moses Moku, Kekumano, and S.L. Desha, Jr., and S.L. Desha, Sr. (Both Deshas were also judges.) From this area came one engineer inspector for the state of Hawai'i and the territory: Isaac K.K. Kapule, my father. Others who came from the village were: Samuel M. Kamakau, the historian and author of *Ruling Chiefs* and *Ka Po'e Kahiko;* Benjamin L. Kamakau, principal and teacher; Mrs. Sarah Kalua, teacher; Mrs. Alice K. Kaolulo Ackerman, teacher; Alice Pakiko, teacher; Mona K. Kapule Kahele, Hawaiian studies teacher and historian; A.P. Kalokuokamaile, Hawaiian teacher for Lahainaluna and a scholar in his time; John Grace, Jr., teacher; Ellen K. Hashimoto Lum, nurse; Charles Au Ani, politician; Walter Panila Kahiwa, teacher; and Walter Kahiwa, Jr., teacher. There were others who were painters, carpenters, secretaries, county workers, and fishermen. Most of these people were educated at the old and new Nāpo'opo'o schools and Konawaena High School. Some went on to college to further their education. Some who went away for more education did not return to the village or any other place in Kona. Now there are only the memories that we leave behind as we continue forward.

Hāwalaʻau

The cove Hāwalaʻau, which means "voice of the air" or "echo,"is not used for beaching canoes due to many big boulders. Not far from this area, there is a springboard put there by the children who live close by. The sea gets so rough, the board is usually gone.

Shellfish, crabs, fish, and sea urchins are plentiful in this area. You even find them in the tide pools here, too. When the tide is high and the tide pools get filled, lots of small fish come in. Most of these fish are trapped in these pools when the tide runs low. People would gather all these fish, otherwise they would only get dried up and the mongooses would have a great meal.

Families who live close can hear what goes on in some of the nearby homes, especially when there is a family fight going on. I used to live close to this cove until the 1960 tidal wave hit and we had to get out of the area. Our house was destroyed and we lost most of our belongings. While living in this place, we got to hear all kinds of family commotion at the next house. Especially at night when the sea is quiet and there are no waves, boy, you can hear every word that is being said, from good to the worst kind of words that really hurt the ears. I guess that is how the world is now.

Kapahukapu

The area called Kapahukapu, or "forbidden box," used to be a big pool. A reef used to run across the pool making it look like it was boxed in. As the tide rose, it flowed over the reef and filled up the pool. It made the water warm when you went swimming. It also made it deeper, but as the tide dropped, only brackish water was left on the inside and the water got so cold. In fact, you can drink the water; it is almost fresh.

In the old days, this pool was set aside for the women of the aliʻi class to bathe in. No commoners or any men were allowed to enter this pool. As time went by, the kapu system was done away with and it became a pool where fishermen would beach their canoes. The reef was such a problem for the fishermen as they would have to lift their canoes over the reef when the tide was low. This was such a humbug that they broke a passage through the reef. That gave them an easy time gliding in, whether the tide was low or high.

On weekends, this cove was filled with all the children of the village. Those who could swim well would swim across to the wharf and get out of the water. The kūpuna used to get all riled up when the children did that, claiming it was dangerous for the children to swim across because they scream and splash so much in the water. Sometimes with all this commotion sharks would appear. So far no one from the village has ever been bitten by sharks. But eels, yes.

There is something strange about this cove. Children or older people who were sick with fever, bronchial problems, or deep colds were taken to this cove when the tide was low and the water very cold. They were dipped into the water several times and then wrapped up and taken home. I know for a fact this method does work as a cure.

Once my grandmother was told that I had asthma. She could not believe that because no one in the family had asthma. My parents wanted to take me to see the doctor, but my grandmother refused. Instead she scooped me up and carried me all the way to the cove. She walked right into the water and dipped me a couple of times in that cold water. All the time I was crying because the water was so cold. For five days she did this to me and after that the nights were just wonderful because I had no more nagging coughs. Other kids in the neighborhood were treated the same way and in the same cove.

My son was about four years old when he began to get very sick. His fever was high and he had a dry cough that didn't sound too good. I took him to the doctor and he told us he had whooping cough. He was given medicine and shots, but they didn't help at all. The doctor told me I had to take my son to the hospital.

During that time we were living in Hilo. On my way home to pick up some things for my son to take to the hospital, wild thoughts were going through my mind. I was so worried about my son, then all of a sudden I remembered how when I was young I got over that asthma. I drove straight to Kona to this cove and dipped my son in the cold water. My parents were angry with me because the water was so cold, but the tongue-lashing didn't stop me from dipping my son in that water. The first time I put him in the water, he screamed and kicked but I was determined to do what I had in mind after coming so many miles to this cove. Every day for a whole week he was in that water. After the second night, I noticed that he didn't cough too much, and the fever had gone down. By the fifth day, he looked much better and wanted to play and jump around. As far as that lingering cough, it wasn't there anymore.

Kapahukapu

At the end of the week it was time for us to return home to Hilo. I took my son directly to the doctor's office to have him checked. Upon doing so, the doctor looked at me and said, "Did you give him some kind of remedy?"

I told him the whole story about the cove. He wanted to know where it was located. I told him. Every year, he would come over with his family and spend their vacation close to this cove. He never stopped coming here until he died several years ago. I remember him taking some samples of the water to be tested, but I didn't get to know the results. All he told me was that this water does have some elements or other minerals besides salt.

Almost every child that is born in the village is taken to this cove for their first cold bath. Colds are rare in the village. The only time someone has a cold is when visitors come or when some of the people go on trips to Honolulu; they bring back colds, flu, and other contagious sicknesses. Other than that, there's nothing so bad that cannot be cured by the kūpuna. My two children were taken to this cove, too, and so were other children after them. Like what my doctor had said, "There may be some healing elements in that cove."

It's very puzzling that only this cove, Kapahukapu, has the secret within its water. So we leave here with the healing wonders and continue on.

Kepuhi

The blower

As we leave Kapahukapu, we continue on to an area where there are many small tide pools along the coastline to Kepuhi, "the blower." Many small fish are in these tide pools. Wana is plentiful during the nights and torchlight fishing is good too. At certain times of the year, some of these fish are caught for eating. You also find some seaweed that is not found in other tide pools along the shores anymore.

Sometimes during certain months if you go to these pools, especially when the tide is running out, you will find transparent sacks like jelly. These sacks are filled with all kinds of baby fish. Some of these sacks will burst open if they brush against the rocks or seaweed. One of those hūpē koholā can fill a bucket with small fish. Usually, these sacks are blown to the shores by the whales (as we children were told) or sometimes they just float in with the tide. Most of the time, the big fish will attack these sacks and eat the little fish in them. Other times, when the waves move toward the shore, the sacks burst open and the little fish swim into the shallow water or into the tide pools. Very few of them will grow to be big fish.

At the point of Kepuhi is a blow hole. Water is always spouting from this blow hole. If an explosion or the sound of rocks rolling under water is heard, the old–timers will say, "We are in for rough and stormy weather."

Sometimes I wonder about all these sayings among the people of the village.

From Kepuhi to Kalaemamo at Kaʻawaloa, it's just like entering through a huge gate. Why? "Because when the sea is so rough, the waves will break at Kepuhi and soon you will see the splash at Kalaemamo." It seems like they break at the same time.

From Hōlualoa to Kepuhi is Kapahukapu but today it has a new name. Now the old name is left out and Manini Beach came into existence. Because of one politician who always goes to this area to cast his net and catches the manini fish, the old name was left out. The old folks who were still living at that time were so angry when they found out. This is what they had to say: "No hea lā kēia piapia a kaulana kēia inoa ʻo Manini Beach. ʻO Kapahukapu ka inoa i kapa ʻia mai kinohi. Keu nō ka mahaʻoi a me ka pōhole." (I think it is best to not translate this saying.)

Anyway, there are so many ʻailona within the village that at times you don't know whether to believe them or not. One familiar sight is when the naiʻa play and jump clear out of the water into the air and splash hard on the surface of the sea. That means the ocean will be very rough. Lights that look like torchlights in a line from the water's edge all the way up the pali between Lepeamoa and Pukaʻana mean a bad storm or tidal wave is about to hit the area. When one end of the rainbow appears on the old Kahikolu Church and the other end on some area that has a home, it means some member that belongs to that church has died. To see a puppy transform into a huge dog means a volcano is about to blow. There are many more such signs and some are just out of this world.

So many of the names of Nāpoʻopoʻo have been forgotten, but some are still in use today. Hurrah for those names.

Here are some family names that are hardly ever heard, except as seen on old maps or from the people who bear them. There are five ahupuaʻa with the name Kalama in the Nāpoʻopoʻo area.

1. Kalama Kū: These were the families of the ali'i and from the generation of Kū. Their job was to tend to the god Kū. (The tax map key uses Ka Lama Kumu but the old-timers say it was Kalama Kū.)

2. Kalamawai'awa'awa: This family lived in this area a long time ago. They were known to be grouchy, mean, and selfish; so, like sour or salty water, they bear this name.

3. Kalama 'Umi: When 'Umi came to visit Kona, this family saw to his needs, especially food. Everything was provided in tens; in other words, ten pigs, ten dogs, ten calabashes of poi, ten of the best fishes, and ten of everything else.

4. Kalamakōwali: In this family, the men did the 'awa chewing and the mixing of the poi for the ali'i. These men also grew the 'awa.

5. Kalamakāpala: They were known as the tattoo family. They were the ones to prepare the dyes for tattoos that the warriors used. They also did the tattooing. They prepared dyes for the malo and the fishing equipment of the ali'i.

How did these names come to be used? Well, all these families belonged to the ali'i clan. One of them had to serve the god Kū. Another was always grouchy, mean, and selfish. The other three served the ali'i. As for their names, they became land names for areas from lower Nāpo'opo'o to the higher slopes. So much for Nāpo'opo'o, the "great dents."

Names of places that were changed

Some names of places were changed while others were just made up to the liking of some people. However, it is disgusting to hear another name used when you know the old name you were taught. Here are some of the names that are seldom heard now among the people who live in these areas:

OLD NAME	NEW NAME
Kapahukapu	Manini Beach
Kapukapu	Kealakekua Bay
Kīloa	Nāpoʻopoʻo Beach Park
Piele	Nāpoʻopoʻo Beach Park
Kalama ʻUmi	Hawaiʻi Coffee Mill
Kuapehu	Captain Cook
Kaiakekua	Nāpoʻopoʻo Wharf
Kapalilua This was a district that ran from North Kona to the end of South Kona	
Lokoliʻiloa	Kālua ʻŌpae

Other names that are rarely heard are as follows:

The very first name of Nāpoʻopoʻo was Kaiakekua. Later because of a legend of the area, it was named Nāpoʻopoʻo: Two other names are also connected to Nāpoʻopoʻo: Waihapakai and Wailapa. These names are also from the same legend.

Hale o Lono was an old heiau. Today a big beautiful house stands on it. Kauluwai is the name of the area where Konawaena is today, and these are also the areas where the name Kealakekua is now used: Keawaiki, Koʻopapa, Kahauloa, Kūlou, Nipoa, Kauluwai, and Keʻei. It is too bad these old names will be lost. There were many more, but now they are forgotten.

Palemanō

MAY 1936

Kūlou

Kūlou was the first name that was given to the people of Palemanō. They were such a humble people that when they were approached by other people, they always had the habit of bowing down. For this habit of theirs, the area was named Kūlou. This area is now called Keʻei Beach.

Keʻei

Kiʻei is the true name of this area according to my kūpuna and relatives. In the old days, people lived in grass huts. Whenever a stranger was spotted, whether on sea or land, the people would retreat to their huts and peek out to observe who the strangers were, or to watch anything that was happening. Because of this habit, these areas were named Kiʻei, the true name of Keʻei.

Note: I questioned my kūpuna about these names. They got so huffy and said, "Dumb ipukea, the trouble is they don't listen good how the people speak, and only write how they hear which is not the correct way." Many times names were written incorrectly. Well, I'm glad I got to know the right name. Thank you, kūpuna. May 1936.

Palemanō

Palemanō, or the "covering of the sharks," is a point that most ships traveling from the Kaʻū side will know. Kealakekua Bay is the next port or haven where they can find a place to anchor their ships when there is a storm on the ocean. It is also a reef that is home to sharks. There is a heiau on the shore too. This heiau is dedicated to the shark god. This is all the information I got from the old timers of that area.

The heiau is in ruins due to people digging and poking around. I have gone to see this heiau and it is really ruined. Some of the rocks were removed. According to some of the kūpuna there, some men came with trucks and took the rocks. They asked these men, "Why are you taking the rocks?"

They answered, "To use for our fishpond."

That was that.

By the way, the ruins of Palemanō heiau are still there if no one has removed the rocks to take along with them for their stone gardens or fishponds.

This is the story that was told by my Tūtū Kala and Tūtū Kaouwinui, who are sisters. My Tūtū Lokalia was also there. She went along with us up to the Kahikolu Church to help clean the cemetery. While up there, Tūtū Naha, Tūtū Kiliona, Aunty Mele Moku, and cousin Kalani joined us and of course I had to take along my small sister Pali. The others were already there, starting to clean up the cemetery. We all pitched in and did our share while Tūtū Lokalia went to pick the dry leaves from the hala trees that were growing up there. She couldn't see the lau hala going to waste; that was part of our livelihood.

Kalani and I picked all the brush that was scattered and put it in piles so it could be burned early the next day. Both tūtū men chopped the 'opiuma trees down and we piled them in one place. This was a hard job because of those sharp thorns. We got scratches and pokes in the fingers until we just wanted to sit and cry. My sister was lucky—she didn't have to do a thing but follow Tūtū Kala to the hala trees. Finally, Tūtū Kiliona called out, "Time to eat!"

He sent Kalani and me to get our lunch by the hall and take it to the front of the church under the kukui trees. We did and went to help our tūtūwahine bring their lau hala, too. When everyone was there in the shade of the kukui tree, Tūtū Naha blessed our food and we ate our lunch.

After lunch, where we were sitting was so cool that nobody wanted to move anywhere. Tūtū folks were just jabbering away and looking down toward Ke'ei, Kahauloa, and Nāpo'opo'o Beach. At that time, there was a big ship way out on the sea heading toward Kailua. Then Tūtū Naha said, "You know in the old days when we were young, you would only see those big ships with sails. Today we see big ships that have machines to make them go fast or slow. Can't beat the old days."

The other tūtū and Aunty Mele Moku all agreed with what he was saying.

Tūtū Lokalia said, "Even though I was a small girl like this mo'opuna, I still can remember when I was brought here to Hawai'i from Portugal. That's the kind of ship we came on. The kind with the sails. But I never want to ride another one as long as I live."

They all laughed to themselves. Finally Tūtū Kala said, "Oh, that's how we have the Spanish blood."

I interrupted and said, "How did we get Spanish blood?"

Then she said, "This is how the story goes. In maybe 1527 or 1600,* a ship with sails was seen coming close to the point of Palemanō. During that time, the ocean was so rough. Maybe they were trying to reach Kapukapu but the ship crashed and sunk out there at Palemanō. It was said that 'the ship all smash on the point.' All the people died except two. The two were children, brother and sister, and they were the only ones who knew how to swim from that shipwreck. They swam until they landed on the sand at Kūlou Beach. They were so tired that they just lay there on the sand. The people began to come near to see what kind of people had landed on their shore.

"The two children were so afraid. They thought these people were cannibals. But the people just wanted to see what kind of children came to their shore. What the two children could not understand was that some of the people were fair-skinned, with light brown hair and blue or gray eyes just like them. The boy made a motion that they were thirsty and wanted a drink of water. They did get the water, but it was brackish because that was the kind of water the people had. They also brought food to the children. The children ate all the food that was brought to them. The people took the children home and they were raised by the ali'i of Ke'ei Beach or the area. Later, when they were all grown up, the girl mated with an ali'i and the brother with a female ali'i. From here on the generations began to have Spanish blood."

We have Norwegian blood, too. The name of the ship (of which I am not sure) was *Laasa* or *La'aka*.

Well, the story was so good that nobody wanted to go back to work. The sun was hot too, so everybody packed up and home we went. As for me, I made sure that I got this story.

The story was from my maternal grandmother, Mary Kahikikalakalani Wahineonamoku 'Auko'o Kaolulo Pakiko. She died September 2, 1945.

Publisher's note: In an oral history transcript dated August 30, 2002 Mona identifies the year as 1525.

Why the Rainbow is in the Sky

[TOLD BY MY MATERNAL GRANDMOTHER MARY KAHIKIKALA ʻAUKOʻO KAOLULO]
JUNE 23, 1936

L ong, long ago lived a beautiful chiefess. One day, a chief was on his way home from one of the wars that had taken place in Hilo. The chief and the warriors were on their way home through the forest to Kona. Tired, hungry, and thirsty, some of the warriors were also wounded.

They walked until they came to a huge tree. The chief, who was named Kalani, called out to his men to stop. "Let us rest a while before we continue."

All his men gathered around him. Chief Kalani chose an area under the huge tree near the trunk. This would be fine, for it was already dark. They thought they would try to sleep until daylight. Little did they know that this huge tree was the home of the beautiful chiefess.

During the night, the chiefess, who was watching these men, came out to see who these men were and if they were really asleep. Upon investigating them, she recognized Kalani as being a chief. Around his neck he wore a feather cape which only an aliʻi can wear. She gazed at his face and saw that he was a handsome young man. She looked around at the other men who were asleep and some of them were wounded. Some pieces of dirty tapa were wrapped on wounds of the legs, arms, and other parts of their bodies. They looked so dirty and needed clean dressings. The other men had ti leaves tied around their arms and legs to cover their wounds.

The chiefess thought to herself, "They must have been to a war and are now returning to their homes. Poor souls, they must be tired and hungry."

She backed away quietly and entered the tree on the other side where there was a door that could not be seen by others who stopped there to rest in the tree's shade.

The chiefess's name was Ānuenue. She sat down on her mat and wondered, "Should I help these men or not? For, if I do, they will know who I am. Oh well, I will help them without them knowing who is doing a good deed for them."

Why the rainbow is in the sky

She stood up and went to the next room to tell her friends what she had discovered and what she planned to do. Ānuenue told them, "We must prepare food and water. Also some pieces of tapa to wrap the wounds of those men who are hurt."

Her friends began to nīele, "Ānuenue, how shall we help them?"

Ānuenue then spoke, "We have to move quietly. We will take water, food and pieces of tapa. Leave it as close as we can to the one who is sleeping near the tree trunk, for I know he is an aliʻi."

Her friends said, "'Auē! What if we are caught?"

Ānuenue replied, "If you will be as quiet as you can, nothing will happen. Lokelani, who loves roses, and ʻIlima, born from the ʻilima flowers, will take the poi in a large ʻumeke and set it down near the one close to our hale. Lehua, who emerged from the lehua flower, and Kekai, who came from the sea, will take the lūʻau that was steamed in coconut milk. Waipuna, born from the spring water, and myself, we will bring all the water we can carry. Now let us begin while they are still sleeping. We will start right now."

Lokelani and ʻIlima went first while the others watched. The two girls took the poi and hurried back quickly. Next, Lehua and Kekai took the steamed lūʻau leaves in coconut milk and hurried back. Now it was Ānuenue and Waipuna's turn while the others watched over them.

Ānuenue gathered all the pieces of tapa bundles, and with a full ʻumeke of water, went out to where she was to leave these things. Waipuna followed with her ʻumeke of water. They made another trip with two more ʻumeke of water. Waipuna returned to the other girls but Ānuenue lingered a while to gaze at the handsome aliʻi. She had so much love for him. At that moment he stirred and turned over on his side. She was so frightened she didn't dare move for fear he would awake and discover her there. It was kapu to look at a sleeping aliʻi under punishment of death. When she saw him breathe evenly, she backed up very quietly until she was safely far from the men, then she turned and entered the tree house.

Her friends were relieved, for they too had seen what happened. They all hugged one another. Finally, Ānuenue said, "Let us go to sleep until daylight, then we can watch them when they awake and find the food and water and tapa pieces near them."

It was nearly daylight when the girls heard the voices outside. They rushed to an opening in the tree trunk to see what was going on. One of the men was examining the tapa pieces. Running his fingers over the designs, he then handed them to two men who went over where the wounded men were. They started to rub some leaves between their palms, then they spread them open and placed them on the wounds, using the tapa pieces to cover the wounds.

Ānuenue was focused on the aliʻi. He still held some pieces of the tapa in his hands, looking at it as if it was something new. Those were her pieces of tapa, and she became so excited but didn't want her friends to see the way she was acting.

The aliʻi laid the tapa carefully on the ground, then tasted the poi and the lūʻau, as if to be sure it was all right, while the men waited. Then he raised his head and said, "Maybe it was the menehune who brought these things or maybe their akua."

Being so hungry and thirsty, they went ahead and ate the food and drank the water, yet they were still puzzled and kept wondering, "Where and who brought these things?"

After their meal, the aliʻi called all his men together and said, "Today we must continue on our trip home, but this time I will be the last to leave this place. There are some herbs I would like to collect before going home."

Most of the warriors returned home with the wounded men. Two other warriors remained with the aliʻi.

Ānuenue and her friends watched the moving of the men, but did not see the aliʻi and the two men enter the lush forest growth. The girls thought, "Well, it is safe now for us to go out in the sunlight and relax. Our guests have left."

They picked the flowers of the lehua trees and the maile vines to make lei to deck themselves.

While the girls were busy making lei, Ānuenue went to a cool shady spot, lay down and gazed at the treetops, watching the birds flitting from one tree to another branch. She kept thinking of the aliʻi. She was about to close her eyes when a shadow fell directly over her face. It was the chief himself looking down at her. Ānuenue was so frightened she jumped up and was about to run away when the chief caught hold of her arms and held her tightly in his hands. "Do not struggle anymore, I will not hurt you," said the chief. "But will you tell me one thing? Where did you come from? Do you know who left food and water and tapa pieces for me and my men?"

Ānuenue put her head down and nodded, "Yes."

The chief told her, "Thank you very much. Now if I let you go, will you let me talk to you? I will not hurt you or tell anyone about you. Maybe you can tell me more of yourself and the things we received this morning. Do you live nearby?"

By this time Ānuenue had calmed down her fears. She answered him, "Yes."

"Are you alone?" asked the Chief.

Ānuenue shook her head and replied, "My friends are with me."

Just by talking and asking questions, she became more beautiful and many colors surrounded her. By now, the chief was falling in love with Ānuenue. He fumbled at his waist in the fold of his malo and brought out a piece of tapa and asked her, "Does this tapa belong to you?"

She answered, "Yes, it does."

"Then it was you who left food, water, and these pieces of tapa. Then you are not a commoner but an ali'i."

Ānuenue bowed her head and said, "My real parents are not of this world. I was raised by Mokiao and Kalili, but they died when the war was at Ka'ū. My friends took me and raised me when my adopted parents were killed. They hid me in the potato field and called their god to protect me. A great mo'o came and brought me here and left me in the care of his daughters. They are my best friends and sisters."

"Where are your friends now?" he asked.

She replied, "Perhaps this minute they may be watching us. Even the birds of the forest are my friends. They will warn me if I am in danger. Now I must return to my friends. I cannot tell you more of myself."

The chief turned to see if he could see her friends, but he couldn't see anyone. When he turned back to say something to Ānuenue, she was gone. It was as if she had been swallowed up by the forest. All he could hear were the birds making so much noise it was as if they were teasing him. He stood up and thought to himself, "I love her very deeply, and I must find her."

He looked and looked and still found no sight of her. "What shall I do? I will never return home until I find her. There is something about her I don't understand. She seems to have a glow around her, and she is so lovely. I wonder what she meant by what she said? She said her real parents are not of this world. Is it that they are dead, or are they gods of another world?"

All these questions kept turning in his mind.

Kalani spent days looking for Ānuenue, but still had no sight of her. One afternoon, he came across a waterfall and heard laughter and giggling. He parted the bushes and there she was, swimming in the pool below the falls with other maidens. The pool was beautiful. There were so many colors that it was hard to describe. He crept closer and closer and closer to observe them.

Suddenly it was like the trees were closing in on him and the birds were making so much noise. He could not see the waterfall, the pool, or the girls swimming. The trees seemed to move so close that they blocked out the sunlight and he was locked in. Everything was so quiet and there was an eerie feeling. Since he couldn't find his way out from between the trees, he sat down to rest after walking round and round looking for a way to get out.

He then remembered that Ānuenue had told him the birds and the forest were all her friends. He looked around him and still he couldn't see the outside—not even the sky—the trees were so thick. Even the bushes and grass were thickly grown. Finally, he lay down, closed his eyes, and hoped he was not in a dream world. "I wonder what manner of place this is," he thought.

After quite a while, he opened his eyes. What he saw made him jump up, his heart beating fast. Everything had moved back to where he first saw them. The trees opened up, the bushes and grass were how he first saw them, and Ānuenue and her friends were nowhere to be seen.

Chief Kalani looked around and decided to go back to the big tree before it got dark. Upon reaching the tree, he was met by his two men. They seemed to be excited and scared because they had something to tell their chief. Kalani sat down with the men to listen to their story. They spoke of seeing some maidens swimming in a pool at a waterfall. "The colors around the pool were just beautiful, and the maidens were very pretty. But one maiden had a glow around her, and we think that's what made the colors around the pool. All of a sudden, the forest closed in on us and the birds sounded so angry. After quite a while, everything was back to normal."

"Ah," said the chief, "I was not dreaming. It was real because that is exactly what happened to me. I think the maidens we saw are kupua."

Upon saying the word "kupua," the forest became quiet and eerie. Not even the birds made a sound. Everything was at a standstill.

The warriors found a banana and were sharing it with the chief when they heard a shrill voice say, "You have stolen our banana."

The men dropped the banana and looked around but could not see anyone. So one of the men picked up the banana and began to eat. Again they heard the same voice, but it sounded a little more friendly. All at once, a pillar of many colors stood before them and from within the pillar came a voice saying, "If you will follow me, there's food to fill your stomach. But first, the chief must remain here until he is called. Harm will come to the chief if you disobey my command."

The warriors were uneasy, but they stood up and followed the pillar of colors even though they were afraid and worried for their chief.

Chief Kalani thought to himself, "I wonder where that pillar is taking my men?"

Suddenly he heard light footsteps. He looked behind him—there stood the girl he had been looking for. Kalani was so happy that he jumped up to welcome her with a big smile. She smiled and greeted him, then sat down beside him. Then she began to speak. First she asked him, "Will you be my friend and stay with me?"

Kalani was surprised because he was going to ask her the same question. But what he had in mind was to ask her to be his chiefess. Anyway, he agreed to be her friend. Then he was in for another surprise when Ānuenue said, "I know you want me for your mate, but if you can bear with me, we will always be together. There are times I must go away for a while, but I will always return to you if you will love and wait for me."

Now in Kalani's mind there was a streak of jealousy. "Maybe she has someone else. I wonder." Right then Kalani asked her, "Why must you go away?"

Ānuenue replied, "To help the people of the lowlands."

The chief did not like that because he was very much in love with her. To be close to her he had to agree with Ānuenue. Ānuenue stood up and told Kalani, "Now that we understand each other, let us join your men and my friends for the evening meal."

They had walked only a little way when they heard laughter and merriment going on. The chief parted the bushes and saw the other maidens. They were just as beautiful as Ānuenue. They were with his two men, eating, talking, and having lots of fun.

When Kalani and Ānuenue entered the clearing, all was quiet and the girls bowed and prostrated themselves, likewise the warriors. Chief Kalani and Ānuenue sat down. The maidens and warriors were asked to sit with them. By custom of the people, the women were not to sit with the men. "But here in the forest where we are alone," Ānuenue said, "we will all sit together and enjoy our eating."

Ānuenue spoke to her women friends and the men, "Today we sit with the men. Be friendly to them. There is only one thing I would like to say to Chief Kalani and his men. You must promise never to reveal our home or us to anyone when you return to your homes and your people. If you do, you will never be able to come through here or have any help."

Chief Kalani answered, "Yes, we promise. My men and I promise and join our newfound friends who helped us when we were hungry, thirsty and tired and also helped our wounded. We thank these wonderful women for the good deeds they have done for us. They have given us strength when we needed it the most. From all who sit here, no harm will come to you. Now I will tell you who I and my men are. My name is Chief Kalani. First warrior is Kimo, and second warrior is Kuwalawala."

Kalani then sat down close to Ānuenue.

"My name is Ānuenue, Princess of the Rainbow. My friends are Lokelani who loves roses, 'Ilima who was born from the 'ilima flower, Lehua who emerged from the lehua flower, Kekai who came from the sea, and Waipuna born from the spring of water."

After all this excitement was over, Ānuenue announced the other exciting news, that Chief Kalani would be her mate forever. His men were so happy for Ānuenue.

Their dinner over, Kekai, the eldest of the girls, stood up and spoke. "Tonight we eat and have fun and are very happy. Tomorrow we have lots to do. We must build new houses for our ali'i."

"Yes, yes!" echoed all who were seated there.

Ānuenue and her friends bid the men goodnight and entered their home in the tree trunk.

The chief and his men were given mats and tapa to cover themselves from the cold air at night. This time they slept in comfort. They remained under that shady tree to spend the night with lots of stars shining in the clear sky.

At the crack of dawn, Ānuenue came creeping to the chief to awaken him, but the chief was already awake. When he saw her, he stood up quietly so as not to awaken his men. Ānuenue beckoned him to follow her, and he did. They walked until they came to the waterfall, then sat down to rest. "This is where our houses will be built for I love this waterfall. This is a nice place," said the chief. "Perhaps I can plant taro since there is lots of water. Maybe we can plant other things too."

They were planning what they would do until they heard their friends calling them to come and eat.

After their morning meal, the girls began to clear an area near the waterfall. Even the birds helped pick all the dry grass and carry it away. The men helped too. They had a lot of fun until the house they were building was finished, then they heard a loud noise. Birds, many, many of them, flew right into the house. They made so much noise, then all was quiet. All of a sudden, the noise started again. This time they all flew out of the house. Even the tiny birds all joined the flock and flew away too.

Everybody rushed to the door of the new house to look inside. Feathers were piled neatly to form a bed. The floor was covered with the soft downy feathers to walk on. All the walls were covered too. Every stick and tie cord that was showing was all neatly covered with feathers. Every color that you can think of was there to see.

Kalani was amazed and tongue-tied when he saw the inside of the house. It was so beautiful. He turned to Ānuenue and said, "The inside of your house is just like your name. The many colors are just like the rainbow in the sky." They lingered in the house admiring the way the birds had set the feathers in place. Then they went out, deeply in love with each other. They both were thinking of what happiness they would have.

It was the call of her friends that brought them out from their day dreaming. Her friends were calling them to take their place at the papa 'aina for it was time to eat. When all the foods were set on the papa 'aina, Kekai, the oldest of the women, announced, "Now that the house is finished, our princess will take her mate. This is a party we have prepared for them. So let us give thanks to our akua, and someone will be here to have the couple married."

When all were seated in place and all was ready to eat, there was a loud tweeting of the birds. They were so happy that they sang their best. Suddenly, there was a brilliant light that moved and stood over Ānuenue and Kalani. Then a voice that sounded like tiny bells said, "My dear daughter, are you taking Kalani for your husband? As you know, you have a duty to perform at all times."

Ānuenue answered, "Yes, my father. I love him so much, and he knows at times I must leave him for a while."

Then he spoke to Kalani, "Do you love her so much that you will not be angry when she must go away for a while? As you know, she is not of this world but was lent to this world for its needs. Love her deeply and trust her. You will never be sorry as a human being. Protection will always be near you. I will be with you and your generations to come forever and ever. Now, thank you, Kalani, for making my daughter happy because she has been a sad girl almost all of her life on this earth. Promise me, Kalani, that you will always love and treasure Ānuenue until your last day."

All Kalani could say was, "I promise," and he glanced over to Ānuenue, smiling.

"I must leave you now," said the voice. He formed a bright rainbow over the couple saying, "Aloha e nā keiki aloha. A hui hou nō, i kekahi mau lā—All my love, children, until we meet again someday."

All Ānuenue could say was, "Thank you my father."

The rainbow faded away. Kekai then said, "Let the party begin."

There was so much singing and dancing and happiness. Even though Kalani was happy and enjoying the fun, he just couldn't get over the words that Ānuenue and that voice had told him, like when she said, "My parents are not of this world." That voice had said, "She was lent to this world." The way she addressed that voice, "Thank you my father." He thought, "Now I understand, that's it! Kāne is her father! No wonder the birds did things for her. Even the forest and the luscious growth, they also do things for her. Ānuenue must be a water baby. I think her friends are moʻo and water babies, too. My goodness, what have I gotten into!" Kalani kept these things within himself because he loved Ānuenue so much, and he had made a big promise that he must keep.

Soon the party was ending. After so much good food and fun, now it was time for all of them to retire for the night. Kekai led the warriors to their house, but they hesitated to follow. Kekai assured them that no harm would come to them. They would be safe, "So sleep well."

There was so much happiness there in the forest for many days, moons, and dark nights.

Finally, one day Ānuenue announced she was heavy with child. Although she was happy about the coming event, her heart was heavy with the thought that it was almost the time for her to go away for a while.

When the time came for her to leave, a rainbow would appear in the sky at a certain place. That meant her father needed her to tame the rain so that it would not cause a flood and destroy the people and their taro patches or their worldly goods.

One beautiful night, with all the stars shining in the sky, Ānuenue's baby was born. There was a beautiful rainbow at the entrance of her house. She knew it was her father and called out, "Oh my father, hello!"

Then a voice was heard, "Hello my pretty flower. You have given birth to a son. Call him Kaleiānuenue—the wreath of the rainbow—because you will be wearing a wreath of rainbow over the earth when the time comes. We will meet again when Kaleiānuenue goes all on fours."

With these last words her father departed.

Kalani, who was so handsome and tall, with a strong body and a broad chest, looked at Ānuenue lovingly and smiled. He said, "Today my heart is filled with happiness. I cannot find the words to express my feelings, but can only say, 'I love you.'"

The days seemed to hurry along so fast for Ānuenue. All that her father had said did come to pass, for indeed they had a lovely son. Even the name her father instructed her to name the child was right. A glow was always around the child. Kalani and Ānuenue were so proud and happy for their baby.

Many new moons passed, then the rains came. Ānuenue began to feel sad, for now the time had come when she must leave her husband and child behind. For how long all depended on her father. The thought of leaving her family behind was so painful she just let her tears stream down her face. Kalani could not bear the thought of her leaving them, but he had made a promise that he must keep. So he tried to calm her down and assure her that he and their child would look forward to her home coming.

That evening she put the baby to sleep and went outside to join Kalani. They sat together holding each other. The rains became harder and harder. Suddenly there was an eerie streak of light that glowed brightly. She turned to Kalani and said, "I must go now, for my father has sent for me. Don't be afraid. Look after our child. Our friends will help you. When I return, everything will be all right."

They held on to each other tightly. Then she looked at her husband, and with tears rolling down her face, she said, "I must go now."

She let Kalani go and she walked to the steak of light. Upon touching the light, she was transformed into the most beautiful bright rainbow. It began to move toward the lowlands.

Kalani watched until it started to arch in the sky. He thought to himself, "She looks very pretty for us here on earth."

Now he began to realize what Ānuenue meant about going away for a while. "Oh, how I miss her so much. But I can see her out there too. Perhaps when the rains stop, she will return to us and come home again."

One day Kalani went into the house to see how the baby was doing. There was a bright glow around the baby, and the baby was being lifted from his bed by someone he couldn't see. It was something invisible. Kalani reached out for the child but it rose higher and higher until only the brilliant glow could be seen. He called and called after the child, but it rose higher and higher up into the sky.

Kalani sat down and cried bitter tears for his child, at the same time saying, "It wasn't enough that Ānuenue had to go away for a while but now my child is taken from me also. What shall I do? Did I do anything wrong?"

Many questions went through his mind. For days, he remained in the same position. He refused to eat or talk to anyone. His men and the women tried to talk and comfort him, but he remained silent and just stared at the sky as if searching for his child and wife.

Just when he was about to give up living, he heard the birds talking to one another saying, "Today is a great day. Our princess was sick, but now she is well and strong, and soon we will see her home again with us. Our princess must come home soon, because our chief is soon to die of loneliness and a broken heart."

Kalani listened, but couldn't believe what the birds were saying. He was thinking he was close to death and must be dreaming. It didn't take long before Kekai came to tell him the good news, the same thing that he had heard the birds talking about. Kekai tried to get him to eat something, but he refused all food, drink, and help. Instead, he remained in the same position.

That night it began to rain. Kalani remained the same and did not even move. The rains came harder and harder and still he didn't move. Then the sky became bright and there was a streak of light from the sky, and the other end was near him. There was a bright rainbow coming nearer and nearer. On the rainbow sat his beautiful wife Ānuenue, holding a bundle close to her body.

When the rainbow got closer to Kalani, Ānuenue opened the wrapped bundle. There was a bright glow around the bundle as she held it out for him to see. Kalani opened his eyes wide. He was so happy, he forgot how weak he was. He jumped up and held his hands out. The bundle was his beloved son who had been taken away from him. In his weakness he reached for the child. Ānuenue laid the child in his arms and climbed down from the rainbow. They hugged and cried and held on to each other for quite a while.

Ānuenue sat down and told Kalani, "To test your love for me and the child, my father came to take the child away from you. When we saw what was happening to you, we knew that you meant it when you said, 'I love you very much.' Are you angry with my father?"

Kalani answered and said, "It did hurt me very much. It wasn't enough with you gone, that the baby had to be taken, too. I was so hurt and lonely, I refused to eat or drink anything. I wanted to die. Anyway, what took you so long to get back?"

Ānuenue answered, "As I told you before, my parents are not of this world. But when we looked down and saw how you were, I asked my father to send word that we were coming home. We saw how much you loved us and of your true faithfulness and we could never let you die. Now let us be happy and the next time when I have to leave home, we will all go together."

They did live happily ever after. When you see the rainbow with the colors so brilliant, that means Ānuenue has Kalani and Kaleiānuenue with her. But if the rainbow is light in color, that means it is only Ānuenue. And so ends this love story of why the rainbow is in the sky.

How Maunalei got its name

How Maunalei got its Name

[TOLD BY MY MATERNAL GRANDMOTHER KAHIKIKALA ʻAUKOʻO KAOLULO]
1938

Long, long ago, when the forest began and the people were clearing areas to plant taro and other things for their needs, everything grew green and luscious. The forest was a beauty to see. Rain was always falling, and this kept the plants growing and full of life.

Suddenly the air became so still. No breeze was blowing, birds were quiet and not a sound was heard. All that day until it was evening, there was an uneasiness in the air.

The farmers said to one another, "The day is so hot, we are due for a dry spell. We will be in great trouble."

Days became hot and unbearable, and people began complaining. Soon, the taro leaves and other plants began to wilt. No more rain fell. Even the people were without water. They began to call out to their gods for help.

Two sisters lived in the forest who were moʻo, or water nymphs. Their names were Lilinoe (feathery rains) and Waihuaʻi (bubbling waters). When they heard the people's cries, they were full of pity.

Then and there, the two sisters decided between themselves, "There is only one way we can help these people. We must seek the help of our mother, Goddess Lea."

While they were talking about their plans, Lea heard them and appeared before her daughters, these two sisters.

Lea then spoke, "Since you have so much compassion, love, and pity for the people, the forest, all creatures, and all the plants around you, I will grant you your plans. You, Lilinoe, will cause the rain to fall but just to wet and cause dampness. When this is done, you will become a pool of water that will never go dry. Every time there is a drought, you will see that water is always there." Lilinoe agreed.

"You, Waihuaʻi, because of your name, will also become a pool of water. No matter how low the water, you will keep bubbling so that the pool will

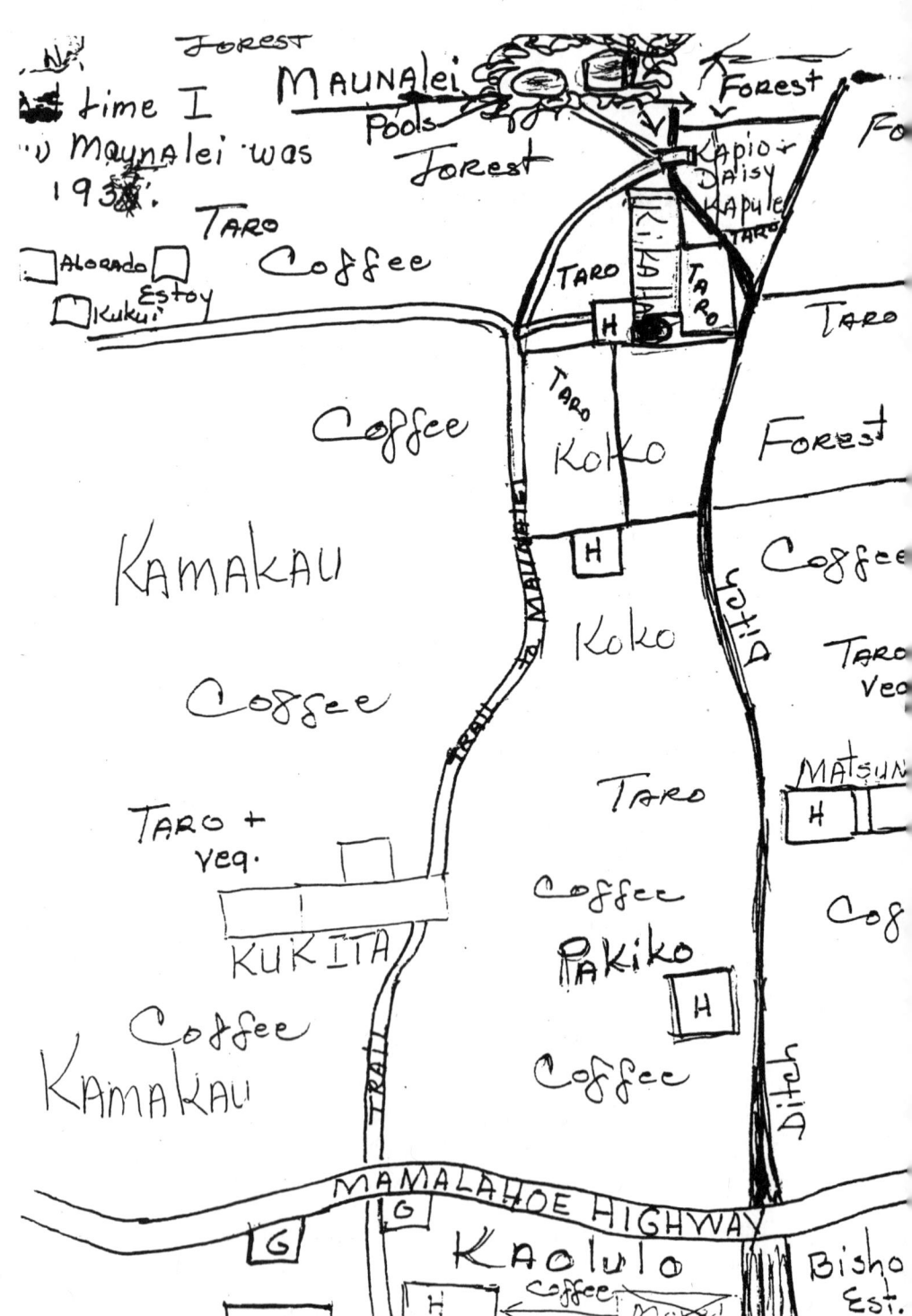

Trail to Maunalei

never run dry. Remember, both of you always have water. Another thing, both of you, because your beauty is beyond description, I will cause the white, sweet-smelling flowers to grow around both of you. This will be my symbol, when these flowers bloom, rain and water are there. When it blooms, it will form a giant lei to show my love for the both of you." Then Lea said, "My daughters, are you ready?"

They answered, "Yes."

Lea hugged and kissed her daughters lovingly, then she said, "Well, the time has come. Lilinoe, your pool will be deeper because of your task. Waihuaʻi, your pool will be shallow because of your bubbling. Neither of you will overflow." Now Lea said, "When I raise my hands and bring them down slowly, you will be transformed into pools of water."

The two sisters stood side by side. With tears in Lea's eyes, she stood between her daughters and raised her hands. As she slowly brought them down, Lilinoe and Waihuaʻi were transformed. Before Lea departed, she made the white flowers grow and bloom with all their might, forming a giant lei around the pools.

When she was satisfied with all her tasks, she stood between the two pools. With tears flowing down her cheeks, she said, "From today on you will be known as 'Maunalei,' not by your own names." At these last words, Lea departed for her home somewhere in the sky.

All that Lea had said came to pass. Above Kahauloaiki, about a quarter mile from the highway, sit two pools side by side. One is deeper, and the other is shallow and keeps bubbling, never overflowing. As for the white flowers, they are white ginger. As the saying goes, when the ginger blooms, there's always water around, rain or springs. Because of the white ginger that blooms around these pools Maunalei came into existence.

The people's cries were answered. To this day, the two pools are still there.

Note: My parents and grandparents and other relatives had their taro patches near these pools. In the sketch there is an old dead lehua tree standing. Lauaʻe plants were growing on it.

As children we used to climb and sit on the branches just to see that giant lei when the ginger was in bloom. Too bad we didn't own a camera in those days or that beautiful lei could have been shared with all to see. The last time I was there, I was about eleven years old.

We used to scoop all the water out from the Waihuaʻi pool only to see it bubble and fill up again. I guess we were just trying to make sure what the kūpuna were telling us was true, about the ginger, the lei, and the water bubbling. Well, it did satisfy our curiosity.

The woman and the shell

The Woman and the Shell

[TOLD BY MY MATERNAL GRANDFATHER, ALBERT K. KAOLULO,
WHO HEARD THIS STORY FROM HIS FATHER] 1938

The people who lived near the beach always depended on the ocean for their daily food. As the women and children caught the smaller fish, shrimp, shellfish, crabs, and seaweed from the tide pools, the men would paddle their canoes out to deep-sea areas where they could find and catch bigger fish. When the sea was calm, deep-sea fishing was productive, and the village had plenty of fish to eat. Now in the village, there was a young man who often went fishing alone. Although no one knew how he caught them, he always returned to shore with a canoe full of all kinds of fish and squid. The best part of it was that he shared his catches with the people of the village.

One morning, the young man started out to sea very early, even before the sun had climbed over the mountain. Floating in his canoe, he waited for the sun to brighten the bottom of the sea. As he looked down in the water, he thought he saw many people walking on the ocean floor. He was so busy watching them that he didn't see some of them climb up the side of the canoe. The people who stared at him looked so ugly and fierce, with sharp teeth like the puhi, and their arms and legs were long and slim like the heʻe. Before he could do anything, they pulled both him and the canoe down to the bottom of the sea. He struggled with all of his might to swim away from them, but they held firmly on to him. When they bit him and tried to strangle him, he somehow managed to escape. He swam for shore as fast as he could, but he was still too far out at sea.

He looked back and saw that those ugly things were still coming after him. Just as he was ready to give up, he felt a hand on his legs. He thought that the ugly things were holding his feet but instead of being pulled back, he could feel that he was being pushed forward. The young man glanced back and instead of those ugly things, he saw a beautiful woman with long hair and a great big fish-like tail.

She let go of his legs and swam alongside him, signaling him to follow her. They swam and swam until they reached a cave. The inside of the cave was as bright as it was outside. He looked around and saw that he was surrounded by fish of all kinds. The fish seemed to form a solid wall, but as they approached it, the mass of fish began to dissipate so that they could swim on through. When he looked back, the fish became a solid wall again.

Reaching a smooth rock, he climbed up to rest. He was so tired from that long swim that he had to lie down on his back and close his eyes. He thought about how he had escaped from those ugly things. All of a sudden, he remembered the woman who helped him. He opened his eyes to see if the woman was still there. She was right there, looking and smiling at him. As he looked at her, he thought, "She is so beautiful. Her skin is white like the pearls and shells on the beach. Her hair is a yellow-green color and is very long. She appears to be human although she has a tail in place of legs."

Finally, the woman spoke. "Kanuha (for that was the young man's name), I saved you from these people of the sea because I am your 'aumakua. You brought offerings from the sea and made sure to share your catches with the people of the village. Now, listen carefully, and I will tell you what happened back there. Those ugly people who attacked you were sent to kill you by someone in the village. He is jealous because of the fish that you catch. You will know who it is when you get back to the village. Take this shell. When you get outside of this cave, blow it three times with all of your might. You, and the people who like you, will not hear the sound of the shell, but the bad one and those ugly things will, and they will be destroyed forever. Then, set the shell down, and it will return to me. Now, place it on the rock in front of you so that it can lead you out of this cave. Follow it and no matter what you hear, do not turn or stop, and do not be afraid. The shell will never leave you until you have finished your task. Remember what I told you and do not tell anyone about this cave or what happened to you, or even about me. When you are old and gray, return to this place, and I will come for you. Meanwhile, I will protect you every time you come out to sea to fish."

Kanuha thanked her. She kissed him on the cheeks, waved aloha, and then slid back into the water. The last Kanuha saw of her was her tail before she disappeared completely into the water. He then turned to look at the shell. It rose and began to float before him, always seeming to move just a step ahead of him.

He had been following the shell for a long time when he suddenly heard the voices of people crying in agony. He stopped, but the shell turned around and bounced itself on Kanuha's chest. Kanuha then remembered the woman's warning. He was never to stop until he reached the end of the cave.

Kanuha and the shell finally came to the end. The shell stopped in midair, Kanuha reached for it, took a deep breath, and began to blow with all his might. He then waited a while to see what would happen. All at once, there was a loud explosion in the water. Turning to see what it was, he saw a black cloud rise up into the sky. Kanuha set the shell down. The shell rose again and circled around Kanuha as if to say aloha. Then it flew into the cave and disappeared.

Kanuha started to walk toward the village when he saw all the people hurrying to the beach. He followed them to see what all the excitement was. When he got there, among the crowd he saw a man lying on the sand as if he were dead. As he looked closer, he saw that it was none other than the kahuna of the village, and his entire body was being infested with, and eaten by, worms. "So, this is the man who wanted me killed," Kanuha thought to himself.

Suddenly, a huge wave came up and crashed upon the kahuna's body. When the wave moved out, he was nowhere to be seen. Even the worms were gone! In fact, the sand was as clean as if there had never been anything there.

Then Kanuha saw his family among the crowd. When they saw him, they hurried to meet him. They were so happy to see him, for they thought that he had drowned. Someone had seen his canoe sink into the ocean, and they searched everywhere for him, but found nothing. Kanuha told them that he had swum all the way to shore, and he was so tired that he had fallen asleep on the beach. It was the many voices of the people that woke him up. He told them this but never once mentioned the woman, the shell, the cave, or the ugly things that wanted to kill him.

Well, Kanuha returned home with his family and lived happily with them for a long time, and every time he went fishing, he never once forgot his offering to the sea or to share his catches with the people. He kept hoping that he would see that beautiful woman with the fish tail, but Kanuha never saw or heard of her again.

Many years passed, and he kept his secret. He began to grow old, gray, and weak, so he couldn't go fishing anymore. One day, however, he managed to drag himself to the secret cave. When he reached the cave, he sat down to rest. All of a sudden, he heard his name being called from deep within. Looking into the cave, he saw two men and the shell coming to meet him. The men bent down, picked him up, and held him tenderly in their arms. Without saying a word, they entered the cave. They seemed to float all the way in as they followed the shell.

When they reached the other end of the cave, there stood his beautiful woman waiting with outstretched arms. This time, however, she did not have her tail, but two legs instead.

She guided him to a smooth rock and told him, "Now I will take care of you." He smiled at her, nodded his head, and then said, "I have loved you from the first day we met." The woman said that she loved him too, and told him, "Now we will be together forever."

Kanuha replied, "I am very happy." With these last words, he closed his eyes and died. The woman had the men lift him up gently. They entered the sea with the shell and disappeared into the water, never to be seen again.

Now, because of this story, every time a conch shell is found in the sea or on the beach, it is said that it is an offspring of that woman's shell.

Short Stories from Keālia to Hoʻokena

Keālia

People in this area claim Keālia is a land section that runs from the sea to the mountain. This is a story I heard about how they named that area Keālia. I think it is such an interesting story.

Chief Kaleipaihala lived in this area and all he did was spend hours and hours watching games like mokomoko, kōnane, and spear throwing. Every day this was all the chief ever did. Whenever another chief came to visit him on some kind of mission, Kaleipaihala would tell him to wait because he was busy watching the games and wanted to see who was going to win. People used to get disgusted and tired of waiting for him. Even when the chiefess told him it was time for them to leave, he would answer in a very angry tone and say, "When the sun sets, then I am ready to go. Now, don't bother me."

Kēōkea

Kēōkea is a land section between Hōnaunau and Kiʻilae ahupuaʻa north of Keālia and Hoʻokena. Some people said that this area was always white like a desert because of the bones bleaching in the sun. It has been said that bones were bleached here in the sun before using them for hooks, kāhili or arrowheads. It is known as a scorching area. No matter what they planted, almost everything dried up.

ʻĀinapō

This is an area or place where all kāhuna congregated to pursue their studies of mostly witchcraft or sorcery. Because they were done in secrecy, most of their studies were done with the utmost care when no other eyes could observe the nature of these studies. In fact, most of these studies took place during the night. Because of these things being done in secret, this place was named ʻĀinapō (land of the darkness).

by M. K. Kahele

Short stories from Keālia to Ho'okena

Kaleipaihala always had the habit of prolonging his visits until the sun set in the ocean, then he was ready to leave. Otherwise, no one could move him no matter what took place.

Because of this chief and his habits, if you prolonged your visit at a certain place or home at Keālia, the people would say, "Oh my, this must be the salt of Chief Kaleipaihala," meaning this must be the descendent of Chief Kaleipaihala.

This is how the name Keālia was made known.

Ho'okena

This is a story of Ho'okena. I heard this story from one of my uncles who lived in this area and was an old time policeman. He had quite a number of stories to tell, and I wish I had taken more interest in them. However, at that time, I was not aware of many other places except where I came from. Anyway, here is the story of how Ho'okena got its name.

The people's welfare rested on the shoulders of the chief of the village. Now the chief of the village lived on the shore of the beach. The people who lived at the beach were fishing people. Those who lived on the higher slopes were the farmers.

All through the land, everything was flourishing. There were lots of fish, and the farmers' production of grown food was all doing well until the dry weather became a threat to the people. The farmers began to worry as their taro and other plants were beginning to dry. The only way they could protect their plants from the hot weather was to get water. There were no springs where the farmers were living. The only means of having water was to depend on the rain, but for several months no rains came. Finally they decided that there was only one thing to do: they must haul water from the beach. The farmers and their families gathered whatever containers they had and began to march down to the beach for water. Now, at the beach only brackish water was plentiful. So they began to haul the water for their taro plants. For days they went about their task.

When the chief found out what the farmers were doing, he felt so sorry for them that he gathered all the beach people together and told them they must help the farmers. At first the people did not like the idea because they said they were not farmers but fishing people, so why should they help the farmers? The chief became very angry and told them they needed the food that the farmers grew and if they didn't help the farmers, the whole land would be without food, for they could not live on fish alone. Still, the beach people would not agree. So the chief laid down his rules and forced the people to do what he had asked them to do. If they would not help the farmers to haul the water for the taro and the other plants, they would be put to death. By this order, the people began to haul the water to the upland for the farmers. The taro began to flourish, and there was more than the farmers could use for themselves, so they shared most of their produce with the chief and the beach people to show their gratitude for the help they had given them. Likewise, the fishermen gave part of their catches to the farmers in exchange for things from the uplands. Due to the chief forcing the beach people to help the farmers, the area became known as Hoʻokena (to quench thirst). And so this story ends.

Pahupahu
KNOCKING

This is an old Hawaiian legend, from the island of Oʻahu, when it was peopled with ghost gods. They lay waiting for persons passing from Kauaʻi to the other islands. They would catch these persons and eat them all up.

One of these demons could transform himself into eight different forms. Each transformation was really ugly. He was hunchbacked, crazy, one-eyed, blind, deaf, and lame.

Living on Oʻahu was a lovely girl who was the only daughter of a Hawaiian couple. This daughter always had lovely dreams of a place named Waipiʻo on Oʻahu. It was a place filled with the natural beauty of the water and a towering pali.

She always told her mother about her dreams. The mother warned her that she must forget these visions or she would be under the influence of Halilili, the king of the evil ones.

The daughter, unable to throw off the evil influence, finally died. Her bones were kept in the home and her spirit would return at times.

Some strangers came one day and the parents told them about the ghost of their daughter. The strangers told them that they must go to see the kahuna to save her.

During the night, one of these gods came to take the daughter as usual to Halilili. He knocked (pahupahu) but the girl, given strength by the kahuna, refused to go. All night long the battle continued, but the daughter stayed away from him. In the morning the spell was broken and the girl returned to life and lived happily with her parents.

Miloli'i Stories

These stories were told to me by my husband's aunt Mrs. Elizabeth K. Kuahuia and Tūtū Mrs. Kipi Keli'ikuli Ka'ana'ana. They knew that I was interested in stories and legends and past events that were never written or recorded. Then they asked me if I would listen to them. I didn't refuse this request because that was down my line. I had a feeling of being honored. My most aloha nui loa mai ka pu'uwai i kēia mau luahine i ha'i mai ia'u nā mo'olelo i pili ana i ko lāua 'āina. Aloha nō. Aia a'e nā mo'olelo e ho'olaha nei e a'u.

Kapalilua

AN OLD NAME FOR THE MILOLI'I AREA

I collected these stories, legends, place names, and Miloli'i events from my in-laws and tūtū, and aunties and uncles of my husband. As I watched and listened to their stories, their eyes and broad smiles seemed to reveal all their inner thoughts, and I could almost visualize those lives of long ago.

The stories they told me were just out of this world. They were fantastic and some stories were just weird. Some events were interesting and I thank all these individuals for sharing their stories and their lifestyle. Being able to understand and converse in the Hawaiian language, understanding them was no problem at all.

Hau'oli Kamana'o built in 1865

166

I first came to this isolated village of Miloli'i in the latter part of 1946. When we left the main highway, we turned off onto a gravel road that was really bad. It seemed like a trail instead of a road. We rode through a thick kukui grove and the road wound down the hill until we were out of the grove. The sun was just about setting. Coming out, we were greeted by the old lava flow. I thought to myself, my goodness, how much farther do we have to travel before we get to the village? The road was just terrible, full of holes and so narrow. I kept wondering how we would let a car pass if we were to meet one coming up. As we passed more lava and curves, I saw housetops far away.

My cousin, who was returning from the service, brought me to Miloli'i. Since I was on vacation from my job at Pier 1 in Hilo, I decided to take his offer. I am not sorry at all that I went along. His mother, my aunt, was the school teacher at Miloli'i, teaching in the one-room school house. That's where we were headed. On the way down to the flats, my cousin showed me where Ho'ōpūloa Village used to be. At that time, there were about three houses built there. I asked my cousin what happened to the people who used to live there before the 1926 lava flow. He said, "Some of them moved to Miloli'i and established themselves there. The rest moved to the upper lands and to other islands."

Finally, he told me we would be entering Miloli'i soon. As we came over the hill, I got a full view of the tiny village. There were lots of canoes in the awa alongside the road before we reached the teacher's cottage.

His mother was so happy to see the two of us home at last. She had waited all afternoon for us to arrive, and we had finally made it. It was just about dark by then. After dinner we all went out on her porch to sit and enjoy the evening breeze. My aunt told me the front property was the school and she was the only one who had a telephone in the village. I noticed that most of the houses were grouped close to one another, judging by the lights I saw.

My aunt then said, "Here there's no electricity, running water, doctor, or anything modern." There were about four houses besides the school that owned water tanks and two places that had cement cisterns: the church in the back and a house on the hill coming down to this part of the village. As for the other homes, they used either wooden barrels or tubs to catch rainwater. Brackish water was for baths and all domestic uses. All around this area there were brackish water ponds. The one-room school was for students up to the eighth grade. After that, some of the students became fishermen or the girls got married. I asked my aunt about the population of the village. She replied, "Counting the children plus the Filipinos who are fishermen we have at least a hundred people."

"Another question, Aunty, how do they survive? And are they all pure Hawaiians or is it like Nāpoʻopoʻo where we come from?"

She answered, "No, most of them are part-Hawaiians, and there were more in the past." Not like us at Nāpoʻopoʻo. Although some of the living conditions are similar, our way was a little more modern than it was at Miloliʻi. "I wish you could stay longer, then you would experience the lifestyle of the people here."

Learn I did, and I am very thankful. I found that fishing was their main source of livelihood. The lifestyle in the village was simple, but traditions were still strong among the villagers in their daily life. Some things they kept well-hidden among themselves. Other than that, the people were loving and very friendly. I have never come across people like here at Miloliʻi. People at my village kept mostly to themselves, but here in Miloliʻi I found the people more warm. They take you into their hearts as if you really belonged to them.

I also gained a husband here, a man who was born and raised three miles from Miloliʻi going along the coastline to Kapuʻa. His family was the last to leave Kapuʻa during World War II. They were asked to move to the closest village as they had no means of communication should anything happen. Being that his parents were elderly and had several grandchildren living with them, they moved to Miloliʻi Village so they could feel closer to home.

My husband and one brother went into the army. The older brother had a family of his own. One brother was a fisherman, another worked in construction, and another was a merchant seaman aboard one of the freighters that called on Hilo and other ports of the islands. Most of the young boys here in the village went into branches of the service or became merchant marines.

On Sundays most everybody young and old went to church. There were only two churches in the village, a Catholic church and a Congregational church that had a beautiful story connected with it, sad and meaningful.

During the afternoons, a volleyball net was strung across the road. This was where all the young men and women of the village passed their time playing ball on Sunday afternoon. The women would challenge the men.

It was great fun watching them play. All the children and the elderly or old-timers were fans. As you watched them, their faces really lit up when the women won.

Traditions were very much carried on. Christianity was also there in the village, but the old ways were somehow still mingled among them, too.

Miloli'i itself was isolated from all other activities or things of interest, yet the village did keep up with whatever else was around in this world. At least two or three families owned radios that ran on dry-cell batteries. Whatever news they heard they reported to all the other villagers. Sometimes by the time it got to the last house, the news had been made into more news than was told by the first informers.

Another thing I noticed on Sundays, you didn't see any canoes or boats out fishing or see anyone mending their fishing equipment. Other days, as long the sea was calm, the canoes and sampans were out fishing.

One Sunday afternoon, I sat with all the tūtū and old timers. They were so warm and friendly. Since I spoke the Hawaiian language fluently, I asked them, "Why is it that no canoes or fishermen from the village are out on the sea on Sunday?" They looked surprised when I spoke to them in their language. For a while they just looked at me as if I had said something wrong.

Finally a tūtū lady—who I later learned was Tūtū Kipi—spoke to me and said, "You are so young and yet you speak the mother tongue so well." She thought I was a city girl because someone told her I was from Hilo.

I told her, "No, I come from Nāpo'opo'o and my tūtū raised me. She only speaks Hawaiian and most of the people and young people there speak Hawaiian fluently."

Then she said, "Not like our young people. Some of them don't speak the language. Some, they speak kāpulu."

I told them that where I came from, in our house nobody was allowed to speak English. My tūtū Lokalia was very strict. She was pure Portuguese and was five years old when she and her sister who was eight years old were brought to the islands by their father. He married a Hawaiian woman from Maui, so Hawaiian was all she knew. My parents also spoke the language, but I lived with my tūtū. The reason I moved to Hilo was because she was sick, and where we lived was too far to walk to the doctor. So we moved to Hilo and I went to school there. When the war broke out, I went to work at a laundry, then went back to school to continue my education. After two years of college, I worked for C. Brewer & Company as a clerk. I was on vacation, so I came to visit Miloli'i with my cousin.

I told them, "It feels so good to talk the language again since all the people I know don't speak Hawaiian anymore, only haole. But here in Miloli'i I can speak with you folks."

They were so tickled that they told me no fishing on Sundays was due to a great tidal wave and this had been the law of the village since then. Sundays there was no fishing, mending equipment, card playing or gambling, good times, or kanikapila. Our talk led to more conversations. I had a million questions to ask them. They were so good to respond, especially Tūtū Kipi and Aunty Kapeka.

I asked them, "Are there any stories of this village?"

They replied, "Yes. If you are interested we will tell you."

I also asked, "Can I write these stories on paper?"

All the tūtū sitting there answered, "Why not? If we die, nobody will know the stories of Miloli'i from one end to the other."

So this is how I acquired these stories.

They told me the story of how the name Miloli'i came about. Milo means to weave, twirl, or twist. Miloli'i was where all the fishing lines were made, supplying all lines down the seacoast. Up ma uka they gathered 'olonā then brought it down. Even coconut husk was used, soaked, and pounded. You twist it. They did the finest weave at Miloli'i.

I became wide-eyed and began to laugh. I told them, "I'm not trying to make fun, but where I come from is also called Kapalilua." They were amazed, because all the time they thought the name covered the area from Ho'okena almost to South Point. They told me there was a little story, a code that was used by a chief to the next chief. By using this code, they knew their enemies were at a certain place and how many warriors were coming. We know 'ulu does not grow at the edge of the sea. The number of warriors was counted by forties. For example, if they said four or five counts, that meant 160 to 200 warriors. Kapalilua is between Mauna Kea and Mauna Loa. So Tūtū Kipi quoted the code and the meaning.

Aia ka 'ulu
Ke pae nei i ka lihi kai o ka Pali Lua
'Ehā paha 'elima ka'au
'Ohi pau loa a māhu.

There's the breadfruit
Landing at the water's edge of Two Cliffs
About four or five counts
Pick all of them and steam them.

Actual meaning of the code:

There are the men
Landing at the edge of the shore between Mauna Kea and Mauna Loa
About 160 to 200 men
Attack and kill all of them.

I thought this was a rather strange code, but ever so interesting. Actually, the translation differs from what these chiefs really meant. It is either a riddle or parable. I asked if they had any idea who the chiefs were who used this code. They didn't know but had heard it from their kūpuna. The stories they told me were interesting, sad, weird, and fantastic.

Note: The real name for the areas before South Point up till almost Honalo was Kapalilua. It was like a district between two mountains.

Miloli'i Malihini

A DESCRIPTION

Miloli'i is a very lonely village, all by itself, isolated and miles away from any other village or town. From the main highway there's a turnoff and you get onto a gravel road that leads down to the beach. The road is treacherous with sink holes and loose gravel—a narrow winding road that leads downhill almost all the way to the village. The road is about seven and a quarter miles, and it takes about half an hour to reach the village.

Observing the village from high above, it seems to sit below sea level. But the land is actually flat when you finally get down and make the last curve. To get to the village you must cross the Ho'ōpūloa Flow, which came from the mountain and buried the entire village of Ho'ōpūloa in April of 1926.

Ho'ōpūloa Village was very active before the 1926 lava flow. It had little stores and a gas pump, a wharf where ships came in once a week or every other week. They took loads of koa logs, loads of 'ōpelu and other things and sometimes some passengers. This is the way the people of Miloli'i and Ho'ōpūloa received their supplies in exchange for the fish, logs, and other things that were sent to Honolulu.

The lava flow left Ho'ōpūloa a wasteland and devastated the entire village. It left the people with nothing but the a'ā. Some of the people moved to Miloli'i, the closest village. As for the rest of the people, they moved to the upper slopes. Some of the people who were fortunate moved to O'ahu. The best part was that no one lost their life, but all personal belongings were lost.

After a couple of years, a couple of families moved back to Ho'ōpūloa to live. The government built homes for them, but in the 1950s the last family moved away. Living conditions were very hard because of lack of employment. Fishing wasn't bringing in enough to support the families, so they had to seek somewhere else to resume their lifestyle.

The road to Miloliʻi is really bad and narrow. When meeting a car coming up from the village, the driver must look for a wide space so the other car can pass. Cars must have good brakes on account of the downhill, winding road.

When you leave the highway and go down toward Miloliʻi, you are going through a kukui grove. It feels cool and fresh. The smell of dampness makes you wonder whether you are in a great forest. As you glance around, there is hardly any sunlight that penetrates through the leaves of the kukui trees. The ground is covered with a soft green moss that looks like velvet. It forms shapes as it covers the rocks—to me, there's life in this growth.

One time when I was on the road, so many things were floating through my mind, things like women folks picking the dry kukui nuts to roast in the cinders and make into a condiment (ʻinamona). As we drove along, I thought of the many uses of the kukui. Looking at the trunks and the roots sticking out in some places, I thought of the dyes that were made from the bark and roots, the leaves and the old rotted trees used for fertilizer, the green nuts and flowers used for medicinal purposes, dry nuts used for condiments or making simple jewelry, old nuts used as fuel to light the stone lamps of the Hawaiians. Oh boy, my thoughts went wild with all the things I could do with kukui.

It is quite a drive through this grove, and then you are greeted with the open waste areas of lava, aʻā type. You can see and feel the heat waves from this aʻā. I was more concerned with the drive downhill because of the lousy condition of the road. Some places it looks like a wide trail. All the way it's aʻā until you reach the village.

Passing the houses alongside the road, children and older people were waving their hands. I looked at my cousin and said, "Walter, are the people here all friendly like this, waving and smiling? I know they're doing that because you are coming home." Such friendly people.

Reminiscing About the Events From the Last Sixty-five Years

[TOLD BY MY HUSBAND ABEL PEPE KALILIAKU KAHELE]

My father was a good fisherman. All he did was fishing all his life. Every day was the same thing: fish, fish, and more fishing for our living. When I think back to those days, it makes me cry. Why? Because when I look around us today I wish my parents were still alive. Maybe things would be easier or maybe they would be cussing everybody and how they are fishing today.

In my family we have two sisters and five brothers. My oldest sister is Kalawae'a. I pity that sister because she had all the most work at home. She had to take care of us the younger ones so my mother can go out help my father catch fish. That is why she cannot write her name or read and write, because she cannot go to school. She had to stay home and take care of us and kaula'i the 'ōpelu.

If she no watch the dry fish and my father them come home, he take the kuku stick and give her good licking. Sometimes my mother try to stop my father, but she get licking too. Why must it be like that? I really no understand. Even my older brothers and my sister Hano cannot do nothing, because they are going to had it too. Me and my brother Nahinu use to run behind the house and hide on the a'ā and cry to ourselves. We can hear my mother and sister yelling. Many times we wanted to take a big stick and stones to hit my father, but my mother always stop us and say that is your father. The worst times is when he come home from Miloli'i or from some Japanese fishing boat all drunk and that's when he gets out of hand. Our poor mother is the one who gets it all the time.

We live at Kapu'a. Near us is the Kaluahalawa family. When they are at home and my father is beating us or my mother, the old lady use to come over with a big stick to clobber my father and ask when he stop. Otherwise we had it.

Every day, as long the sea is mālie, that canoe is always out on the sea. Either my brothers or my mother always go out with my father. My sisters and me and Nahinu we stay home and get ready the palu for the next day or sometimes for the same day.

'Ōpelu fishing was our main fish. We have to get the taro and olo until we think that's enough. If no more taro, we use the pumpkin or my mother and my sisters go catch the red 'ōpae in the pūnāwai behind the house. With this 'ōpae, my father mix with whatever palu he get left. As for us who stay home, we have to dry the 'ōpelu. Every day kaha, salt, and kaka the fish for kaula'i. When all the fish dry, we pack 'em in the barrels and my father and my brothers take the barrels to Ho'ōpūloa to send to Honolulu for sell. Get one Pākē and he get big store and he order the fish from my father. My father order the salt by the bags and cracker, flour, and sugar for us. The balance money they send to my father. This is how we get our living.

Ho'ōpūloa had wharf before and that's how we get our ukana. Sometimes the sea gets rough and we had to walk three miles to Miloli'i then walk again to Ho'ōpūloa wharf. We get whatever ukana we can carry and walk home to Kapu'a again. My father and my older brothers stay back at Ho'ōpūloa wait for the sea come mālie so they can bring the rest of the ukana home, especially the salt. Sometimes when they come back, no more money cause my father use to buy drinks and drink with the family there.

Sometimes, when I think back those days, make me cry and I get real mad because when I look at the kids today, so easy for them and yet they make more trouble than make themselves useful. So much for them to learn and do yet instead they go get in trouble.

Me, even though I was young, I pity my mother, because she always gets the works from my father. You know, we use to go fishing all the way to Kaulanamauna. We stay there sometimes two weeks or until we get enough fish, then we come home.

Get one place at Niua'u where the ko'a stay. At this place get the fish kū'ula, and that's where my father every time go before he go out fishing and when he come home, oh boy, plenty fish. Get one stone over there and he always take one nī'au with him when he go to this stone. Anyway, get one puka on this stone, and what he do, he put the nī'au in the puka and he sit there and watch how the shadow of the sun and how the wind blow the tip of the nī'au. By that way, he can tell when the good time to go out fishing or not. The tip of the nī'au tell him about the weather, if windy or going be good day. He tried to teach me and Nahinu how to watch that nī'au, but we were real young that time. I know Nahinu can read that because he was older than me. At that time I was only six years old, but I still can read that nīʻau. My father was the last one to use that sundial. That stone stay in the heiau ma uka side of the beach of Niuaʻu. That's the kūʻula too, for the fishermen.

Someday I like go back there and see all where we use to go and stay. That's why my brothers wen born all different places. Even me too, I born at Kaupō, not too far from our house at Kapuʻa. One brother born at Kaulanamauna, one born at Kapuʻa and the others born at Kaʻū, some place in Pāhala.

You know, my mother don't know how to swim. But every day when my father go out on the sea, she always have to go whether she like it or not. Even us brothers too. One time my father get bone head cause my mother was kind of slow to throw the kaʻai. He get mad with my mother, whack her with the paddle and throw her in the water. My mother hang on to the ʻiako and more my father get mad and try to crack her with the paddle. I cry, cry, and cry for my mother, but my father give me one heavy slap. Had some people fishing outside us, they came and pull my mother out of the water. When we get home, I tell my sisters and my brother what my father wen do to our mother. They get real mad, but they cannot do anything because that's our father and he more old then all of us. So instead, they would ask my father if they can go with him just to save my mother from him. I tell you, honey, he was real mean. But those were the days we had to live through.

When we go fishing, we have to go up ma uka for cut the kukui bark for cook hili for the ʻupena ʻōpelu. That's the best time we ever get because we can pick guavas, ēlama berries, ʻūlei or kukū ʻupena and the berries for us to eat. Sometimes we find some pīlali on the kukui trees. Us boys, we pick all this kind things while my father and mother go find the kind plants for medicine. When we get enough, we go home down to our house.

When Tūtū Lohiau come down, he always bring us sugar cane, papaya, banana, taro, ʻulu, and guavas, big kind and sweet. We all go catch fish, ʻopihi, limu, and when the wana fat, we get that, too. By the time he go home, he all loaded with his horse.

A Fisherman's Wife

My father-in-law, whom I never met because he died before I came into the family, was a great fisherman according to the stories I have heard in the village. Even my own relatives who live in Nāpoʻopoʻo told me about Abel's father. His story was told over and over from one fishing village to another, from one fisherman to another. The only thing that was really heartbreaking was when and how he died. At that time, my husband Abel was only nine years old. A great school of akule was surrounded at Honomalino Bay. Many fishermen came to help catch these fish. They came with sampans and canoes all the way from Nāpoʻopoʻo, Hōnaunau and other fishing villages along the coast to Miloliʻi. It took a couple of days to land the fish. The school of fish was so huge they had to let some of the fish go free.

After the fish were divided, they had a drinking party. Liquor was supplied by the Japanese fishermen who came all the way from Hilo to help with this great catch. It was already getting dark when Abel and his dad started home for Kapuʻa. They were almost outside of Kapuʻa when Abel's father fell into the water from the canoe. The father hung onto the side of the canoe while Abel tried to help his father, but he couldn't get him up. His father was a big, tall man. Because his father had had so much to drink, he couldn't get himself up onto the canoe. He told Abel to paddle the canoe home and he would swim to shore and walk home. Abel tried to get his father close to a rock so he could get on the canoe from there. He did see his father get onto the rock, but all of a sudden a big wave washed over it and that was the last he ever saw of his father.

Abel cried, yelled, and paddled the big canoe to the awa, at the same time yelling for his mother and brothers to help look for their father. They searched the area with lights until they reached Honomalino where all the other fishermen were resting for the night. After hearing what had happened, everybody turned out to look for the father till daylight. There was no sign of him anywhere. They even dove in the water, into caves in the areas where he had fallen in and where he was washed off from the rock, but they didn't find anything, not even a shred of clothing. Finally, the search was given up after many days spent looking for him. This all happened on May 30, 1929. From that day on, no akule was seen there anymore. I think this was a tragic thing that happened to this family.

The father was a strong believer in the fish gods. Nothing could change his mind. His kū'ula is still somewhere along the Kapu'a seacoast in a spot only his family knows. Almost all his children and his wife died with that secret and only Abel and one living sister know, but they will never talk about it, or tell where it is. They had made a promise and they intend to die with it.

I have often wondered how things would be had he lived. Those questions have bothered me all these years. He was a good provider for his family, but was also mean to them. He would rather buy liquor with his money than see his family get hold of it. Yet in his own way, he was a good man to everybody who knew him. His wife tried to raise his family by having the older ones help out with the fishing to keep them going. When the younger ones were all grown up, she got married again. This man, also a fisherman, moved her to Miloli'i to live with him. Later, the rest of the family also moved to the little village, yet they always went back to Kapu'a to live. When their own children were ready to go to school, they moved back to Miloli'i. It was much closer to the school. They couldn't see their children walking over the hot lava, or a'ā, six miles to school every day, three miles there and three miles home. They had done it, but that was not going to happen to their children. Abel and I raised our son in Hilo and the other children did the same. As for my daughter, she was raised in Kona. Like her brother, everything was convenient for her. Abel couldn't see them being brought up like him. Peter moved to Hilo, to have his children grow up knowing better. William moved his family to Honolulu for better surroundings, but was sorry he did that. He came right back to Miloli'i to live and go fishing. Abel is now retired and also goes back to Miloli'i to fish. Ellen also moved out and her children had the same treatment like the others. Hannah also gave all her children a city life. But every school vacation, all these children came back to Miloli'i like how the 'ōpelu schools appear at the ko'a. Miloli'i is just like the ko'a of the people. No matter where they go, somehow they always return.

Going back to before Abel was born, his father and mother traveled from one fishing place to another, following the fish. They spent a few days in each of the places they went. All they did was catch fish. They salted and dried their fish and when they had enough to load their canoe, they would head for Miloli'i, then on to Ho'ōpūloa to ship their fish to Honolulu. When their supplies arrived on the ship from Honolulu, they would head down the coast again. This is how they made their living. They stayed at Kaulanamauna and a son was born there. They moved on to Kaupō, and that's where Abel was born when the 'Alikā lava flow went down to the ocean (1919). Manuka, another son, was born there. At Kapu'a, another son was born. They went on to Ka'ū, and two daughters and a son were born there. They migrated wherever the fish were to be found.

The father of my husband's family really was a hard worker. Sometimes when I get to thinking of all the hardships this family faced, I think most of us were more fortunate.

The father was long dead before I came into this family. I was welcomed and made to feel at home by them. They took me in as their own youngest sister and I was called Kaina. They never called me by my own name unless they were talking to someone else outside the family. Maybe it was because I could speak and understand the Hawaiian language that they made me feel at home. My mother-in-law was a tall, strappy blonde and a sweet woman. In her own way, she reminded me of my own mother. I later learned she was part Norwegian. I often wondered how it was she got that blonde hair and very light, smoke-colored eyes. Two of Abel's older brothers had eyes like hers, but a little darker in color; the others had light brown eyes like their father's. None of them had blonde hair like their mother, but some of the grandchildren had light-colored hair that was in fact 'ehu or a light reddish color. Most of the family are six feet in height or taller. Kahele, the father, was a full-blooded Hawaiian.

Coming from a farmer's family, there were many things I had to learn. First was their different living conditions, to which I adjusted well. I had to accept the culture they were accustomed to. I learned to prepare fish to be dried, how to pack the fish in ice, and I learned the trade of fishing. This was to be my husband's and my life as well. My husband didn't expect me to master their way of living, but to me, being a fisherman's wife was my part to learn. It was hard, but I managed to get by and enjoyed it very much. In the beginning, my mind was a whirl. I got so frustrated and disgusted that I just wanted to run and run and forget all these monstrous chores that went on without end. Sometimes I was so filled with emotion that I wanted to quit everything and go back to my job in Hilo. Other times, I drowned my emotions in tub after tub of fish that I had to clean, salt, and dry. Maybe I was full of self-pity, but thinking of my husband out on the ocean, trying hard to catch whatever fish he could, gave me second thoughts.

One Sunday, I had gone to church and the sermon for the day was about the beatitudes. It really set my eyes wide open and my mind wide awake. A second chance was all I needed to set everything right.

I had read the Bible over and over and yet I had failed somewhere along the line. I guess my mind was not set at that time. After that sermon, I had no more doubts, emotions, or depression. I guess every woman has at one time gone through the same depressed feelings I had but being a fisherman's wife is an experience that cannot be forgotten.

The evenings were spent singing and dancing. The young people would pick up their musical instruments and just sing their hearts away, like there was nothing in the world that could touch them. All the tūtū would join in and sing along too. Sometimes when I sat down at the beach waiting for my husband to come home, I often wondered if this is what my life would become, too. Many a time I was caught in my own web of dreaming for the best in life.

Here in the village I learned that most of the people lived with a fear of witchcraft and superstitions. And they lived by the moon calendar and studied the stars, tides, clouds, the currents, and the habits of certain kinds of fish. I also learned that whenever the men were out fishing, you could not lift mats to sweep out the dust underneath for fear the sharks would open their mouths. To argue at home with your neighbors or household meant hard luck for the fisherman. To play cards or commit adultery was also an offense. Most of all, a woman who was having her menstrual period was never allowed to go near any fishing equipment or to help clean, salt, or dry the fish, or go near a kūʻula for she was considered hard luck for the fisherman. I think this is the only time that the women were free from all these tedious chores.

Certain times of the month nobody went out fishing. These were nā ʻOle. These days were mostly spent mending nets or just staying at home resting. At these times, fishermen also tended to their kūʻula, worshipping and leaving food and tobacco there, too. They believed in kahuna. If anything unusual happened, they would run to a kahuna for some kind of answer. If a comet was seen flying in the sky on a clear night, someone would say "Oh my, somebody is sending this akua lele to hurt someone." I have often heard people in our household let out a piercing scream. I questioned my mother-in-law about these kinds of phenomena. She told me whenever you see the akua lele flying in the sky or over the village, scream all you can, and it will break up and fall to the ground in ashes. By doing this, the ill intent of that akua lele will not be able to hurt anyone. I thought that was rather weird.

Another phenomenon is Pō Kāne. I have not seen an akua lele or heard the music of the night parade in all the time I have lived at this fishing village so I cannot say I do believe in these fantastic and weird beliefs. In my heart I know there is a God Almighty, and I worship Him above all things, so there is nothing that these people could do to make me one of them.

The funniest part is, they do go to church and praise God Almighty, and yet, they also bow down to their heathen gods. I really can't understand them. The fear of witchcraft is very strong in this village. There are so many things that are hard to explain and so many things I hadn't heard of in my life except here in this village. Sometimes I think it is all a fantasy. They had something like 'ailolo or 'unihipili. Where I grew up, I had never heard of such things. Maybe my people did have those too, but they were never spoken of within our ears' reach, so that is why it was strange to me. I had heard words like kepalō, kahuna, kū'ula, 'epa, or 'ailona, but nothing like what I had learned about during my stay at Miloli'i.

I asked my own mother about matters like this and she said, "When I was young, they did have people who did things like that, but when Christianity came in stronger, all that dwindled and most of the people turned to their Bibles. Moreover, all those who used to do all those things have died, and so have their talents and evil doings." I'm thankful for that.

Life must go on. I think I must have been a little more nosey than anyone else. I could not understand their serving so many gods, yet they did know right from wrong.

Today the young generation has taken over and things are very different from their tūtū's time, though fishing is still their main concern. Most of these young people own boats, trailers, and trucks to haul their fish to market in Hilo or to the small markets in Kona. They also have television sets run by car battery or by generators. There are radios in every home, as well as telephones. Lights are run on generators. Every family owns a sedan. There is also a little store and gasoline pump. You hardly ever see anyone paddling a canoe to go out fishing because everyone owns an outboard motor. But water is still a problem. This village hardly ever gets rain. Sometimes it's only one heavy downpour and that's all for the whole year. Otherwise water has to be hauled in containers from up on the highway where there's a water tap opened by the county. Before, they didn't have this and the people had to depend on brackish water for their use. I know my in-laws used to live on this water. It is all right to drink it directly from the wells as it does not have too much of the salt taste. I remember when I first drank that water, I was so sick that I thought I would have to go to the doctor. After the first couple of days, I was all right. My husband told me that when you get used to it, it won't give you any troubles again. It sure didn't, and I'm glad I had a part of that past style of living too.

Most of the families here are on welfare, food stamps, and assistance. I wish they had had this kind of support when the older people were young, especially when the ocean was rough and the fishermen couldn't go out to fish. Some families went without food during the rough weather. They lived on dry coconuts or some kind of herb that they concocted into a brew that would satisfy their hunger until they could go after some fish to eat. I think these younger generations are really fortunate today, but they take it for granted. As long as there is some kind of help, it's easy for the taking.

The road to the village is paved, all the way from the highway and through the village until where the park is today. You see all kinds of cars and people coming down. Some are tourists, movie stars, VIPs, and more. The most discouraging sight is the litter, but these people would not see their village cleared of the litter along the roadside. I made some suggestions about this but the answer I got was, "Iā 'oe ia wahi." It was like being shot in the back! Well, I guess that's the way they want to be.

The only clean areas are where the little store is located and down at the park. The rubbish dump is right along the roadside as you enter the village. It is a bad sight and the animals get into this rubbish pile and drag the rubbish onto the road. A couple of times we had to stop our car to pick up all the rubbish. Sometimes even the little kids get into the rubbish and bring things out like discarded toys that some family had thrown away. There are lots of things that an able-bodied man could do to beautify the village instead of spending time drinking, gambling, or smoking pakalōlō.

The village now is made up of four or five families, and everyone is related to each other except the Filipinos who live there. Most of the young people married their cousins or in-laws. Maybe if the old people could see them now, they would turn over in their graves.

Sundays are never kept sacred anymore. Everybody goes out fishing regardless of what day it is. I happen to have a small lot down there and we keep it as clean as we can. We built a little shack on it, but it is quite comfortable. We intend to build a new home if the state will grant the approval to build on this lot; the state is still the owner of the land. There are several of us who took out lots and are still waiting for state approval. Some of the owners have already built their homes, but others haven't, including us. In the meantime, a shack will do. My husband is now retired and spends most of his time there. Fishing is still in his blood. As the old saying goes, "Once a fisherman, always a fisherman."

Another thing that the people have there is a boat ramp which is always busy. People come all the way from Hilo, North Kona, and South Kona to launch their boats here because the fishing grounds are good. Most of the ʻōpelu and ʻahi koʻa are close by.

I guess people will never apperciate the good that is set before them. They take it as if the days really belong to them. Never do they set aside a time or day for the Creator of all things on land, sea, or air. I feel so sorry that in times to come, Miloliʻi will not be a place where you can find solace and contentment. The culture is falling apart.

Milolii Store
ROAD-WAY
Milolii
GROCERY Store
Road way

Miloli'i Store

Miloli'i

When I visited Miloli'i in 1946, there were about ninety-five people plus children. There was a one-room schoolhouse at the end of the village, and a teacher, Mrs. Sarah Kalua, who taught grades one to eight. The school grounds were covered with sand and this was the playground for the children. A cottage was next to the school, and this was where the teacher lived. There were no more than twenty students at that time. The school was also used as a meeting house or a place to hold big lūʻau.

The village was a place where there was no prejudice against nationality or religion. The villagers' lifestyle brought them close together. Just being near them made you feel as though you were being drawn to them like a magnetic force. It was their way of aloha that made you fall in place with them.

Their livelihood was fishing. Morning till night it was fishing. Whatever fish was caught and brought to shore was packed in ice and trucked to Hilo where it was sold on the auction block. If the price was good, the fisherman made money, but if the price was down, they took what came. Sometimes the market was flooded with cleaned, salted, and dried fish. Dry fish was good to sell, but too much of a job to do. When the trucks came back from Hilo, they brought back ice and food.

The road to Miloli'i was terrible. There was no electricity, running water, television, or anything that I know would be handy to have. For lights, they had kerosene lamps or gas lanterns. Water depended on how much rainfall they had had, or else they used brackish water. All the people there raised pigs and chickens for home use.

Mrs. Kalua tried to raise vegetables with some of her students. They used sand and the dry leaves of any kind of foliage that grew on the beach and mixed this into the soil. Whatever vegetables grew were shared with all the people there who liked to eat them. Most of them didn't care for vegetables and said they were Japanese food. (You find these complaints among the older people. They will accept the tomatoes and green onions but nothing else. Poi and fish is their daily diet.) Fish was eaten raw, dried, broiled over hot coals, boiled in water with salt, or cooked in coconut milk. This I really enjoyed as I was also raised on fish. The only time I have seen cakes and soda or other good things was when there were lūʻau. As for fruits and candies, these appeared only during Christmastime, or when relatives came for visits. I somehow fit into this pattern because I had come from almost the same way of living, only that my folks were farmers and I was now among fishing people.

The thing I found most interesting was how happy they seemed to be. Sunday was a day of taboo when everyone had to go to church. No one went out fishing on Sundays, not even to mend their nets or repair their canoes. That day was kept very sacred. Church services were held at the Hauʻoli Kamanaʻo Congregational Church every Sunday morning with Mr. Eugene Kaupiko, the deacon of the church, conducting the services.

During Sunday afternoons, they would go visit one another or sit on the beach watching the sea or the little keiki swimming. As for the older boys and girls, volleyball was their favorite game. The tūtū chatted or exchanged stories that I thought were real fantastic. I caught on to one of their stories and recognized it right away as one I had read in a storybook. I thought that was rather cute, their being in a remote area but they still had the outside world around them. The story was about Kū a Pākaʻa. To listen to it told in the Hawaiian language was something else. It sounded so interesting that you could almost visualize what actually took place in that story. They had other stories and legends of certain places that sounded so weird, like fairy tales.

When the sun was just about setting on the horizon, they would all go to their homes. Everywhere got so quiet, the only voices you would hear were the babies crying or a mother scolding her children. Sometimes on days like those I got carried away and wished that that kind of life would just live on and on.

The next day—Monday—was a working day for the fishermen. Every family owned canoes, ʻōpelu nets, and other fishing equipment. They loaded their canoes with the ʻōpelu nets and palu, and paddled out to the ʻōpelu koʻa and tried to lure the fish into the net by feeding them the palu. Sometimes when the catch was good or they caught enough fish to fill their canoes, they would paddle for shore. The fish would either be packed in ice or cleaned and dried. As soon as there was enough fish to make a truckload, it was all packed in ice and loaded on the truck. They left for Hilo in the cool of the evening so the ice would not melt and the fish would be kept fresh until it reached the market. Fish had to be on the auction block first thing in the morning so it could be sold.

While the fathers and older boys and girls were out fishing, mothers at home prepared more palu for the next day. Food had to be prepared and little ones tended to before the fishermen came home with their catches. There was much to do before it got dark. Some of the fish were given away to those who helped carry the canoes on land and helped unload the fish from the canoes. Of course, the tūtū always got their share, too. Before it got dark, all or most of the fish was packed in ice or cleaned and salted, ready to be dried the next morning.

When the fish was dry, they were packed into bundles of forty—a ka'au—and was sold either to the markets or to people who placed their orders. Every day it was the same routine. On dark nights, certain fish were caught. On moonlit nights, different kinds of fish were caught. All these catches were sold on the auction block in Hilo. Other times, when they went out night fishing for 'ū'ū, they caught so much that shovels had to be used to get all the fish out of the canoes or sampan hatches. I have actually seen this; I hadn't realized how many fish the fishermen could bring in on one trip.

When World War II broke out in 1941, most of the young men were drafted or volunteered for the service. Things got hard for the people of the village. They had to face regulations, blackouts, curfews, and permits for gasoline for the trucks. It was quite a while before the fishermen could go out fishing again. They could only go out to a certain distance and had to be home before dark. There was nowhere the people could turn for help so they kept on fishing as long as they could make a living.

Trucks were loaded with fish and ice and left for Hilo early in the morning so they would not be caught by the curfew. During that time, martial law was in effect; you had to abide by that law or be arrested. It was tough for the people, but somehow they managed to get along.

A war bond drive was on and the village participated in it. This little village won an award for buying the most bonds. Secluded as they were, they still made it through the war years under the leadership of Mrs. Kalua, fisherman Frank Manalili, and the other fishermen who made headlines in our local newspaper. Mrs. Kalua is now gone, but her wonderful deeds linger on. She was a helper of those in need, from being a family consultant to patching someone's wounds. In her way, she was wonderful.

When the war was finally over, the boys came home, including the son of Mrs. Kalua. He became a substitute teacher for Miloli'i School and taught grades five, six, seven, and eight, preparing those who were to continue on through school. Those parents who could afford to send their children for more education sent them to the Kamehameha Schools or to schools in Hilo.

Miloli'i School

Miloli'i School

This was the school most of the children attended. It was a school that held many memories, a one-room building with a little room adjoining the porch that was used for a library. The ground outside was covered with sand and this was used as the playground. Most of the books were old but they served their purpose. The school had one teacher who taught first through eighth grade.

There had been another structure before this one. It was torn down and this school was built in its place with the library added and the ground filled in and covered with sand.

Today the school is no more. It's been torn down and cleared away, even the water tank. In its place is a parking lot for cars, campers, and boats. As for the rest of the grounds, they have been turned into a park. The basketball court is still there as well as the pine trees which line the front near the beach.

This place is now known as the Miloli'i Park. Children today go up the hill on buses to Ho'okena School. Those who go to high school ride the bus all the way to Konawaena High School in Kealakekua. They leave home at 6:00 a.m. and return between 4:30 and 5:00 p.m. Children there have a better system of education than they ever had before. They get to meet students and teachers from different ethnic groups and the books they have are just out of this world. The best part of all is having different teachers or classrooms for different subjects and not staying in the same class waiting for the teacher to get around to them. Although they had to adjust to new methods, the children made it in their way.

Great Tidal Wave

[TOLD BY AUNTY E.K. KUAHUIA AND TŪTŪ KIPI K. KAʻANAʻANA]

On February 5, 1898, there was a great tidal wave that destroyed the entire village of Miloliʻi. Although homes, canoes, fishing equipment, and other things belonging to the people were all lost, they were thankful that not one life was lost, human or animal. The people never lost hope and began living by their same patterns again. The land had extended farther out but now there was deep water there and the sea had moved inland.

The little Kalawina church used to be where the pine trees are today. The church was lifted up by the wave and set down many feet from where it had stood before. (Where it stands now is only a few feet away.) Not one board was broken by the wave and everything was just the same except the foundation. The church bell rang and rang until the building settled down and everything was quiet. Only the regular sound of the waves could be heard then. Everything on the beaches was neatly cleaned.

It seemed to the people like it was the end of the world for them. They were cold and hungry. To keep warm that night they all gathered close together near where the little church was set down by the wave. They gave their most heartfelt prayers of thanksgiving to God Almighty for saving their lives. Even though they were hungry, they praised the one Maker of all mankind.

During their prayers, they heard voices calling and torch lights coming from ma uka. At first the people were frightened because they thought maybe it was the dead coming to claim them. They huddled together more closely to protect the women and children. But as the lights came nearer and the voices kept calling out to the people, some of them recognized the voices of their ʻohana who lived up ma uka.

The ʻohana brought much-needed food and clothing. There was much crying, hugging, rejoicing, prayers, and thanksgiving.

The eldest in the village gathered all the people before the little church with all the food and clothing which had been brought to them. He told the people to kneel down with heads bowed, then he called out to the Father Almighty to bless the things which had been brought to them, and to bless the 'ohana who had brought these gifts. He thanked Him for saving them and giving them another chance to live and flourish.

From that day on, a rule was made to keep Sunday a sacred day and February 5, 1898, a day that must never be forgotten. The day must be respected and be a memorial for all to remember what water can do, and that God Almighty is much stronger. So from that day on, Sunday and the Hau'oli Kamana'o Church became a symbol or a shrine for the people who were there during that great tidal wave.

The little church was originally built in 1865 under the direction of the Rev. John D. Paris.

Note: According to Tūtū Kipi Ka'ana'ana, at the time of this great tidal wave, she was a young girl and was there when this event took place. There also is a song written for this event called "Lā 'Elima" sung by our own Diana A. Aki.

Miloli'i Area People

JUNE 1946

These were the people I met the time I first visited the Miloli'i area.

At Kalihi

Kalaniweo Kuahuia (husband), second husband of Malaea H.N. Kahele Kuahuia, mother of Abel Pepe Kahele (wife: Mona K.K. Kapule), Henry Nahinu Kahele, William Kahele (wife: Maria Kalua Poaha), John Keola Halena Kahele, Peter Kahua Ka'i Kahele (wife: Rebecca Laniawe), Hannah Koanohano Sesson, and Ellen Kalawae'a (husband: David Fernandez).

Abel Kahele's family was the last family to live at Kapu'a. His brother William and his family moved to Miloli'i to live. His brother Peter and his family also later moved to Miloli'i. His sisters Hannah and Ellen each married and their children lived in Ka'ū because their husbands were plantation sugar workers.

Abel and his brother Henry went into the army. His brother John left Kapu'a at the age of nineteen to join the Merchant Marines. He didn't come back until he was retired. Then he came to visit Miloli'i for two days, returned to San Francisco, and died. His ashes were returned and buried in the Kalihi cemetery.

William and his family later moved to Hilo where he worked for the Defense Department. Then he was transferred to Honolulu where he worked for a construction company as a crane operator.

Peter was a merchant seaman, returning later to become a fisherman until he died of an illness.

John Halena Kahele, Sr. was the father of these children and the first husband of Malaea H.N. Kuahuia. He died May 30, 1929, lost at sea and never found.

At Omoka'a

An old Korean man lived in the first house at Omoka'a. He was known by the name of Pakini.

The next house belonged to Manuel and Lokelani Malama and their daughter, Lokelani, Jr.

In the next house lived John and Nancy Apo and their children Alex, Violet, Elenora, Genevie, and Charlotte.

Leaving Kalihi and Omoka'a, next was the Hau'oli Kamana'o Church. Across from the church was the Miloli'i School and Cottage. The school was a one-room school for grades one to eight. The cottage on one side of the school was a home for the teacher.

The teacher, Mrs. Sarah Kalua, lived with her children Emmaline, Albert, and Walter.

Across the school grounds was another home where a retired teacher lived with his daughter and another man and his son: David Kaupiko (retired teacher from Ho'olana), his daughter Healani, John Wailanai, Sr., and John's son Mitchell.

Leaving the school grounds and going up the road was Pohina Estate (two empty houses).

In a house further in on a high area lived Francis and Lili Chang, their children Kamela, Sonny, Eugene, Loke, Abel, Clement, Earl, and Winnie.

Kalanihale was the next house.

In the next lot most of them were fishermen: Tranquilino and Pake Manali'i, three children, John Hulama, and Antonio, a Filipino fisherman.

There was another house in the back where Mahina Waiwaiole who was called "Kuku" lived.

In another house lived two elderly brothers, Junior and Martin Kaupiko.

In the next lot was another house where Alorado and his wife lived with Baldo, Rafile, Tomas, and others whose names I don't know. All these people were Filipino fishermen.

In the next lot lived the Kaupiko family: Kaimana, his wife Malaea, and their granddaughter Ukuli'i.

In the next house lived Eugene and Kapela Kaupiko and their children Kalani, Winona, Naomi, and Willie.

Across from Eugene Kaupiko was a little store belonging to J.B. Siu and his wife. Next to this little store was the biggest awa where all the canoes were kept. From this awa up to the next couple of houses was called Waikini.

As you travel up the hill on the road, on the ocean side was the Magoon home where Elvis Presley made the movie "Girls, Girls, Girls." No one was living in this home. Below this home was the wharf with a warehouse on one side.

Next to the Magoon home was the Ka'ana'ana home. The oldest people of the village lived in this house. They were refugees of the 1926 lava flow of Ho'ōpūloa, where they had owned a very large home and an ahupua'a. (This is where Tūtū Kipi and Auntie Kapehe lived.) The household included Kepano Ka'ana'ana (husband), Keli'ikipi Ka'ana'ana (wife), Melekule (mo'opuna), Louis Kuahuia Ka'ana'ana (mo'opuna), Edward Ka'ana'ana (mo'opuna), Kukulu Kuahuia and Kapeka Kuahuia (husband and wife; she was the niece of Ka'ana'ana), Kepano Kuahuia (mo'opuna), and Louis Kuahuia II (mo'opuna).

Across the road on the ma uka side was another home belonging to James Akana and wife Julia.

Next was the Catholic church and cemetery in back.

In the next lot was Antone and his wife Amoy, and their children at that time: Amoy, Louis, Dora, Pualani, Raymond, Leilani, Kepano, and Becka.

The rest of the lots were lava fields. There was a house on the road going toward the wharf; this was the home of Llanes and his wife Sarah. At that time she had her children with her: Sarah Paulo, Maggie Paulo, Pauka'a Paulo, Edward Paulo, Peter Paulo, Jr., and Louis Paulo.

Just before leaving the village, there was a last house and that was the Peter Paulo, Sr. home. Filipino fishermen lived in this house.

These were all the people I knew when I first came to Miloli'i.

Miloli'i Traditions

Traditions are closely followed here. It is a wonderful feeling knowing that traditions, culture, and local wisdom are still in use.

The old methods of fishing, equipment, and lifestyle remain. I came from another village and did not witness things, like the canoes all lined up side by side on the beach. Ever since I came to Miloli'i, there have hardly been any canoes on land. Most of them are out on the sea along the coastline, fishing.

When they return home, some of the canoes are so loaded with fish that you can only see the parts where the outrigger is lashed. This is a very exciting sight because you see families all helping one another unload the 'ōpelu from the canoes into tubs then cover them with chipped ice ready for the truck to haul to the market in Hilo. Even bystanders are given fish. By the time you go home, you sometimes have about a ka'au of 'ōpelu.

Here also, as I listened and observed the people, I found words that were in great use by the people of Miloli'i, words like 'auē, ke aloha, laulima, kōkua, 'imi aku, ho'olako, and ho'oponopono. The word ho'olako was a commonly used word. With almost everything they did in the village the word ho'olako was used, like when there was going to be a lū'au the elders would say, "'O 'oe ho'olako mai ka pua'a" (You provide the pig). Or, "Ka po'e no kahakai ho'olako nā mea o ke kahakai" (People of the beach provide all things from the beach), especially fish, 'opihi, wana, he'e or any other things. Ka po'e o uka e ho'olako mai ka lā'ī, mai'a, kalo, pala'ai a me ka 'uala, a me ka 'ulu" (People of the uplands provide the ti leaves, banana, taro for poi, pumpkin, potatoes and 'ulu.) Other families would provide the cakes and all the other things for a party. This method is still used in the village but today it is called "potluck." Those who drink liquor furnish the liquor, or whoever wants to ho'olako.

There were even boats named *Ho'olako* and the name was truly a good provider. In fact ho'olako was an everyday word in the daily lives of the people. There was always something to be done with each family in the village and it was such a wonderful sight and feeling. I wonder where else you can find a lifestyle like the one here in Miloli'i. There were so many things I have learned, listened to, and cherished, especially the language. Hawaiian was very much spoken here, I guess because of all the elderly people.

There was a stamina that could be felt within the village and a warm feeling of welcome. There was also another feeling within the village: of resentment. This unspoken resentment was silent and mysterious. This was alongside togetherness, or as we say, lōkahi.

Other than that, everything else was love, caring, and togetherness here in the village. Perhaps the younger generations would like to introduce methods they may have learned on the outside and bring them into the village, but the elders will not accept these methods. Who knows what will happen in the years to come.

Historic Sites

MILOLI'I

From Kaumuloa all the way to Ka'ū there are many historic sites including heiau, caves, and kū'ula (fish shrines). Within Miloli'i there is also a very amazing navel rock, Pōhakupiko, hard to describe unless you see it. As you travel or walk along the sea coast there is much to see. Many archaeologists and others have come to the area to study and observe these sites. Some of the sites have been destroyed by bulldozers, animals, or campers. More will be lost if development takes over these lands.

The most perfect hōlua slide is still there at Pu'u Hinahina. The bottom part of the slide has been cut away for a road plus some nasty people drove their four-wheel-drive trucks up the slide and caused more damage. Some parts of the trails have been cut away to form roads for cars. Kahua hale are still there too as well as places where potato was planted. The pu'u are still there.

Our club, the Pa'a Pono of Miloli'i, has taken action to preserve all these areas. What a sad, sad plight it would be should the Hawaiian people lose their culture or have it destroyed. What the first Hawaiians left should remain as a symbol to show every generation what Hawaiians and Hawai'i are all about.

I hope generations to come will see all these facts and sites and be proud that they are Hawaiian. To have Hawaiian blood is to be Hawaiian, but to love one another whether Hawaiian or any other ethnicity is also to be Hawaiian at heart. To be born in the islands is your culture, no matter what you are.

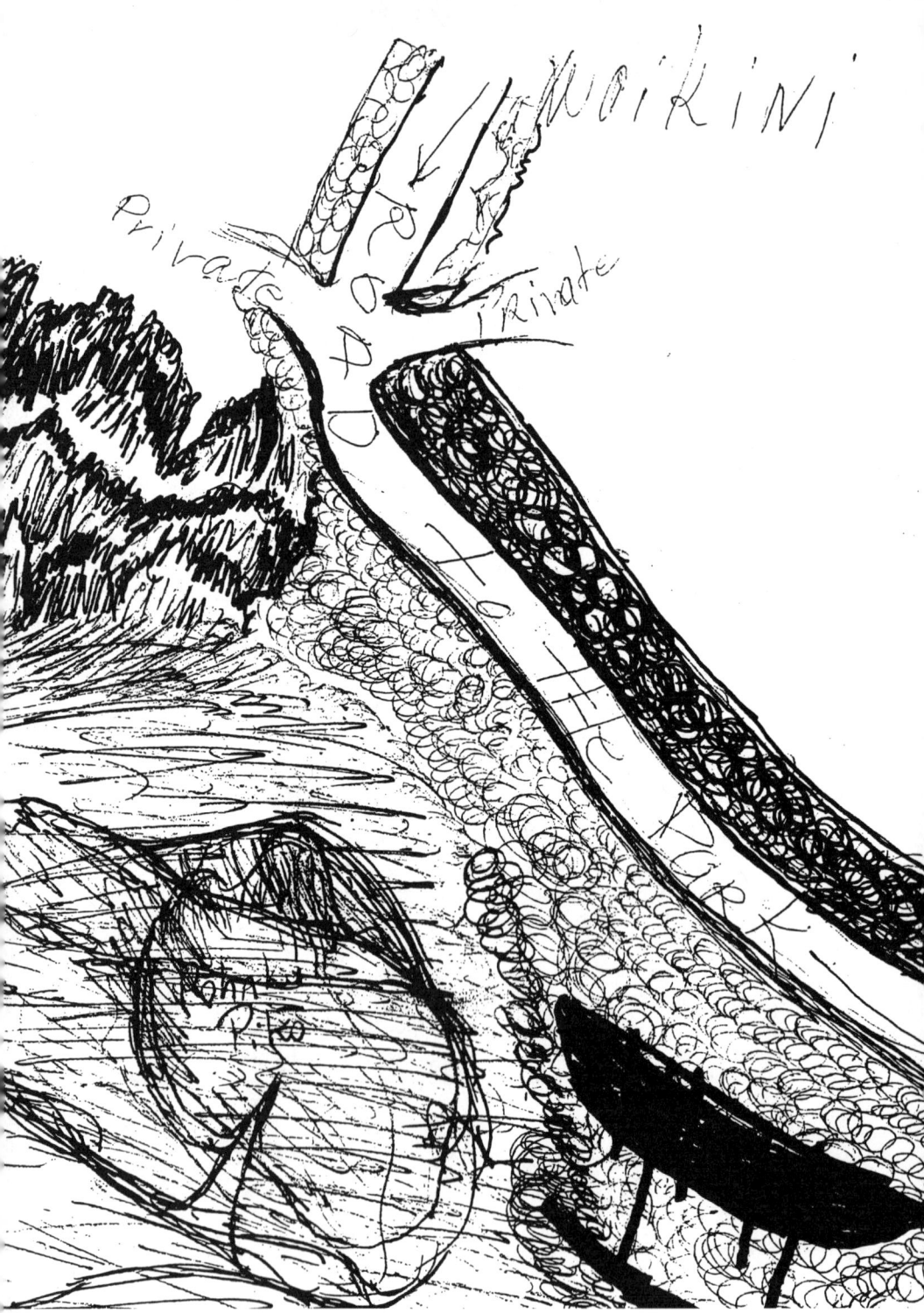

Pōhakupiko

Pōhakupiko

NAVEL ROCK

Across from Eugene Kaupiko's house was a little store belonging to J.B. Siu and his wife. There was also a little market where some of the fishermen sold their catch. The market belonged to the same owner of the little store. This is where the people of the village all gathered during the day or late evening to hear the latest news from other fishermen. Usually the news was about fishing, how far out or how close in to go to the fishing stations to catch certain fish. During that time, 'ōpelu was the most popular catch of the village, sold to the markets or dried and sold to individuals who ordered dried 'ōpelu.

Next to this little store was the biggest awa where all the canoes were kept on the beach. There used to be lots of canoes there with sometimes not enough space for another canoe. All these people paddled their canoes. Two years later they began to use outboard motors that were faster for going out and coming home. Little by little, paddles were put aside. Now only the old timers still paddle.

There's an interesting rock in this awa that is located right about in the center of the awa. According to the people in the village, it is called the Pōhakupiko (navel rock). Whenever a new baby was born in the village and the navel dropped off from the baby's stomach, the mother took this piko and placed it in that rock. If it was a single piko, only one hole would be found. The piko was placed in the hole and the hole was plugged with a pebble. In three days no hole, pebble, or any mark would be left. This Pōhakupiko balances on another flat rock and rocks only when the waves come in. When the ocean is rough or there are high seas, all the other rocks will be thrown on shore, but this particular rock just stays in one place.

When my son was born, his piko was also placed in this rock. I, for one, did not believe what the people told me until I experienced it with my baby. My husband, who belongs to the village, took the piko and placed it in a hole and covered it with a pebble. Three days later, we went back to see what happened. I couldn't find a hole or pebble anywhere. I searched all over that rock but found nothing. I related this incident to the elderly people there and they told me that meant my baby was accepted. If the child was not accepted, the hole would be left open and a crab would be found in its place. I don't know what to believe. All I can say is, it is very strange.

Clouds of the Past and Present

When I look back on the number of years I've been going in and out of the village, I feel as though I have missed a lot of the changes in the people and the environment surrounding the village itself.

The people are different now. Since being outside the village, they have adopted the modernized world and modern lifestyle. They have a new attitude of ignoring the culture and the values that were taught to them by their kūpuna. It is a very sad plight that traditions cannot be handed down to this generation and the next generation to come.

However, there's one person who really has her heart set on some of the cultural values. A tradition has been handed down to her in the form of music, words, and dances. Who is this person? It is our own Diane Aki. She is young, but in many ways a talented person, and dedicated to her cultural values.

I think the people of Miloliʻi should be proud of Diane's goals. I, for one, am proud of her work and I try to help her whenever she requires any help. I am no professional but I have gained much knowledge in my lifetime. My help circulates to all who need it. Diane is also a winner of the Nā Hōkū Hanohano and Haku Mele awards, the only winner from this moku nui o Hawaiʻi, and she is from this isolated village of Miloliʻi.

As a kupuna, I am proud of all Diane's efforts to perpetuate and learn the lore of the music and lifestyle of this little village of Miloliʻi. When she sings songs she has composed about places she has visited, it's like looking through a picture book or mirror at those places. I wish there were others of our younger generation who might learn and share some of this knowledge. Who knows, maybe someday we may have another artist develop here in the village.

Many changes have come to Miloliʻi and the people are getting more modern in their lifestyle and daily living. New homes have sprung up. There are more homeowners and almost every household owns automobiles, telephones, TVs, stereos, etc. What is outside the village is here too. We have no electricity but solar power is here, as well as generators. There is no running water but every home has its own water catchment tanks for water to drink and all other uses.

The land is state owned, and the people have long leases for their lots (sixty-five years). It took fifty years or more to accomplish what we have today. Friends who were involved in politics and those who were not helped us very much. To them goes our heartfelt thank-you and much aloha.

Soon we will have our own water system here in the village. Right now when water is needed, water is hauled in from up ma uka to fill the water tanks. Almost all the people in the village own trucks so they can haul water and haul their fish to the markets to sell. Fishing is still going on here at the village, whether it is to put food on the tables, for lū‘au, or to give away. Some of the fish are dried and saved for future use.

Some of the young people work at the macadamia nut company above the village. Others still go out to catch fish for their livelihood. There are about six elderly retired people who live here. Both my husband and I retired and came back to live the rest of our lifetime here in the village.

I was sitting here watching the sunset. The horizon was painted in the most beautiful colors so hard to describe. I don't think the most talented artist or painter could really capture these brilliant colors and pastels. The most vivid colors are to be seen on the horizon.

My mind began to focus on the mystery of life. I began to imagine myself being with God Almighty, watching Him create this world and universe, placing everything where it should be: the colors of each flower, the different greens for the trees, leaves of plants or grass, the different colors for the hills, crags, gulches, valleys and the mountains, the different creatures or animals of land and sea, and how the water was drawn back to where it was born.

The next thing was to divide darkness from the daylight, and the number of hours to be put between night and day. The great light that was called the sun was to brighten the world in the day. The moon and the stars were to shine when the world was dark, which meant night.

As I kept watching the sun sinking down over the horizon, wild thoughts were going through my mind as if there was a fight going on between the light of day and the light of night. It seemed like the sun was always the winner because after only a little while of darkness the sun was already climbing over the mountain. Such a wonderful creation this is, yet all these wonders are taken for granted, or wasted.

The more I looked around me, the more I loved our Creator. I wished all humanity could be thankful for what was around them.

There are so many things and thoughts I would really like to capture on paper, but I just cannot find the right words to explain my feelings.

Now when I look at the village, there are so many changes that I never dreamed of. Many new homes have sprung up and taken the place of the old houses or shacks that were there. Through the help of our village club, Paʻa Pono, and some individuals and friends, we were able to get a long lease from the state of Hawaiʻi. It took us three years to get Governor Ariyoshi to sign the bill. He flew by helicopter to Miloliʻi to sign the bill for the second phase of home construction. With the help of our Almighty Father in Heaven, we were able to accomplish this task.

Next came the houses to be built. This is where other help came in from the state and the Hawaiʻi County Economic Opportunity Council handling the project. Materials were brought to the village but self-help was the main labor. Only one contractor was hired and another hired to handle other matters. Our self-help project was a tremendous work, with all the village young people pitching in and going from one lot to another to help build the houses. It was good teamwork and everything went as planned.

In all of these projects, the Paʻa Pono Club played the most important part in establishing the whole program. The legwork was done by Gilbert Ka-hele, a nephew, and others who got involved in this whole project. There were other important people who helped with the financing and other aspects that had to be taken care of before the project went ahead as planned.

We were very much concerned for the people of the village. In the past, people lived in a close-knit ʻohana with two or three families in one household. Some had only a pāpaʻi hale but there was much happiness and aloha within this lifestyle. When all the kūpuna passed on, the lifestyle changed.

The children became different. Drugs and pakalōlō were brought into the village. Alcoholism became a problem in the lives of our young people. Firearms of all sorts were also brought in. Some of the adults learned these things outside of the village. These things that were not known to the people here before are now out of control among the young people and some of the adults. One murder has already been committed. The one that committed the murder came from outside, but married a girl from the village. I do hope that someday all these habits can be abolished from the village. Alcohol use is heavy among the young people. Nothing can curb this menace. I hope and pray they will change someday.

Fishing using both old and new methods is active here in the village. Old methods still do exist. This sustains the life of the people. This is a part of the lifestyle that continues for both the old and young.

Here in Miloli'i, there was no such thing as electricity or running water. Water tanks were the most important item in every home. Water to drink was like a precious jewel. When the rains came, water was collected in every container available, and of course in the water tanks. If there was no rain for a long time, water was hauled in by water trucks to fill the tanks. The cost of a thousand gallons was at least seventy dollars a load. Drinking water was so needed that the hurt was not there when you had to pay the cost.

When I came to this village and had my first glimpse of life here, I thought it was a real forsaken land like something I had read about in books. Getting to meet the people and walking the shoreline for miles, I had never known there was a place like this. I was enchanted with everything that I saw. I felt as though I was at home. I didn't have any idea that this village would become my home and life forever with the people all becoming my 'ohana. Being married to a man from here was just wonderful. We had our ups and downs during our years of being married, but I was never abused, slapped around, neglected for companionship, or two-timed in over forty years. We are still as one and we hope to live that way all our lifetime as the Lord in heaven allows us. Although our health is poor, we manage to sail over the aches and pains that always cross our paths, and put them behind us. We are parents to a son and a daughter and ten grandchildren whom we love very much. Now my husband and I live in the village.

Kanaka Mahi'ai

[TOLD BY MY UNCLE HENRY LESLIE, SR., MY FATHER KAPIO KAPULE, AND
KŪKŪ NAHA, WHO WAS THE ELDEST IN THE VILLAGE] 1934

There was a farmer who liked to grow things, especially taro, sweet potatoes, pumpkins, bananas, sugarcane, and ti leaves. Taro and sweet potatoes were the main crops, as they were staple foods. Banana, sugar cane, and ti leaves were planted along the borders of the farm.

The farmer's wife also had a part in the farm. She helped with the planting and harvesting of the crops when they were ready. With the help of their two children, they harvested and loaded their taro, sweet potatoes, pumpkins, and bananas on their donkey and went to the beach to trade with the fishermen for fish and other things from the sea.

The people of the fishing village depended on the farmer for their staple foods. They traded their fish with the farmer.

The farmer and his family were happy. They did everything together. And so this is the story of a simple farmer and his crops.

Miloli'i Legends

The Story of Kamapua'a and Pele's Son 'Ōpelu

[A LEGEND THAT IS HEARD MOSTLY BY FISHERMEN, TOLD BY THE OLD-TIMERS OF MILOLI'I] JANUARY 1947

The son of Kamapua'a and Pele was named the god of thieves. All this son did was steal and steal and steal or damage whatever he came across. Kamapua'a and Pele could not calm him or discipline his actions. He made so much trouble that the people cried out to their gods for help. He ravaged the people's taro patches, potato fields, pumpkins, and anything green that was edible.

This son was doing the same thing his father Kamapua'a had done. Because of this behavior, the gods had named him a god of thieves. There was nothing else that Kamapua'a and Pele could do so, their son was changed into a fish like no other kind of fish in the ocean. He was then named 'Ōpelunuikauha'alilo.

So when you saw a ho'olili or a school of fish, it was said 'Ōpelu was out thieving. He and all his followers were changed to 'ōpelu. The 'au'a, his spies, would go out and taste the palu, and if it was good, the school of fish would congregate and eat the palu, and they would be caught in the nets.

Taro, pumpkin, or potatoes were used for palu, because that's what 'Ōpelu used to ravage from the farms. This is how 'ōpelu came into existence.

211

Legend of the Empty Sea

[TRADITIONAL, FROM MILOLI‘I]

I n ancient times, the Hawaiians had gods for everything. They had gods from the earth to the heavens.

Kū‘ula was known as one of the gods of fish. He could transform himself into a man and mingle with the people. Because he was known to be very good at doing this work, the Shark Chief made him the head of all the fish, sea creatures, and fishermen. The fishermen all respected him and always called for his help. Never was there a time when he turned a deaf ear to the people.

However, there was a bad god who did not like Kū‘ula and who was mean and jealous. Some people who were also bad were his followers.

The bad god ordered his followers to capture Kū‘ula, his wife Hina, and their son ‘Ai‘ai and burn them to death. But Kū‘ula found out about the plot and he and his wife Hina escaped. They took with them all the fish and sea creatures but left their only son ‘Ai‘ai and four magic items. They left their son behind because there were some good people and ‘Ai‘ai could help them. Kū‘ula told his son to use the magic items if the time came to help the good people.

Pili was a young boy and a very good friend to ‘Ai‘ai. One day the good people asked Pili to ask ‘Ai‘ai to help them as they needed food, especially fish and things from the sea.

Pili went to ‘Ai‘ai and told him of the request. ‘Ai‘ai said, "I can help them but they must do what has to be done." Pili went back and told the people what ‘Ai‘ai had said: they could only take what they could eat, and they must learn to conserve so they would have fish all the time. The people agreed to the terms.

‘Ai‘ai took the magic items and walked to the beach.

The first item was Kū‘ula's bait stick. ‘Ai‘ai set it in the water and all the fish came. Next, he took out a special lure which was a cowry shell. He set it in the water and all the he‘e appeared. Then he took out four washed, polished pōhaku and dropped them in the water. They became homes for the fish. 'Āweoweo, 'ū'ū, and other red fish appeared. Last of all, 'Ai'ai placed a small stone image of Kū'ula on the rocks on shore as a shrine. All the crabs, 'opihi, and other sea creatures appeared.

From that day on, the sea was never without fish or sea creatures. The people also learned about conservation. They had listened and so they had what they asked for.

Moku Nai'a

[TOLD BY MY MOTHER-IN-LAW HALEAKA NUNUHA KAHELE]

The sky was clear and blue, and the sea was calm. The only movement was the rippling of the water in the gently blowing breeze. It was all so peaceful. Never had such quietness fill the air.

Suddenly, out of nowhere came a great splash that interrupted the calm surface of the sea. Pretty soon there were more splashes and porpoises leapt in and out of the water. These fish were playing a game—competing for the biggest splash. The game continued for quite some time as the fish proceeded with their leaping and splashing on the sea.

Finally, the splashes ceased and a formation of porpoises could be seen swimming away. No one seemed to know where they went. While they were playing, however, they were being observed by two young men.

Moku, the younger man, turned to his cousin Kama and said, "I wonder where these fish go from here? No one seems to know their destination. They come and then leave when they are through playing."

Kama, the older cousin, replied, "You know, when the nai'a play, swim, and splash in such a way, it means that the sea will become rough. That was the sign to our people."

"Come on, Kama," Moku said, "let's go see what's going on in the village. Perhaps there is something we can do."

The boys strolled back to their homes. Entering the lānai, Moku heard his mother call out to him.

"Where have you been, Moku?" his mother yelled. "Your father waited and waited for you to come home, but you never came back. What is the matter anyway?"

Moku replied, "Kama and I were on the beach watching the nai'a play. Kama told me that their playing is a sign that the sea will be rough. Is that really true?"

Moku Nai'a

His mother answered, "If you will sit down and listen, I will tell you the story my grandfather told me when I was a young girl." Moku sat down, and his mother began to tell him the story.

One day, a little boy who was also named "Moku" went down to the beach for a swim. While swimming, he felt something touch his side. When he looked in the water, he saw a great big fish. He was frightened and tried to move away, but every time he moved, the fish would swim closer to him.

Eventually, the boy began to pat the fish's head, for it seemed like that's what the fish wanted. They began to swim together and soon became good friends. "I will keep this fish as my best friend and will never tell anyone about him," he thought. He walked up to the beach and looked back to see if his friend was still there, but he was nowhere to be seen.

The next day, the boy went for another swim and there was his friend alongside him again. Knowing that his friend would always be there to meet him, the boy went swimming every day. They swam and played together in the cove each day until it was time for the boy to return home.

This went on for many days. Soon the boy named his friend "Nai'a" because when he swam the water looked so smooth and bright.

One day the boy told Nai'a that there was another awa where no one ever went. He swam with Nai'a until they reached this secluded cove with high rock cliffs on both sides. He asked Nai'a to remain there so that he could play with him every day.

The boy left Nai'a in the cove and went home for the day. Every day afterwards was the same—swim, play, and then home.

One day, the boy's father told him, "Today you must not go swimming. You must go with me to the uplands and gather olonā bark for more cording."

The boy did not answer, for at that moment his thoughts were of Nai'a. He felt so disappointed because he could not swim with Nai'a that day, but he followed his father anyway. As father and son traveled to the uplands, the father noticed a red glow in the sky.

He turned to his son and said, "We cannot continue uphill anymore, because Pele is coming down. Let us return home." The boy was very happy for he could be with Nai'a after all.

Then his father said, "Let us look for a high place, so we can see where the flow will be heading."

They climbed atop a high rock where they could see the village and where the lava flow was going.

"Alas," said his father, "it is going to flow close to the village. We must hurry home to warn the people."

As they looked to see where the flow was heading, the boy began to worry, for the little cove where Naiʻa was waiting was in the path of the flow. He could not keep his secret any longer, so he told his father about Naiʻa.

His father looked at him and said, "You must hurry and warn your friend to move out away from that cove."

The boy ran down the hill as fast as his little legs could carry him. Before he left, his father told him to swim with his friend toward the deep water until they reached the other side. They would be safe there. By the time the boy reached the cove, however, part of the lava flow had entered the water. As for Naiʻa, he was still there at the cove waiting for his friend. The water was getting warm and dead fish were floating all around. The boy kept hoping that Naiʻa would swim away, but by the time he reached the beach, Naiʻa was still there. He yelled to Naiʻa to swim out, but instead, when Naiʻa saw him, he moved closer to shore, thinking the boy would swim with him. As soon as he was about to swim to Naiʻa, the lava flow covered the boy. Naiʻa screamed and jumped in the air to splash water on his friend, but it was too late, for the boy was covered and had turned to stone. At last, Naiʻa knew that his friend would never swim with him again, but he would not leave his side. Naiʻa moved closer and closer and with one loud scream, his nose and head turned to stone. Finally, his entire body was completely solidified and there the boy and porpoise have remained to this day. Because of them, this area is now known as Moku Naiʻa, and porpoises are often spotted there.

Moku looked at his mother and asked her, "Is it from this story that the people have the ʻailona of the naiʻa?"

His mother answered, "Yes, from that time on, whenever the naiʻa play, jump, and splash, people have taken it to mean that rough or stormy weather is in store."

Therefore, when you see the naiʻa playing, you will know what to expect, too.

'Ōlelomoana

[TOLD BY AUNTY KAPEKA KUAHUIA AND TŪTŪ KIPI KAʻANAʻANA]
OCTOBER 1946

*This story is about the fishermen of ʻOpihale, South Kona and how the name
ʻŌlelomoana (words from the ocean) came about.*

Long, long ago fishermen lived at ʻOpihale beach. There were two
men named Kino and ʻUhai who were good fishermen. They caught
a lot of fish and shared their catches with the people there.

Every day Kino and ʻUhai would take their precious fishhooks, get in their
canoe and head out to the fishing grounds. They always caught a lot of fish.
People wondered how they caught so many fish whenever they went out.

Finally one day their precious fishhooks broke off the line. Kino and ʻUhai
were so disappointed and angry with themselves for not being careful with
their fishhooks. Kino looked at ʻUhai and said, "Our hooks broke and we
don't have any others like them. We might as well go home. We cannot
catch any more fish."

ʻUhai answered, "Yes, might as well. It's useless anyway."

Before they paddled for home, ʻUhai told Kino, "Eh! You know, when we
get home we can make some more hooks. Remember the two old men
who died and were buried? Their bones will make good fishhooks because
they were old and we can have good strong hooks. Our fishhooks broke off
because we made our hooks from a young man's bones. This time we can
make better and stronger hooks."

Kino replied, "Yes, good idea."

Now all this discussion was taking place way out on the sea. The fishermen did not realize that their voices had traveled over the water with the
wind and were heard on land. Their voices were heard by the spirits of
two ʻelemākule, the ones that Kino and ʻUhai were talking about. One
ʻelemakule told the other, "We better run away and hide somewhere or
else those two fishermen who lost their hooks will come home to take our
bones to make fishhooks."

The other old man replied, "How are we going to run when we can't even walk? When we were alive we could hardly stand or walk. Now how are we going to run?"

"Well," answered the other old man, "since we cannot run, we will crawl. Let us head north, and maybe we'll find a place to hide so Kino and 'Uhai cannot find us. Now since we are going to crawl, we better start before we're too late getting away!"

Crawl they did. The old men started toward the north and got a couple of miles away from the beach where the fishermen lived.

No sooner had the two 'elemākule left the area when Kino and 'Uhai returned home from out at sea. As soon as they landed on shore, they headed straight for the place where the old men were buried. Upon trying to locate them, they became angry because they were nowhere to be found. The fishermen knew they were digging in the right place but no bones could be found so they gave up and went home.

As for the two old men, they found a safe place to hide. They crawled all the way to this new place, so the area was named Kolo. The area where they were first buried, which was also the home of Kino and 'Uhai, was named 'Ōlelomoana. Remember, the fishermen's plan was heard on the land, so if you plan to do anything on land, be careful. Someone will tune in to your conversation. This ends the story of 'Ōlelomoana and Kolo, South Kona.

Omoka'a and Okoe

'AI KANAKA (CANNIBALISM)

[TOLD BY TŪTŪ KIPI KELIIKULI KA'ANA'ANA]

Long ago there were two brothers who lived in this village. One of the brothers was kind, considerate of others, and was a hard worker. The other brother, who was older, was lazy, didn't want to work and didn't care about 'ohana or other people.

The good brother was known as Kamiki. He always went out fishing and always shared his catch with whomever didn't have any fish. As for his brother, he was just lazy and went from house to house to eat. This angered Kamiki very much.

Finally the day came when the brother had to move out of Kamiki's home. This brother's name was Omoka'a.

Omoka'a moved to the edge of the village and made his home there. Now travelers who were passing on their way to Kona or Ka'ū somehow never reached their destination.

Every time a traveler came by, Omoka'a would kill the traveler and bake him in the imu. This became his food. Omoka'a met a girl in the village and she too had a desire for baked humans. They became husband and wife and lived together.

When travelers came by, they would coax the travelers to come into their lānai and rest a while. After walking in the hot sun, the travelers would accept the offer of water to drink. While they were drinking the water, Omoka'a would club their heads. He had a hot imu going. He baked the travelers and when they were cooked, he and his wife ate their meal. Smoke was always seen at Omoka'a's place. The people wondered, "Maybe now Omoka'a is a good worker and has an imu going."

Somehow some of the villagers became suspicious. They didn't say anything, but they shunned Omoka'a.

Now Kamiki was waiting for some 'ohana who were to visit him, but these 'ohana had not arrived at his home. Kamiki decided to visit his brother who lived at the edge of the village. He had heard the gossip about his brother and wife, but he didn't want to believe it. So he went to Omoka'a's place. When he got there his brother and wife were not at home. He waited and waited then stood up to look into the house. In one corner of the house stood a big calabash. He walked over to where the calabash stood, lifted the cover, and there was the smell of kālua pig. Upon taking a peek inside, what he saw made his stomach turn: there was a human hand, legs, and other body parts. On the other side of the calabash there was a pile of human bones and skulls. He was sick just looking at the sight. While standing there, he heard his brother coming home and looked around for a place to hide. The only place he could hide was behind a bundle of folded tapa cloths. He had only just moved in the back of the bundle when he heard his brother lifting the cover of the calabash. Kamiki watched from his hiding place to see what his brother was doing. The brother brought out part of a leg and began eating it. His wife reached in and brought out a hand. Like her husband, she ate too.

Kamiki was sick and raving angry. Just at that moment he saw a tapa cloth that almost popped his eyes for he recognized the design as belonging to his 'ohana. He waited until his brother was almost asleep then he pounced on him with fury and nearly killed him. As Omoka'a and his wife pleaded for their lives, Kamiki told them they had eaten their 'ohana for he had recognized the tapa by the design. To save their lives, they promised Kamiki that they would never eat another human being again.

Kamiki told them they must go away from the village. His brother moved toward Miloli'i and lived there. Because he lived there, that place was named Omoka'a (murderer). His wife moved down the coast a few miles away from Omoka'a. This place was called Okoe (murderess) because she lived there. True to their word, they never ate or killed any more human beings.

That's the end of this weird story.

Kaumuloa

THE REAL NAME FOR HO'ŌPŪLOA

[TOLD BY TŪTŪ KIPI KAʻANAʻANA AT KALANIHALE AWA] JUNE 1946–1947

One hot and tiring day, a young couple stopped at a little village. They were thirsty and hungry. The young man turned to the young woman and said, "Let us go and ask the people if they would offer us water and some food."

The woman looked around then replied, "This place looks so dry. There are no coconuts on the trees and no other plants around. All the people that we see seem to be sick and tired. The funny part is, no one seems to care whether we are here or not."

There was a little boy playing in the sand and they decided to ask him where they could get a drink of water. But as they neared him, the little boy stood up, looked at them with wide eyes, and ran to an old man who was sitting in the shade of a coconut tree. The couple followed the little boy until they stood where the old man was sitting.

They greeted the old man and asked him if they could have some water to drink and some food to eat. "We have come on a long trip. The day is so hot and we are thirsty and hungry."

The old man stood up, looked at them and motioned for them to follow him. He had them sit in the shade of a hale and replied, "Wait for me. I will be back."

It was quite a while before the old man returned. In his hands he held a gourd of water, one fish, and a small potato. The old man offered them these things and said, "I am so ashamed because this is all I have in the house. Please accept these gifts. In this gourd is water but we have only brackish water. I am so ashamed because I have only a little to offer."

The young man took the food and the gourd of water and bid the old man to sit with them and eat. But the old man declined and said, "I must go see what my grandson is catching at the beach. Both of you sit down and eat. I will be back, perhaps with something fresh from the sea."

Kaumuloa

Before the old man began to walk away, the young man asked him, "Where are the people of the village? How come the coconut trees do not have any fruit?"

The old man began to tell a story.

> One day a man came to the village. He didn't seem like a kind man. There was something sinister about him. He demanded coconuts. Since there were only old men and women in the village, none of them could climb the coconut trees so they offered him a very dry coconut with no water in it. They said, "That is all we can offer."
>
> The man took the coconut, but he was very angry. He turned around and told the old people, "From now on your trees and food will be scarce in the village."
>
> With these words he left the village. As days went by, the coconuts on the trees began to rot and could not be eaten. Even the pigs would not eat them. The potatoes and all the other plants began to dry up. Fresh water in the springs became salty. The people starved and were forced to drink the salty water.
>
> Fish began to disappear from the reefs. Sometimes no squid or shellfish could be found. You do not see the people in the village now because they are in their homes too weak to move around. Just my grandson and I can move around and help people with what we can.
>
> People from along the coast would sometimes pass here and would stop to offer whatever they had. I would keep just enough for my grandson and myself, the rest of the food I would try to share with all the village.

"Grandfather, grandfather, hurry! Come and help me! I caught lots of fish in my net."

The old man excused himself and hurried to the excited yelling of his grandson. On reaching the beach where his grandson was struggling to pull the net up, the old man's eyes were wide and he couldn't believe what he saw, for the little net was full of fish. He jumped into the water and began pulling the net to shore. He and his grandson picked out all the fish that were in the net and had a great pile to feed the village.

The old man was so happy that he cried and cried, hugging his grandson, "You know the gods have been good to us and gave us all these fish."

225

Even when he looked at the shore, fish of all kinds were jumping in the water. "I gave the only food we had in the house to some strangers. Oh my! We must take all this fish and go home, for I left them eating food there."

He was so happy when he told his visitors he had many more fish to offer them. The couple smiled and said, "We are already filled. You must sit with us and eat. We will take care of the fish you caught."

The old man answered, "I would like to share them with you and the whole village."

The couple smiled and replied, "That is most kind of you, but for now, call your grandson and sit here. You'd better eat now before the sun goes down."

When the old man returned to the shady area where he had left the couple eating, he was stunned and could not say a word. There on the mat was a large ipu full with poi, steaming sweet potatoes, cooked lū'au leaves, raw fish, steamed fish, and steamed squid. The little boy turned to his grandfather and asked, "Grandfather, where did this food come from? Did our gods bring them?"

Grandfather only mumbled, "Yes, I think the gods brought all these foods. They must have heard my prayers. Let us call our friends to join us."

But the couple was nowhere to be seen because they were busy giving every house some of the fish the old man and his grandson had caught. The couple made sure the people had poi, too. They were a strange and friendly couple, but no one guessed or knew who they were. Not even the old man knew.

The old man and his grandson sat down to eat and suddenly the people in the village started all coming to his place yelling thank you's and blessings for the fish and the poi. The old man was so surprised that he couldn't say a word. Only tears of happiness flowed from his eyes. Seeing how happy the people were and how they were not hungry was the best thank you. The couple had returned by now and was sitting there with the old man. The little boy reached for the gourd to drink water. "Grandfather!" the boy yelled, "The water tastes very good! It is not salty anymore."

The old man reached for the gourd and drank some water too. He was speechless and took another long drink. All he could say was, "Strange... strange."

The young couple didn't say a word but smiled at the old man and his mo'opuna.

226

Finally the old man spoke, "Would you like to stay with us for a while? We have much here to eat. My grandson and I would like to share our good fortune with you. Since you came, so much has happened. I think you brought the luck, so abide with us as long as you want."

The young man then spoke, "Mahalo no kou lokomaika'i e komo mai iā māua e noho i kou hale. Thank you for inviting the both of us to stay at your house. The sun is setting in the sea, we must rest. But before we fall asleep, I have one request you must help me with so that your village will never go without food or fresh water again. Tomorrow you must go to every house in the village and ask the men to help you. They will come. You will see. A huge umu must be dug. Being that this house is the first, the umu must start from here and go until it reaches the last house in the village. It must be dug before the sun dips into the sea. When the umu is finished, everyone must go into their houses and not come out until the sun comes over the mountains. Then there will be more work to do. The umu must be opened. The house that faces the umu, when it is opened, all that is in it is theirs to keep. Do not ask me questions. I will explain when the time comes. The umu must be dug ho'okahi anana, deep and long like a kahawai, to the last house. I will need the log that you have there by that wall."

The old man replied, "That is a koa log."

"I know," answered the young man.

"You can have it," answered the old man. "Now let us sleep."

The old man told the couple to sleep inside the house. He and his mo'opuna would sleep outside on the lānai.

The young man said, "Tonight we will sleep inside. Tomorrow night you must sleep inside and we will sleep outside for it will be our last night with you. At sunset on that day we must leave you and be on our way. We have a long way to go before we reach home."

When the old man lay down, his grandson was fast asleep by his side. He looked up at the sky full of stars and thought about all the good things that had happened. "What does it mean? What will happen tomorrow? Will the men help us? Why such an umu? Umu are usually deep and round. Why this long? Who is this couple? Where did they come from? Why did he tell me to do what he asked and to not ask questions? Why, why, why?"

With all these questions in his mind, he fell into a deep sleep. At the first crow of the rooster he was up. The food was all set out on the eating mat and the couple was sitting there waiting for him and his mo'opuna. Approaching them with his moʻopuna, he still had many questions but had been told not to ask questions so he greeted them and sat down to eat. It didn't take long before the first rays of the sun began to peek over the mountain.

The old man stood up and went to the houses in the village. Not one man refused to help. They all followed him and he told them what they must do. All agreed and started to dig. They did not stop until it was almost sundown and then each man went home. By the time it was dark, all the people were in their houses. Not one sound or light could be seen.

The couple walked to the start of the umu then the woman began to walk in the umu all the way to the last house and back to where she started. As she returned, the umu became covered wherever she passed. By the time she reached where she had started, the entire umu was covered. Who had done it? The young man took the log to the edge of the sea and transformed it into a canoe. It was a beautiful canoe. Then the couple returned to the sleeping mats. Just before daybreak they were up. The young man stood at the start of the umu and raised his hands up. The earth began to move and uncovered the umu. Foods of all kinds were there for each house. Then he turned to the lands surrounding the village and the trees and plants began to grow and flourish. He turned to the coconut trees growing along the beaches and all bore fruit in great bunches. New trees grew and bore fruit the old people could reach.

The sun was coming out over the mountain. The young man shouted in a loud booming voice for the people to come out. The surprise in their faces could not be described for everything they needed was there from food to growing things. Even the water in the pūnāwai was fresh with lots of fish jumping in the sea.

The old man and his grandson stood speechless. The young man told the old man to tell the people they could take the food in the umu for it was theirs to have. They would never again go without food. As for the men, every time they went out fishing, if they threw the first fish they caught back into the sea, they would always catch fish. As for the women, they would always have lots of plants for medicine and food.

The old man looked at all the people along the umu and repeated all that he had been told. The people all yelled, "Mahalo!" and said the gods of the old man had been very good to them. The people began to pick up all the food that was in the umu. After they were done, the men began to cover the umu again. This time they flattened the top so no one could tell that the long umu had been there.

Then the couple took the old man and his grandson and they walked to where the canoe lay.

"Kupunakāne, I know you have many questions in your mind for I looked into your thoughts last night before you fell asleep. Now I will answer all your questions but before I do, you must promise never to tell anyone who we are and do not say a word as I answer your questions.

"First, our names. Mine is Kū'ula. Her name," he said, pointing to the woman, "is Hinapukui'a. We heard all your cries and prayers and came to help you. Yes, we are gods. We caused the other people to stop and offer you food. We made everything happen in this village because of you and your kindness. We knew that was all the food you had and yet you offered it to us even if it meant you and your grandchild would be without. I filled your net at the beach. Your net will always be filled every time you go to the beach but don't forget to give back some of your first catch to the sea so there will be more fish to come. Now it is time for us to leave you. Tomorrow morning you will find this canoe here. It is yours to keep. It will always take you where the fish are."

Kū'ula and the old man lifted the canoe and set it on the water. Kū'ula and Hina got in while the old man and the little boy stood by and watched. As they left the shore, Kū'ula stood up and said in a booming voice, "From today on this place will be known as Kaumuloa, the long umu."

And they sailed out to sea until the old man could not see them anymore.

The next morning the canoe was sitting on the sand as was foretold. So ends our story of Ho'ōpūloa.

Kalepeamoa

Story of Kanika'ō

THE STORY OF THE MERMAID AND THE ROOSTER

[TOLD BY MALAEA NUNUHA KAHELE KUAHUIA] NOVEMBER 1946

L ong, long ago lived a boy who spent most of his life in the forest. How he got there no one seemed to know, but he was the son of a kupua moa of the forest.

All this boy did was roam the forest helping people find their way home whenever they got lost. The boy had a habit of calling out to people who were lost, so they named him Kanika'ō. He would yell, "Who-e-e-e" until the people found their way out of the forest by following the sound he made.

One day, Kanika'ō heard a wee voice in the forest. It sounded like someone was in awful pain. He followed the sound until he came upon a great tree. The sound got louder and louder. He crept close to the tree to see who was hurt. He moved to the side of the tree trunk. What he saw was a pretty girl with both of her legs cut off. He moved over to where the girl was sitting and touched her. She looked up at Kanika'ō and smiled. She seemed to know him well but to Kanika'ō, this is the first time he had ever seen this girl. He asked her, "What is your name?"

She answered him and said, "My name is Mahana and I know your name is Kanika'ō."

Kanika'ō smiled at her. Then he asked her, "How come both of your legs are cut off?"

Mahana looked at him and said, "You know, in this forest there is a cave that leads all the way to the sea. I come from the beach. One day I found this cave and learned it leads all the way up the hill and the opening is in this springwater pond. When I tried to get up on a rock, my legs got caught in the roots and were torn off. That is why my legs are gone. I was crying because I miss my home and family so much. I cannot return home until I have new legs."

Kanikaʻō looked at her and said, "Well, I will think of something."

Mahana replied, "No, in time my legs will return, but I cannot return to my home until my legs grow back."

Kanikaʻō was puzzled and thought to himself. Finally he remembered what Mahana said, "...when my legs grow back." He realized that only a lizard grows back its tail.

To test what she really was, he asked her to go swimming with him at the spring. She refused and said, "Some other time. For now let us just sit and talk to each other."

Kanikaʻō built a grass shack so Mahana could rest and without suffering from the cold of the mountain, the cold winds, and the sudden rains that often drop on the forest.

Every day, Kanikaʻō would visit Mahana. They would exchange stories. He would tell her how he helped people who were lost find their way out and other stories of the forest. Mahana would tell him all about the beach and her family and the ocean, but she never revealed that she or her family lived in the ocean.

One day Kanikaʻō was on his way to visit Mahana at the spring when he heard her singing. He moved nearer and nearer until he saw her happily dancing and singing. He noticed that both her legs were there, just as perfect as could be, like they had never been cut off. He didn't want to disturb her singing and dancing so he remained hidden in the tall weeds. As he listened to her singing, it sounded like she was telling him how much she loved him—so much—but that she could not live in the forest anymore. The time had come for her to return to her home by the sea. Just then, he couldn't stay hidden anymore as he longed to hold her and not let her go, for he was deeply in love with Mahana.

On seeing Kanikaʻō, Mahana stopped her singing and dancing and ran to his open arms. They hugged one another and held on to each other for quite a while before separating. With tears flowing down her cheeks, Mahana told Kanikaʻō what she must do. They both walked to the spring for a drink of water. Kanikaʻō said, "I will come for you when my father returns from the other islands."

Mahana looked at him and said, "Let me tell you this: There is a bay where I live. An old man who likes to feed people lives there also. Do not accept or eat any food from him. Call for me and I will come to you. I live on the right side of the bay. Do not go to the left side or harm will come to you.

Now I will tell you how I got my legs back. I am a mo'o of the sea, but when I get to go home my legs will become a tail to help me to swim. You, Kanika'ō, are a kupua. I know that your father is a kupua moa of all the forests on all the islands."

Kanika'ō was stunned and could not answer her because she was right.

Mahana turned to Kanika'ō and hugged him saying, "It is time for me to go home for now the tide is high."

She kissed Kanika'ō, then turned and dove into the spring water. When she reappeared, she waved her tail then disappeared into the water and never came up again.

Kanika'ō was so downhearted and lonely that he just sat by the spring and stared at the ripples on the water where Mahana had dived in, hoping Mahana would come out again. But she didn't. Then he remembered Mahana saying, "There is a cave that leads from the sea to here."

"This must be it!" he said. He stood up and dove into the water. Swimming around he saw there was a dark hole. Moving closer to the hole, he saw it was bright, just like daylight on the outside. He swam back to the edge of the spring and got out, all that time thinking how much he missed Mahana.

Every day he thought of her. Finally, one day his father returned from his trip. Kanika'ō told his father all about Mahana, how he loved her and wanted to go to her. His father answered, "If that is what you want, I cannot stop you. Only remember that you are of the land and she is of the ocean."

Kanika'ō went to the spring and stood there thinking, "Should I go after Mahana or not?"

He looked at the trees he knew so well and all the luscious growth in the forest, then he said to himself, "Am I in my right mind to leave all of this for the girl I love?"

He turned to the trees and waved aloha. Kanika'ō ran to the open arms of his father who was watching him and hugged him. With a warm hand, he held his son in a loving way and said, "When you are in trouble, you need only to ō mai and I will come to you."

With these last words, Kanika'ō turned and dove into the spring. He swam underwater until he saw the cave ahead. It was all lit up and bright as daylight. He swam and swam until he felt as though he had been sucked down into nowhere. All of a sudden, he could taste salty water and he rose up to the surface. He looked around and saw many houses and people. He recognized the faces of some of the people because he had helped them find their way out of the forest when they were lost.

Kanikaʻō swam for the nearest rock and climbed up to rest. While sitting there, an old man came to him with poi, fish, and water. He was about to eat the food, then he remembered what Mahana had warned him about. He backed away and refused the food that had been offered to him. The old man began to get angry and replied, "So Mahana warned you about me? I can cause you to lose your life if you refuse to eat my food."

At that moment Kanikaʻō began to call out for Mahana. She did hear the call, but she didn't believe it was Kanikaʻō because the call came from the wrong side of the bay. She thought it was the old man, for he had fooled her once and that's why she had lost both her legs when she had found the cave to the mountain.

"It cannot be Kanikaʻō because he called me from the left side of the bay," she thought so she didn't listen to the call. The second time she heard the call, it sounded like it was coming from the bay again and still she did not respond to the call. Finally, she decided to go see what was causing so much movement in the sea. She swam close to shore when she saw that Kanikaʻō was trapped on a huge rock, while the old man had become a huge eel and was pulling Kanikaʻō into the water. Without thinking of her own life, she swam to help her friend. She bit the tail of the eel until it let go of Kanikaʻō.

Hearing the commotion, the people on shore came to help Kanikaʻō. As soon as Kanikaʻō reached the huge rock, he shook himself till he became an enormous giant. He reached down into the water, caught the eel by the head, and smashed it between his hands until it was dead. He then took hold of the eel and stretched its body and tied it into an impossible knot, slowly turning the eel into an island. Where the head used to be, he shaped what looked like a rooster with the head and tail showing. This eel was the bad old man and Kanikaʻō wanted to remind all eels what would happen if there was an attack again. After all this was done, he sat down and began thinking of the home he had left and all the good things he missed—the shade, cool air, and most of all, his father and the forest. Then he thought, "I might as well go back where I came from since Mahana did not come to me when I called her."

He looked up toward the mountain and he could see the forest. "Now I will walk up the hill, but the sun is hot. I wonder where Mahana lives?"

That's when he realized he was on the wrong side of the bay. So he dove in the water and swam to the other side. He climbed out of the water and walked on the sand. He thought to himself, I will try and call Mahana again. He shook himself dry then began to call Mahana as she had told him.

Mahana was watching his every move, but she could not come to him until he called her. As soon as she heard him calling her name, she popped out of a pool close to him. She climbed out of the water and ran to Kanika'ō. They were so happy to be together again. They swam and played, and she taught him how to fish. They were so happy.

Finally, one day when Mahana came back from a swim, Kanika'ō was nowhere to be found. She looked and looked but could not find him, so she went to her pool and cried bitter tears. She was broken-hearted, and every day she would go to this pool and just cry her heart out. She loved and missed Kanika'ō so much.

One day at the pool, she was weeping so much that she didn't turn around or hear anyone behind her. All she saw was the shadow of a huge rooster. She was afraid and wanted to turn around to see who it was, but a voice told her in a very heavy, demanding way, "Stay as you are and do not say a word. I am the father of Kanika'ō, and I know you are a mo'o and must live in the water. I come to take you home to Kanika'ō. He is sick and lonely. Perhaps you can help him. As you'll see, the heat of the beach has drained his body and now he is dying. You need not worry about being in the water, for I have prepared a pool to your liking near him."

Mahana then spoke, "Kind father of Kanika'ō, tell him I will come to him but I must wait until the tide is high. You will know when I am there."

The father of Kanika'ō told her, "I know the way you will come. I have made it safe for you, so you can always come to the beach whenever you want. But please, will you come?"

Mahana said, "Yes, I promise. I love Kanika'ō very deeply."

The man said, "And now I bid you aloha, my daughter."

The shadow then disappeared. Mahana turned around and there was no one in sight. All she saw were footprints in the sand, prints she had not seen before. Mahana was so happy she dived into the sea and headed to her family to tell them the good news.

They did not like the idea, but she had promised her heart, so there was nothing else to do but let her go with all their blessings.

Mahana replied, "The tide is getting high, and I must go now."

They followed her to the cave and bade her aloha. She turned and caught the first wave that was going up with the tide. Her swim was shorter now because she was so eager to get to Kanika'ō. Finally, she reached the pool. As she got to the surface, she saw a man lying down at the edge of the pool. He looked so frail and weak. She knew then it was the man she loved. She moved over to where he was lying and knelt down to stroke his face. Upon opening his eyes and seeing her, he was so happy that he hung onto her. He told her he had come home because he was sick. Now he would be well since she had come, yet he doubted her.

Then Mahana said, "I have come to live with you forever." Kanika'ō was happy to hear her words.

Every time they both went to the beach, they always came back with the tide. They lived happily all their lifetime.

The island of this tale was named Lepeamoa and was made into a symbol of Kanika'ō defeating the eel who was the bad old man. The bay was named Kapu'a because whenever Kanika'ō and Mahana went to the beach, Mahana went swimming and Kanika'ō would sit on Lepeamoa and watch. Whenever he saw someone coming, he would whistle to warn Mahana. Even today, if the whistle (ka pu'a) is heard from Lepeamoa, it is a warning that the sea will be rough or a storm will come.

As for the area named Mahana, the water is always warm because she cried so much for Kanika'ō when he was taken to the forest that the water became warm from her tears. Today Mahana is still warm and Lepeamoa still whistles.

This is where all good things come to an end.

Ha'alelekeiki

CHILD WHO WAS LEFT BEHIND

[TOLD BY MY MOTHER-IN-LAW AND HUSBAND] JANUARY 1946

This is a traditional story of the people who lived along the sea coast from Miloli'i, Okoe, Kapu'a, Kaupō, Kaulanamauna and so on to the place where this story originated.

Long, long ago at a place near Kaiakekua lived a mother with her child in a little village with other people.

Now this mother's child was very sick. It just so happened that on this day she decided to go to the next village, or fishing hamlet, at Awake'e. The mother was going to look for some herbs for her sick child which grew only at Awake'e. The child was drooling so badly that there was always a thick slime on his mouth, and wherever he crawled, he left a trail of this thick slime, the hā'ae from his mouth.

All the people had left to go up ma uka to do some mahi'ai. The mother could not find anyone to watch her child while she went for the herbs. Her child fell asleep, so she thought she would leave him home and go for the herbs and be back before he awoke. She left him behind and went to Awake'e.

When she returned home, her child was nowhere around the home. She looked and looked and called for the child but there was no answer. By this time, other people were returning home from up ma uka. Upon learning what had happened, they began to search all over the place, along the cliffs and beach, but they turned up nothing. Some of the people and the mother followed the trail of slime and found themselves at the end of a cliff where it dropped down into the sea. There was a ledge down below. On this ledge there was a big black eel coiled up, drooling badly at the mouth. When it saw them, it began to slither and dropped into the sea. It left a trail of slime where it slithered into the water. The mother felt maybe the child had been taken or eaten by that huge black eel. The mother and the other people left that area and went to their homes. Though the mother was sad and cried and cried for her child, there was nothing the people could do to help her.

What actually happened was that when the mother left home, a black eel had slithered to her home. Upon seeing the sick child sleeping and alone, it stayed there to watch the child. When the child awoke, the eel played with the child.

The eel saw that the child was drooling and decided to take the child to the beach to clean him up. But when they got to the water's edge, the eel realized the child could not swim. The child wanted to go into the water very much. The eel was a kupua, so he changed the child to a black eel. The child had a lot of fun swimming.

Finally, the child slithered up on the rock to rest. At that moment he heard his mother calling. He looked up and saw his mother and some of the people with her. He made up his mind, "No, I will not return to her. When I was with her, I hated some of the children and other people because when my mother was not looking or was busy, they would tease me and call me a loli because I was always drooling at the mouth. Everywhere I crawled there was a trail of slime. I was happier today swimming and playing with the eels."

At this thought, he slithered down from the ledge into the water and disappeared.

As for the mother, she believed that her child was changed into an eel because she saw that the eel was drooling. If only she had known that she was right! The people named that place Haʻalelekeiki (child who was left behind). Black eels are numerous at this place. So ends this story.

Fishing Traditions

Fishing Traditions in Our Village of Nāpoʻopoʻo

[TOLD BY THE ELDERS OF OUR VILLAGE] 1934

T he ancient Hawaiians used their own calendar based on moon phases. The fishermen of the old days did all their fishing in relation to the various moon phases.

Each day and month had its own characteristics and some were favorable and some were unfavorable. Even today, many Hawaiian fishermen observe this ancient method of fishing. It seems like fishing and its rules were a tremendous mainstay of the people: the study of the moon, tides, winds, sun, stars, and other planets. Hawaiians had names for each one of the planets and they kept a close watch on how they appeared in the sky.

Certain fishes have been studied to learn their habits, how they feed, and the best season to catch them. The abundance of certain fish in tide pools tells fishermen that a certain type of fish should be ready to catch.

There are certain rites of ceremony to be performed by fishermen before they go for bigger gains.

The winds, tides, and currents do play a very important role for fishermen. They observe all their signs before leaving shore.

Koʻa = coral or certain coral heads

1. Fishing grounds are usually identified by lining up marks on land or shore.

2. A shrine consists of a certain stone that is set in an area with its own altar. Shrines also consist of coral or stones built at a certain area along the shore or near ponds or streams where they are used in ceremonies to make fish multiply.

Some birds play an important role, too. Certain birds are observed when they are seen circling above the water. This will tell the fishermen a certain fish is ready to be caught. Preparations are readied and out go the fishermen with certain types of hooks, lines, or nets. A fisherman's occupation is very interesting because of all the traditions that must be learned.

Nā Akua o Nā Po'e Lawai'a

[TOLD BY TŪTŪ NAHA] 1932

'Ai'ai — Ka po'o o nā akua o ka po'e lawai'a. 'O ia ke keiki o Kū'ulakai.

Kū'ulakai — Ka makukāne o 'Ai'ai. (God of all the fishermen of the Hawaiians. All fishermen have stone images and heiau were named for Kū'ula.)

Hinapukui'a — Ka makuahine o 'Ai'ai. 'O kāna hana e ka'apuni i nā moku a pau a ho'onoho i nā ka'a i'a. (Goddess of all the fishermen of the Hawaiian people.)

Ko'a — Fishing station or mark

Kū'ula — Altar or shrine

Hina'ea — Goddess of the sunrise and sunset of all fishermen

Hina — Prostrate, represents the females. Faced to the setting sun so its realm includes the earth, heavens, and all generations born or unborn.

Kū — Upright, represents the males. It also represents the power of the rising sun.

Wa'ula — 'O ia ho'i, kapu loa ka mea 'ula'ula. The color red was kapu near a kū'ula, or shrine, on the ocean. Used on fishing trips on the ocean or for shoreline fishing by the Hawaiians. Red belongs to Kū'ula or to ali'i.

Akule Fishing

[TOLD BY MY UNCLE HENRY LESLIE, SR., MY FATHER KAPIO KAPULE, AND KŪKŪ NAHA, WHO WAS THE ELDEST IN THE VILLAGE] 1934

For akule fishing:

1. Nets

2. Canoes

3. Paddlers

4. Divers and splashers

5. Men to let the nets go and form a ring around the fish that had been surrounded.

6. Someone to make sure that the nets were really set the way the head fisherman wanted them to be. This is where the divers and splashers did their job. Divers dived down to check the nets because if big fish ripped through them, schools of smaller fish could escape through the holes. Next, the ring of nets with thousands of pounds of fish in them were moved to shallow water near the shore. The splashers took their places around the nets so the fish would not jump out. The splashers would slap the water every time a fish rose to the surface. This would send the fish down and get them tangled in the nets.

7. Helpers from the shore were usually the villagers, from adults to children. This type of fishing needed so many hands. After most of the fish were loaded and taken to the market to be sold, the men who went out on the canoes—the paddlers, divers (the main men), and head fishermen—got paid.

Fish that were still in the nets or tangled were divided among all the families in the village, those who took part in pulling the nets to shore, and those who untangled all the fish from the nets.

Sometimes it took two or three days before all the fish were taken out of the nets. It was lots of fun, but also lots of work. The pay for every child, and even myself, was a bundle of fish to take home. Sometimes we could hardly carry the load of fish that was given to us to take home.

This was done only once a year when the akule fish were caught in the nets.

Fishing Tricks

[TOLD BY TŪTŪ NAHA AS HE HAS DONE]

These were the kinds of fishing that I could not understand, but I wrote them down. In later years when I married, my husband tried this method and found it worked.

For koʻa (or station) fishing for big fish and some reef fish.
ʻAhi
Ono
Ulua
40 ʻanana or fathoms to 45 or 60 fathoms with stone and palu (chum)

ʻUlaʻula
ʻŌpakapaka
Aʻu
ʻĀhua (tombo)
Otherwise 600 feet or 100 fathoms for deep-sea fishing

The Four Seasons (were for four goddesses):
1. Kanono
2. Paʻupoula
3. Haehae
4. Hanakaula

Kumukahi and Palemo — Chiefs who were brothers

Kamono and Paʻupoula — Were both wives of one chief by the name of Kumukahi

Haehae and Hanakaula — Were both wives of another chief by the name of Palemo

The Hawaiians of the past believed this is where the seasons came from.

Fishermen's Beliefs

[TOLD BY KŪKŪ NAHA; WHAT MY COUSIN KALANI APANA AND I HAD TO DO]
1934

The hīnālea is called a scavenger fish. Most fishermen, especially women folks, will observe hīnālea along the seashore, reefs, or tide pools during certain periods of the year.

When the hīnālea are in abundance, the women folks pick morning-glory vines to make hīnaʻi or fish traps. Then you hear them say, "Ke kau nei ka hīnālea. Ua momona ka wana," meaning, "The hīnālea are many. The urchins are fat." As you know, the urchin, when it is full and fat, is the favorite food of the hīnālea and other scavenger fishes like the triggerfish.

My cousin Kalani Apana and I would have to go along with our grandmothers to gather the wana. After the spines were cleaned off, we would break the urchins and take out the fleshy parts to take home. We would then put the teeth parts in the traps and set them in the water where the hīnālea were. It was great fun watching the hīnālea go into the traps to eat the wana parts. We used to catch buckets full of hīnālea. Our tūtū woud clean and cut the fishes into small bite-size pieces, then add in the wana. They would let it sit for a while and then we would eat this for our lunch or dinner. It tasted so good because the fish meat was soft, and mixed with the wana, boy, it was tasty. We grew up on this kind of food.

Most people do not like this kind of fish, but in our village of Nāpoʻopoʻo, almost all the people like it. They are so easy to catch, with traps, nets, or with rods and hooks.

Other fish that are in abundance when a lot of hīnālea are around are as follows:
Humuhumunukunukuʻāpuaʻa (triggerfish)
ʻŪʻū
ʻĀweoweo
Maomao
Moi
Akule
Uku
Kaweleʻā

When there is an abundance of hīnālea, the fishermen get ready and go after these fishes.

The whale is another belief. When the whales are passing by, there is another type of fish that is known as ʻōhua. These are tiny fishes of all kind that live among the corals, the reefs, or in tide pools. Our tūtū get their ʻōhua nets and start out early in the morning when it is still dark, the tide is still high, and the tide pools are overflowing. They wait until the tide goes down and the water is not flowing. They enter the tide pools and sometimes find big bubbles, like balloons, full of fish. This is called hūpē koholā (mucous of the whale).

The main idea is to reach these bubbles before they touch the shore, because once they touch seaweed or sharp stones, the balloons will burst and you have to corral the fishes into a narrow gap so you can catch them with the scoop net. What we do is, when we see a bubble, we pass our bucket right under it and scoop it up.

Those bubbles have a lot of fishes: one of the bubbles can fill a bucket, enough for two households. The bubbles sometimes never make it to the tide pools because the big fish attack them and eat the tiny fishes. But some of them do escape and reach the tide pools. Today these type of fish cannot be caught. It is against the law.

There are many more beliefs, but I'll get to them someday.

Where large heads of coral are found, manini, lāʻīpala, pākuʻikuʻi, mao, kole, hīnālea, and other small fish are also found, especially in shallow water. Even the red flat-spined urchins (hāʻukeʻuke), the black sharp-spined urchins (wana), and other types of urchins like the hāwaʻe or ʻina are found in areas like this or in tide pools.

Rocky shorelines that have a pink hue from the cover of coralline algae show in large part where ʻopihi, purple hāʻukeʻuke, and ʻaʻama crabs live. They survive because of the rich growth of brown algae. Even tiny shellfish like pipipi, pūpū, and other sea life are found in areas like this. Whenever you see seashells or snails around areas like these, you will know there are algae around for them to live on.

In some areas at the bottom of these shallow waters there is a deep mat of red algae. In these places you will find ʻopihi of the flat and larger species, known to Hawaiians as the ʻopihi kōʻele. They taste different from the dark gray or black ʻopihi that cling to the sheer cliffs where the sea washes over them and where there are algae growing. Sometimes you cannot see algae growing in these places, but if you run your hands over these areas, they are smooth and slippery. You will then know algae grow there. Seaweed like kala and 'aki'aki usually cover these areas. There are a lot of varieties of limu growing that are edible. When the sea gets rough, especially in the winter months, the people watch the sea. Sometimes rough seasons last for three or four months. As soon as the water calms down, the people go out and gather the limu pāhe'e. This sometimes brings a lot of 'opihi and other shellfish. It somehow forms algae and this becomes food for the 'opihi.

Reef fishes are in abundance when limu pāhe'e grows, as it is part of their food. Gather a handful of this limu and let it go in the shallow water. All kind of fishes in the shallows or the reef will go for it.

I have experience of this kind and have watched fish swim to the surface and gobble it all up. To me it seems very funny because if you drop other kinds of seaweed in the water, the fish just swim by and never try to nibble them. But drop the pāhe'e and they will attack it. Why? I don't have the slightest idea.

There are many other beliefs, but I couldn't get them on paper because at the time I ran out of writing papers. But I'm not sorry because I got some of the things I grew up with. I never understood what beliefs were. To me I thought they were "musts" I had to learn. As a rule, a child must never ask questions when with an elderly person unless asked to do so.

Old Hawaiian Counting

[FROM THE KNOWLEDGE OF MY STEPFATHER-IN-LAW, KALANI KUAHUIA]
1947

Hawaiians counted by fours and in multiples. The highest expressed number was four, a hundred, a thousand, or a count as a lost number.

Forty is counted by fours, or as 10 fours. This method is mostly used among fishermen and it is still in use.

Example:
Four = 1 kāuna
10 kāuna = 1 ka'au (or kanahā)
10 ka'au = 1 lau
10 lau = 1 mano
10 mano = 1 kini
10 kini = 1 lehu
10 lehu = No limit, or as they say, nalowale, or a lost number

But if you multiply ten lehu that gets you the number of fishes you will have.

Nā Hui Hōkū

GROUPS OF STARS

[TOLD BY TŪTŪ NAHA, 1932. HE GAVE ME THE HAWAIIAN NAMES ONLY
IN LATER YEARS. I DID A SEARCH FOR THEIR MEANING.]

1. Huihui o Makaliʻi — The Pleiades, or the Seven Sisters, makes its appearance in the eastern evening sky in November. This marks the beginning of the year and a season of great feasting.

2. Nānā Mua — "Going ahead" (Castor)

3. Nānā Hope — "Following after" (Pollux)*

4. Nā Kao — Orion, the familiar belt and sword we all see in the sky.

5. Nā Hiku — The Big Dipper

6. Hōkū Paʻa — Polaris
   Hōkūhoʻokele Waʻa — "Steering or guiding star"

7. Kau — The Milky Way or summer season.

8. Newe — The Southern Cross.

When voyagers went south they used these groups of stars to steer their canoes. All the stars mentioned above were important to the Hawaiian people.

Compass:
Koʻolau = North
Kona = South
Hikina = East
Komohana = West

Publisher's note: Mona indicated that Castor and Pollux were twins.

Universe of the Ancient Hawaiians and Their Beliefs

[THANKS TO MY COUSIN KUANA ʻIOLANI LUAHINE AND MY FATHER ISAAC KAPIO
KAPULE, SR.] 1939

1. Ka lani — The heavens

2. Kumuhonua — Earth's foundation

3. Ka lā — The sun

4. Ka lā kau — Where the sun lodges, and the resting place of the sun on the ocean.

5. Ka mahina — The moon

6. Ka hōkū — The stars

7. Ke alanui nā ʻawe a Kanaloa — The much-traveled path of the god Kanaloa

8. Ke alanui polohiwa a Kanaloa — The black shining road of Kanaloa

9. Ke alaula a Kāne — The bright road of the god Kāne

10. Ke alanui polohiwa a Kāne — The black shining road of Kāne

---

Kāne Hūnā Moku — The god Kāne's hidden land. This is where great clouds are driven about the sky by the winds and periodically visit the earth.

Lewa Nuʻu — "Suspended in the upper heavens," where the clouds float. Heavens cannot be seen with the eyes but are a space directly below where the gods live, where stars are sprinkled, and where the sun and moon travel.

Lewa Lani — "Suspended in the heavens," also called a "floating heaven."

Lewa Hoʻ omakua — "The parent air," "suspended in the air," as "lewa" is suspended.

Haehae — "To rend or tear asunder." Curtains of night parted at the coming of the sun.

Milo — Under earth's foundation. It is a great subterranean place of dim light and is ruled by the god Milo. It is also the destination of souls who do not deserve to go to heaven. They lived dull lives without love or affection. Some of these are taken to heaven after a period of time in which they are purified.

Chart of the universe of ancient Hawaiians

Calendar of Seasons

[FROM BEN L. KAMAKAU AND AUNTIE MELE MOKU] 1938

Hawai'i has two seasons: ho'oilo and kau. The months are on a lunar count. For example:

December 2	Makali'i
January 3	Ka'elo (beginning of ho'oilo)
February 4	Kaulua
March 5	Nana
April 6	Welo
May 7	Ikiiki
June 8	Ka'aona
July 9	Hinaia'ele'ele
August 10	Māhoe Mua (beginning of kau)
September 11	Māhoe Hope
October 12	'Ikuwā
November 1	Welehu

In 'Ikuwā on our lunar calendar the Pleiades (the Makali'i) are seen from the east. If they stand overhead it means lots of fish but also stormy weather. This means the big fish are running, and catches should be good.

Makali'i season:*

Welehu	March – April
Makali'i	April – May
Ka'elo	May – June
Kaulua	June – July
Nana	July – August
Welo	August – September

Ho'oilo season:

Ikiiki	September – October
Ka'aona	October – November
Hinaia'ele'ele	November – December
Hilina Mā	December – January
'Ikuwā	February – March

Note: Ben Kamakau's calendar differs in sequence from the one listed by Malo in the newspaper Ke Ao 'Oko'a for February 10, 1870. Kamakau gives the dates, beginning with the latter half of March, as listed above.

Publisher's note: Also known as " Kau."

Calendar of Days

1938

The day starts at noon and ends at midnight.

The month starts at the rising of the new moon as it travels across the sky from the east and sets in the west.

There are thirty days in the moon calendar and one extra day when the points of Hoku are darker (called Hoku Palemo) and the edges of the moon are not fully round before Māhealani appears.

Hilo — Starting of the new moon at which all things are new

Hoaka

Kū Kahi

Kū Lua — The kapu days and nights, held strictly for ceremonial purposes

Kū Kolu

Kū Pau

'Ole Kū Kahi — These days are not considered good for planting or fishing.
('Ole means no, nothing, or none.)

'Ole Kū Lua

'Ole Kū Kolu

'Ole Kū Pau

Hūnā — To hide or the leaves will hide the fruits

Mohalu — Good

Hua — For plants with fruits

Akua — Good day

Hoku — Good, except for Hoku Palemo; fruits will not be held

Māhealani — Good for anything; farmers and fishermen look forward to this moon

Kulu — Fruits or flowers will drop if planted on this day

Lā'au Kū Kahi — Anything with trees is planted at this time

Lā'au Kū Lua

Lā'au Pau

'Ole Kū Kahi – Days of nothing; farmers rest during these days

'Ole Kū Lua

'Ole Pau

Kāloa Kū Kahi — Time to plant anything with vines like ipu, pumpkin, watermelons, potatoes, or flowers on vines

Kāloa Kū Lua

Kāloa Pau

Kāne — Night begins to get dark

Lono — Night when you get ready to stick something in the ground

Mauli — Darkest of all the nights; no stars

Muku — Darkest but for half a night, then the new moon rises and stars are out

Publisher's note: Mona listed Kulu as Kū Lua in her manuscript.

Glossary

Hawaiian terms and phrases as they are used throughout the text

a'ā lava

'a'ahu cape

ahi fire

'ahi tuna fishes, especially the yellow-fin

'ahi ko'a 'ahi fishing grounds

'ahu cape

'āhua young fish

ahupua'a land division typically from mountain to sea

'ai to eat

'ailolo traditional ceremony marking end of training

'ailona sign, symbol

'āina land

'aka'aka to laugh

aku bonito, skipjack tuna

akua god

akua lele flying god

akule big-eyed scad fish

ali'i ruling class, chief

ali'i nui high chief

aloha love, greeting, good-bye, compassion

anuanu cold, chilly

ānuenue rainbow

'ao'ao side

'a'ole no

'āpiki cunning

'āpōpō tomorrow

a'u swordfish

'au'a spy

auē oh dear! too bad!

'aumakua family god or guardian

awa harbor, cove

'awa kava

'awa'awa bitter

'āweoweo Hawaiian bigeye fish

'āwili to mix

'ehā four

'eha'eha pain

'ehu light, reddish-blonde hair color found among Polynesians

ēkoa koa haole, false koa

ēlama endemic ebony

'elemakule old man

'elemākule (plural)

'elima five

'epa deceit

hā'ae saliva, drool

ha'alele to leave, abandon

ha'i to break

hale house

hale ukana storage shed

hāli'i covering

hānai to adopt, to feed

hānau to give birth

haole foreign, foreigner, Caucasian

hau lowland tree

he'e squid [local term for octopus]

heiau place of worship

hewa mistake

hili bark dye

hīna'i fish trap

hīnālea wrasse fish

Hilina Mā month of the year

hoe paddle

holoholo to go out for a ride/walk

holoi to wash

hōlua Hawaiian sled, hill for hōlua sledding

253

ho'okahi anana one fathom
ho'olako to supply
ho'olili school of fish
ho'oponopono to make right
huehue a feeling, hunch or intuition
hupe koholā jelly-like sack of
    baby fish
i'a general term for fish
'iako outrigger boom of a canoe
'ike to see or know
'Ikuwā month of the year
'ili'ili pebble
'ilima native flower
'imi aku to seek out
imu underground oven
'inamona kukui nut relish
ipu gourd
ipukea Caucasian
ka'ai 'opelu net
ka'au forty
kaha to slice
kahakai beach
kahawai stream, gulch
kāheka tide pool
kāhili feather standard
kahua hale house foundation
kahuna priest **kāhuna** (plural)
kai sea
kaina youngest sibling of the same sex
kaka rinse
kākou all of us
kalo taro
kālua baked
kama'ilio conversation
kamali'i children
kanaka man, person
kanapī centipede
kani to sound, crow
kanikapila play music
kāpena captain
kapu taboo
kāpulu careless
kaula'i hang up to dry

kauā slave
kēia this
keiki child
kēlā that
kepalō devil
kīkēkē tap, knock
kīloa put away for safekeeping
kinikini marbles
koa largest of native forest trees
ko'a fishing grounds, shrine
kōko'olua companion
kōkua help
kolo to crawl
kolohe nasty, mischievous
kōnane traditional Hawaiian checkers
kuhilani boss, to boss around
kuhina nui regent
kūkae feces
kuku kapa beater
kukū thorn
kūkū grandparent
kukui candlenut
kula open country, school
kulikuli be quiet [literally "deafening"]
kūpaianaha surprising
kupua demigod
kupuna grandparent **kūpuna** (plural)
kupunakāne grandfather
kupunawahine grandmother
kū'ula stone shrine
lā day
lā'ī ti leaf
lānai porch
lapa'au medicinal
lau hala pandanas leaf
laua'e a type of fragrant fern
laulima cooperation
lau niu coconut leaf
lehua flower of the 'ōhi'a tree
lei garland
limu seaweed
lo'i kalo taro pond
lōkahi unity

lokelani pink rose
loli sea slug
lōlō crazy, slow
lomilomi massage
lūʻau feast, young taro tops
mahalo thank you
mahiʻai farming
maiʻa banana
maile fragrant native shrub and lei
ma kai toward the sea
makaʻainana commoners
makahiapo oldest child
make to die, dead
mākou we
mālie calm
malo loincloth
mamo Hawaiian sergeant damselfish
manini convict tang fish
manu bird
ma uka toward the mountain
māua the two of us
menehune mythical small people
milo to twist
moa chicken
moana horizon, ocean
mokomoko hand-to-hand fighting
moku island
Moku nui o Hawaiʻi Big Island
moloā lazy
moloā ʻino extreme laziness
moʻo lizard, water spirit
moʻolelo story, history
moʻopuna grandchild
muʻumuʻu loose gown
naiʻa dolphin
nānā to look
nīʻau coconut leaf midrib
nīele curious
niho claw, tooth
ō mai to yell out
ʻoe you
ʻohana family
ʻOle night of poor luck

ʻole none, lacking
ʻōlelo word, speech
olo grate
ʻolo gourd container
olonā native shrub
ono wahoo fish
ʻono tasty
ʻōpae shrimp
ʻōpakapaka blue snapper
ʻōpelu mackerel
ʻopihi limpet
ʻōpiopio young
ʻopiuma Manila tamarind tree
ʻōpū stomach
ʻōpua rain cloud, waterspout
paʻakai salt
pahu drum, box
pakalōlō marijuana
Pākē Chinese
palaoa ivory pendant
palaʻai pumpkin
pālau pudding
pali cliff
palu fish bait
papa ʻaina dining surface, eating place
pāpaʻi hale temporary shelter
pau finished
pāʻū skirt
pia arrowroot
piele to trade, skin eruptions
piko navel
pīlali hardened sap
pō night or dark
poʻe people
pōhaku stone
pōhaku kuʻihili stone where kukui bark is pounded
pōhaku paʻakai salt bowl
pōhuehue beach morning glory
poke small chunks, especially of raw fish
puhi eel

255

puka hole
pulu husk
pulu ʻono a variety of coconut
pūnāwai spring
puʻu piles or hills
puʻuhonua place of refuge
tapa bark cloth
tūtū grandparent
tūtūkāne grandfather
tūtūwahine grandmother
ʻuala sweet potato
ʻuhane spirit
ʻuhaʻuha to squander
ukana luggage, bags
ʻula red
ʻulaʻula red snapper
ʻūlei native shrub
ʻulu breadfruit
ulua jack fish
ʻumeke bowl
umu oven
ʻunihipili spirit of dead person
ʻupena fishing net
ʻūʻū soldierfish
wahine woman
wahine hoʻokamakama loose
    woman
wai water
waikōʻihi waterspout
waioleka violet
waipuʻilani waterspout
waipuna spring water
wana sea urchin

Manawa

[MONA K.K. KAHELE] 1941

No ka manawa i haʻi mai nā mea a pau	*For time will tell of everything*
Ua ʻike nō kākou he manaʻo nō e hiki no kekahi mea	*We know that it can mean something*
Inā hiki kākou ke huli ka manawa i hope	*If only we can turn time back*
E mau ana loa ke kīkēkē nā puʻuwai a kākou	*Our hearts will forever beat*
He aha nō lā ka lawehala ʻana	*What can be the worst*
ʻAʻole nō e ʻuhaʻuha wale	*Will not always waste away*
ʻO wai ka mea e ʻike ai nā hana hiki o ka manawa	*Who knows what time can do*
Aia hina kākou a laila e ʻike ʻia	*Until we all turn gray to know*
ʻO ka lā, hūlali nō ʻo ia ma ka lā	*The sun shines by day*
A ʻo ka mahina a me nā hōkū, kōnane nō ma ka pō	*The moon and stars by night*
A me ka ʻenaʻena, nā pohihihi ma luna o kēia ʻuhane ʻuhaʻuha wale ia	*The glow of mystery upon this wasting soul*
Pehea hoʻi lā, hiki nō paha o ka manawa e kali iā kākou	*Can time wait for us*
A ʻo ka ʻae a me ka hōʻole, he mau panena ʻike ʻole ʻia	*Yes and no, are answers unknown*
ʻO ka ʻuni o kākou, ʻinā e hiki ke hoʻohālikelike me manawa	*I wish I could be time*
E mau ana nō ka manawa ma laila nō	*For time will always be there*
I hea ana ʻoe ke hiki e huli	*Where else can you turn*
ʻO ia hoʻi, i ka manawa ʻai no ke kali nei i loko o ka hoʻokela	*Of course, to time that waits in vain*
Ke waiho nei nā hoʻomanaʻo ʻana	*And so it leaves only a memory*
Me ke aloha pau loa iā manawa	*To all who love time*
No nā ʻāpōpō a pau loa	*For every tomorrow*